Social and Behavioral Statistics

Social and Behavioral Statistics

A User-Friendly Approach

SECOND EDITION

**Steven P. Schacht and
Jeffery E. Aspelmeier**

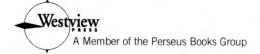

Westview
PRESS
A Member of the Perseus Books Group

Copyright © 2005 by Steven P. Schacht and Jeffery E. Aspelmeier

Published in the United States of America by Westview Press, A Member of the Perseus Books Group.

Find us on the world wide web at www.westviewpress.com

Westview Press books are available at special discounts for bulk purchases in the United States by corporations, institutions, and other organizations. For more information, please contact the Special Markets Department at the Perseus Books Group, 11 Cambridge Center, Cambridge, MA 02142, or call (617) 252–5298 or (800) 255–1514, or email special.markets@perseusbooks.com.

A Cataloging-in-Publication data record for this book is available from the Library of Congress.

ISBN 0–8133–4168-X (pbk.)

The paper used in this publication meets the requirements of the American National Standard for Permanence of Paper for Printed Library Materials Z39.48–1984.

10   9   8   7   6   5   4   3   2   1

Contents

Preface to the Second Edition

I, like my coauthor Steve Schacht, began teaching statistics while in graduate school. When I taught my first behavioral statistics course, I had one section with sixty students and, quite frankly, it scared the @#$% out of me. In my search for the right textbook, I contacted my former professor, long-time friend, and future coauthor to see if his cartoon-based statistics book, *Social Statistics: A User-Friendly Approach*, was ready. I looked it over and immediately knew it was the book for me.

Although it was written as a text for the social sciences, the cartoon-based examples were just as applicable to the behavioral sciences. It worked out quite nicely—the students' ratings of the textbook were phenomenal. I was hooked, and have continued to apply this cartoon-based approach to teaching statistics at both the graduate and undergraduate level. Later, I came to Steve with suggestions for a revised edition and, unexpectedly, he suggested that I join him as coauthor.

Those familiar with the book will find that all of the content and material from the first edition is presented in this revised and expanded second edition in the same easy-to-follow, step-by-step manner. We also have made some significant changes. As indicated by the title, *Social and Behavioral Statistics: A User-Friendly Approach*, we have partially changed the focus of the book. Also, we have included new content—specifically, a chapter covering Factorial (Two-Way) ANOVA.

Although this text has been adapted to appeal to those in the social and behavioral sciences, especially sociology and psychology, those teaching or taking statistics in criminal justice, education, political science, social work, and other fields will find this book equally suited to their courses. Statistics courses are also required in an increasing number of service-oriented master's programs, including school counseling and public administration—these students often have severe aversions and phobias regarding statistics. The anxiety reduction features of this book will appeal to students and instructors alike.

This second edition was partly inspired by our desire to correct some typos and clarify points that some students found ambiguous. Invariably, there will be new typos and new points of ambiguity in this revised edition. We encourage you to report any errors you might find (*jaspelme@radford.edu*). Corrections for these and other issues that may have arisen can be found at *www.radford.edu/~jaspelme/statsbook/Social_and_Behavioral_Statistics.htm*.

It has taken a while for our project to finally reach completion and, unfortunately, Steve passed away in November 2003. He became too ill to oversee much of the work on this second edition, but it is my hope and my belief that the revisions made to this book remain true to his original vision.

Steve never got the chance to write acknowledgments for this edition, and I am sure that he would want it dedicated to the love of his life and soul mate, Lisa Underwood, the person with whom he finally found a home.

On behalf of Steve and myself, I would like to thank the people at Westview Press, especially our editor Jill Rothenberg, who showed tremendous commitment to and faith in our project, and Steve Catalano for picking up the pieces in the wake of the company's reorganization. Extra-special thanks goes to Rachel Parrott, literally the best graduate student I have ever worked with. Without Rachel this book could not have been finished on time (if at all), and with my sanity intact (at least arguably so).

For my part, I dedicate this book to my wife, Kim. She continues to inspire me to be a better teacher and student. I would also like to thank and bid a fond farewell to my colleague, friend, and mentor Steven P. Schacht. You are missed.

—JEFF ASPELMEIER
July 9, 2004

Preface to the First Edition

When I began teaching statistics nearly ten years ago in graduate school, I did so with excitement and apprehension. At that time I eagerly sought out any opportunities that allowed me to teach, and as a first-year Ph.D. student I was thrilled to be teaching my fifth different course as an independent instructor. On the other hand, however, from my own experiences as a student and experiences other instructors shared with me, I knew all too well that I would face a generally hostile student audience. That is, I could expect many of the students in a statistics class to have insufficient math backgrounds, to be experiencing fairly high levels of math/statistics anxiety, and, in general, to be in attendance only because, as one student put it, "Some academic jerk requires it for graduation." Moreover, unlike the previous subjects I taught that seemed to have an inexhaustible supply of supporting materials, there were virtually no materials available to assist me in preparing a statistics class. In sum, after successfully teaching numerous courses, I was now faced with a subject that was generating instructor anxiety.

In previous courses, like many instructors I knew, I often used newspaper cartoons wherever controversial subjects that might provoke student anxiety were addressed. This teaching technique always worked well for me. Since many cartoonists present social science topics in a humorous light, I felt cartoons could be used both as a way to lower student anxieties and as an actual framework to investigate social phenomena. From that very first cartoon I used in a class, student response has been overwhelmingly favorable. Through personal research and from written comments on my student evaluations, I have found that students not only report this to be a fun, novel teaching technique but often cartoon examples are also seen as more applicable to their own lives, easier to understand; overall, they do appear to reduce student math/statistics anxiety.

Although I used a textbook the first couple of times I taught statistics, these materials seemed to be largely written for instructor instead of student needs. As such, I found that most statistics textbooks are of little pedagogical value to the average student (this is especially true for social science students) and I have only used one twice in the 15+ times I have taught this class. (Please see accompanying *Teaching Sociology* article on textbooks in statistics.) In place of a textbook, I have created a rather extensive set of take-home exercises for my classes based on cartoons. Moreover, all of the quizzes and exams in my classes are based on cartoon examples, as are most classroom presentations. This textbook is quite simply an outgrowth of this material.

There are three distinct features about this textbook that differentiate it from others. First, although this textbook is a comprehensive survey of statistical techniques found in most texts, it is still written at a level that the average behavioral or social science student can understand. Second, using cartoons in a statistics textbook not only makes traditionally dry material fun, but in many cases it actually reduces student anxiety. Finally, as an outgrowth of the first two features, I believe that this is one of the first statistics textbooks written with the student explicitly in mind. As such, I hope this textbook and the pedagogical techniques it advocates assist in the creation of a successful learning environment for both the instructor and the students.

I thank Brad Stewart for his editorial assistance on Chapters 1–6 and truly wish he would have been able to see this project through to its completion. I also thank professors Dan Pence of Southern Utah University, Robin Franck of Southwestern College, Diane Pike of Augsburg College, Michael Lacy of Colorado State University, and Victoria Swigert of the College of the Holy Cross for their detailed and thoughtful reviews. Their comments were quite helpful in my attempt to make this a truly user-friendly text. Special thanks are due Professor Ken Berry of Colorado State University. Although he was not directly involved in this project, many of his ideas and techniques for teaching statistics are found in this text.

—STEVEN P. SCHACHT

1
Introduction

We are willing to bet that you and many of the students in your class may read this first sentence with a fair amount of disdain. After all, statistics is often viewed as one of the most unpleasant and, in some cases, most difficult of all the required college classes. As such, and as reflected in Cartoon 1.1, perhaps many of you are also math atheists.

In many years of teaching statistics, we have found that these two adverse attitudes toward statistics—that it is an unpleasant and difficult subject—are a result of several misperceived notions that many students hold. Not all students despise the thought of having to take a statistics class, however, and some, believe it or not, actually look forward to taking this class.

Through research and classroom observations we have found several common themes for why most students do not look forward to taking a statistics class. First, many students in the social and behavioral sciences often view themselves as incapable of undertaking anything but fairly simple mathematical operations. In fact, many students select a major in the social or behavioral sciences because of the belief that they are inept at any mathematically oriented subjects. Correspondingly, because of this attitude many students also experience math anxiety and, not surprisingly, try to avoid any classes that will elicit this feeling.

Further, students who have not taken a statistics class often question the utility of such a course to their "academic learning experience"—often believing that its only value is

Cartoon 1.1   CALVIN AND HOBBES

that it fulfills a graduation requirement. This general adversity to statistics is also a result of the widespread student attitude that statistics have very little applicability to other college courses, to the students' careers, or to life in general. Perhaps this explains why so many students postpone taking statistics until their senior year. Of course, this often causes students to have additional anxieties: "If I fail this class, I won't graduate this term." In total, these sentiments often lead to an overriding attitude that a statistics course will be a potentially painful and basically worthless experience.

Why Learn Statistics?

The rest of this textbook is written to dispel these negative *myths*, but some preliminary arguments about the utility of statistics are warranted. If you agree with the adage that "there are lies, damn lies, and statistics," then you already have a very good idea of the potential value of taking this course (this paraphrased sentiment was initially put forth by Mark Twain). Regardless of your chosen career, you constantly will be presented with statistical information. Your boss might want you to review a recent statistical report on the demographics of the county to estimate future social service demand, for instance, or the instructor for your theory class may require statistical evidence to support a research paper you are writing for his or her class.

Whenever those who are not knowledgeable in statistics come across any statistically based information, they have to either unquestionably accept what others have concluded from it (assuming they even understand this) or find someone to interpret the data for them—which can be quite expensive. Either way, they run the risk of being deceived or even outright lied to because of statistical ignorance. As summarized by another paraphrased saying: "Figures often lie and liars often figure." Such ignorance potentially can be costly to both an employer and a career. Quite simply, being knowledgeable in statistics is an asset to anyone's career aspirations.

Outside of our workplaces, moreover, we are bombarded daily by statistical information. Like it or not, we live in a statistical society. Everything—from your car insurance rates, opinion polls, weather reports, and crime rates to consumer information—is based on statistics. Being conversant in elementary statistics makes each of us a better consumer who is less likely to be "ripped off" in a purchase. Additionally, and perhaps more importantly, statistical knowledge makes us better-informed citizens and allows us to view more rationally the social issues that confront us.

In summary (and at the risk of sounding redundant), like it or not, we reside in a statistical world and we are also users of statistics. Thus, regardless of one's chosen major or career, having a basic, rudimentary understanding of statistics is an asset to anyone who hopes to get ahead—or even stay even—in today's society. With these preliminary thoughts in mind, we now turn to the goals of this text and how they will ultimately make the task of becoming statistically informed a much easier accomplishment than you probably ever thought possible.

Goals of This Textbook

Research has found that social and behavioral science students often dislike statistics because they suffer from math/statistics anxiety. After all, as reflected in Cartoon 1.2, certain majors (e.g., humanities and social and behavioral sciences) are supposed to minimize the number of math-oriented classes a student has to take. Math/statistics anxiety usually takes the form of students fearing that they will do poorly or fail a given statistics class because they are incapable of doing the required math—a fear that often becomes self-fulfilling.

Students suffering from such anxiety, regardless of how mathematically inclined they are, almost always experience more difficulties learning the material than those who do not have this affliction. Moreover, people who suffer from high levels of math anxiety often try to keep their feelings secret. This, unfortunately, precludes students from seeking help from classmates and teachers. As many of you have probably guessed, extreme cases of math/statistics anxiety that are not recognized and dealt with in some meaningful manner can often result in student failure.

Not surprisingly then, often students' math anxiety also frustrates instructors. Some instructors' inability to recognize this very real classroom problem leads them to wrongly conclude that these students are lazy and unprepared. Such a false impression combined with students' real anxieties (albeit these, too, almost always are unfounded) creates a vicious cycle where a negative learning environment becomes an unfortunate—but inevitable—outcome. Although the problem of math/statistics anxiety is often quite real for both the student and the instructor, fortunately it is always unnecessary.

The first goal of this textbook, therefore, is to reduce each student's statistical anxiety. As noted, this book approaches statistics far differently from any other. Not only is this text written in a manner that addresses students' anxieties, it utilizes a specific medium that we have found successful in dealing with this problem: cartoons.

Humor is an excellent way to deal with anxiety. For instance, have you ever noticed that people often laugh when they are nervous or uncertain about something? Such laughter serves to reduce tension and anxiety. This same principle can be applied to math anxiety. Specifically, we use cartoons, such as the two presented here, to make humorous the statistical presentations that are often perceived as boring, intimidating, and difficult.

Cartoon 1.2   FRANK AND ERNEST

FRANK & ERNEST reprinted by permission of Newspaper Enterprise Association, Inc.

We have found that being able to laugh at the given material with a cartoon almost always reduces the amount of math/statistics anxieties present. Reducing anxieties ultimately allows students to more easily learn and retain statistical principles and operations that are in reality—at least at the introductory level—not that difficult. Approaching a subject such as statistics by using humor can actually make learning the material a fun experience.

Further, in an attempt to reduce any remaining math anxieties you might have, it should be noted that since this is an introductory statistics course, a strong math background is not required or assumed. If you are comfortable with the basic mathematical operations of addition, subtraction, multiplication, division, how to square a number, and how to obtain a square root—all operations found on the most basic of calculators—you should not have any problems with the math found in this textbook. Moreover, all of these basic operations are comprehensively and contextually reviewed in Chapter 2.

In sum, with cartoons serving as a common medium, this textbook is concerned with offering each student an introduction to statistics. Fundamental ideas and concepts (formulas) that most statistical analysis is based upon are presented in a basic, systematic, and—we hope—humorous manner. The presentations are structured so that each student will gain an understanding of the practical, applied nature of statistics. Almost every presentation begins with a non-intimidating, often absurd, cartoon example typically followed by a real-life example. In other words, the overall goals are twofold: (1) to reduce each student's potential anxieties about statistics, and (2) to demonstrate the utility of having a working knowledge of statistics.

This is not to say that this is a watered down, overly simplistic textbook. It is not. All concepts found in similar introductory statistics textbooks are comprehensively covered in this text. Unlike every other statistics textbook that we know of, however, this textbook is truly and explicitly written for you, the student. Assuredly, one of the reasons your instructor selected this text is because of its student emphasis, so we are guessing that you will not find this course to be the painful, basically worthless experience you might have expected. Rather, we are willing to wager (with the odds definitely in our favor) that you will find that statistics are a meaningful, sometimes funny way of describing and understanding our world.

What Are Statistics?

The foremost goals of the social and behavioral sciences are to *describe* and *explain* different types of social, psychological, and behavioral phenomena. That is, social and behavioral scientists ultimately strive to understand how individual characteristics relate to and potentially affect each other. Individual characteristics also are called variables. As the word implies, variables are characteristics that vary (*vari*ables) in some measurable way from unit to unit.

When relationships between variables are explored, one characteristic (called the *independent variable*) is often viewed as the cause of change in another characteristic (called

> **Box 1.1   Beer, Taxes, Pirates, Gambling and Watching the Grass Grow: The Origins of Statistics**
>
>
>
> Sorry, but despite the authors' numerous requests there is no beer contained within the pages of this book. Without beer, however, modern statistics would be very different—although it is not because doing statistics drives people to drink.
>
> Research statistics, as currently used in behavioral and social research, is of fairly recent origin. The roots of the study and practice of statistics, however, truly can be traced to beer, gambling, pirates, war, and taxes. The term statistics itself is derived from the Latin word for "state" (*stato*) and literally means "state-math." Romans first used basic descriptive statistics (Chapters 3, 4, and 5) to keep track of the population size and resources. Such information was used in taxation and the planning of wars. More sophisticated methods were employed by people who insure maritime trade (throughout Europe) in estimating the costs of providing insurance against accident and piracy for ocean-going cargo ships. Much of our modern probability theory (Chapter 7) comes from studying games of chance. Further, the basic assumptions of hypothesis testing (Chapters 9, 10, 11, 12, and 13) were developed by William S. Gosset (1876–1937), an employee of the Guinness brewing company, to test the quality of grain used in making beer. Finally, many a statistics student has argued that only someone interested in watching grass grow would be interested in statistics. While this is certainly not true, it is true that modern statistics have been greatly refined by researchers in the agricultural sciences to track the productivity of crops and the influence of various farming practices.

the *dependent variable*). Independent and dependent variables are extensively discussed in subsequent chapters. At this point, however, it is important to realize that we explain and understand most social and behavioral phenomena in terms of relationships and causes.

An independent variable (or variables) quite simply is seen as bringing about change in a dependent variable (or variables). In other words, independent variables are seen as determinants of dependent variables. Examples of simple independent/dependent variable relationships are (a) years of education seen as a determinant of income, and (b) one's gender (and sexist attitudes) seen as determinant of one's major. While there is an infinite array of variables and possible relationships, they almost always are described in terms of independent and dependent variables.

Additionally, variables (individual characteristics) in the social and behavioral sciences are seen as occurring in one of three basic forms. Using Cartoon 1.1 and Calvin as a backdrop, we can describe these three types of characteristics as (1) *personal characteristics*, such as gender (Calvin is a male) or religious background (math atheism), (2) *attitudes*, such as the degrees of like or dislike of mathematical subjects (he has an apparent animosity towards math), and (3) personal *behaviors*, the way a person acts (apparently he also avoids mathematically oriented topics).

Then again, because the focus of any social scientist's research is that which is *social*, we are obviously not interested in how only one individual thinks and acts, but rather how a multitude of different types of people think and behave. For instance, it is funny and somewhat interesting to note that Calvin is a math atheist who doesn't like this subject and probably avoids it at all costs. But beyond Calvin, and his typically tortured existence reflected in this cartoon, who cares?

As social and behavioral scientists, however, what if we knew that numerous people in our society (including members of your class) were math atheists who avoided this topic at all costs? Not only would this be of great interest to us but to learn anything further we would need some meaningful way to describe and attempt to understand this phenomenon. This is what statistics enable us to do. While statistics as a scientific tool empowers us to do many things, at its most fundamental level it allows us to summarize quantitatively and to generalize social and behavioral phenomena so that we may better understand their occurrence and possibly control them.

Often, social phenomena are indicative of a social problem; here, math anxiety. Statistics can be used to describe and better understand nearly any social problem. So, while math anxiety is detrimental to student learning, the use of humor appears to reduce such anxieties. Moreover, new-found understandings almost inevitably lead to innovative ways of dealing with the social problem to be proposed and tested—like creating a cartoon-based statistics textbook.

All of this is not to say that statistics is the only meaningful, or even the best, way for social and behavioral scientists to gain new insights and understandings of phenomena. Studies using statistical analyses, however, are the most widely used and accepted form of research undertaken in the social and behavioral sciences.

Thus far, the term "statistics" has been used rather loosely without a formal definition being offered. Figure 1.1 (below) helps explain what statistics are and are not. Often it is easier to define what something is by first recognizing what it is not. As such, we first define what populations and parameters are and this, in turn, enables us to gain a more complete understanding of statistics.

Populations

To begin with and as reflected in Figure 1.1, statistics are obviously not populations. A population can be defined as nearly anything. Examples of things often defined as populations are: everyone in the United States, all the students at a given university, or a class-

Figure 1.1   Population Parameters and Sample Statistics

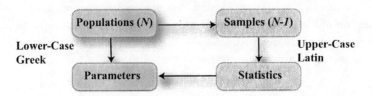

room of students. In practice, a scientist's research question usually dictates the population he or she is studying. If you were doing a study on the level of students' math/statistics anxiety in a given statistics class, for instance, then your population obviously is not students currently enrolled in an anthropology course. Rather, your population is students currently enrolled in the statistics class of interest. Students from one statistics class or several classes could be defined as the population, but only these types of students could be considered because that is what your research question dictates.

Once a population has been defined, then every unit within it is treated in an equal manner. Referring back to the statistics class example, if there were 30 students in the class and you defined them as your population, then all 30 students' math/statistics anxiety levels would have to be measured.

When a population is used, the answers to accompanying mathematical procedures (such as an average attention span) are called parameters. If in the present example, however, you excluded even one student and only measured twenty-nine subjects' anxiety level, then you would no longer have a population parameter but rather a sample statistic. In other words, measuring *anything* less than your *total* defined population no longer equals a population of values but instead a sample statistic. Before samples and statistics are explored, however, the math associated with populations first must be discussed.

Parameters

Referring back to Figure 1.1 and as just noted, the mathematics associated with populations are called *parameters*. Potential examples of parameters are averages, proportions, and percentages. The key to understanding a parameter is that every unit within the defined population must be utilized. So, again, if we defined our population to be 30 students in the hypothetical statistics course of interest, measured the math/statistics anxiety levels of all 30 students, and then calculated an average, the resultant answer would be a parameter. The mathematical notation typically associated with population parameters uses lower-case Greek letters (with the notable exception of N, which indicates the size of the population). Mathematical notation is defined and discussed in detail in the next chapter.

Additionally, population parameters are considered *descriptive*. That is, every element within the given population is considered, so any resultant summary measures—parameters—are correspondingly used to *describe* all members. For instance, building upon our previous example, let's say that on the first day of class we measured each student's level of math/statistics anxiety (for all 30 students) and found the class averages to be 8 (on a scale of 1 to 10; averages/means are discussed in detail in a subsequent chapter). Because every element (student) was mathematically considered, the reported value of 8 is an exact, single summary measure—description—of the entire population.

While statistics can also be used descriptively, more importantly they enable us to make *inferences* and to test *hypotheses*. To understand what these terms mean, we must finally turn to the task of defining samples and statistics.

Sample

As noted, a sample is defined as anything less than the entire population. Mathematically, a sample is expressed as $N-1$, where N equals the total number of elements within a given population. Almost always, however, a sample is a much smaller portion of a larger population. Using the statistics class example ($N = 30$), Figure 1.2 graphically demonstrates how a random sample can be drawn from a population. The term "random" and its importance are discussed below.

There are three primary reasons why social and behavioral scientists usually conduct research using a sample instead of a population. The first reason is that gathering data from even a small population is extremely *expensive*.

In the social and behavioral sciences we are often interested in large populations. Let's say, for example, that we are interested in the average income of a hypothetical community of 100,000 households. To obtain a parameter average income value we would have to interview every household—all 100,000 of them. Actually doing this would be extremely expensive, and quite unnecessary considering that a sample can give us a precise estimate of any parameter value. In fact, a sample of 400 households and their average incomes would give us a fairly accurate estimate of all 100,000 households for a fraction of the cost of obtaining the parameter average.

The second reason for using samples is that to obtain complete information from even small populations is not only expensive but also an extremely *time*-consuming process. Samples are often used because it simply takes too long to gather data from a complete population.

Using our same example of 100,000 households and assuming that we had the resources, it would take dozens of interviewers months to obtain every household's

Figure 1.2   Drawing a Sample from a Population

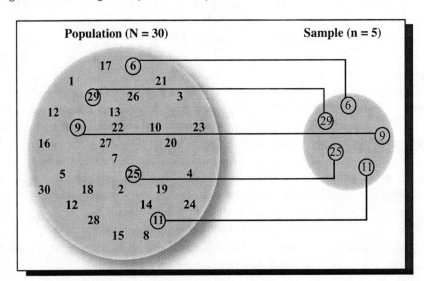

income. Additionally, over a period of months each household's income could drastically change due to inflation, unemployment, or other circumstances. This potentially could render any final parameter obtained meaningless, because it may no longer be true.

The problem of time constraints is even further compounded with attitudinal surveys. For instance, let's say we are interested in approval ratings of the current president. Obviously, however, sentiments on nearly any issue vary over time; with topics such as the president's approval ratings, they sometimes change literally overnight. In other words, a position initially expressed may no longer be true even days later. Exactly because of time constraints and the adverse effect they can have on findings, most political polls (samples) are conducted overnight or within a twenty-four-hour period.

In sum, since social scientists' research subjects are actual people who are constantly changing, most data collection efforts must be completed in a timely manner. A sample is a far more efficient way (sometimes it is the only way) of rapidly collecting information on a population of people.

This leads us to the third related reason for samples: it often is *impossible* to gather a population of information. Even in situations where we might have the money and time to guard against the possibility of changing sentiments, we could not expect to reach all potential respondents. People might be at work, out of town on business or vacation, in the hospital, or simply unavailable. Moreover, these potential availability problems don't even take into account people who might refuse to participate in the study. In other words, when people can't be located or if they refuse to participate we are left with a sample by default ($N-1$). In total, not only is it usually impractical due to time and financial constraints to interview everyone in a defined population, but it is often impossible.

This is equally true in other fields. When you have a blood test at the doctor's office, would you rather have a sample or a population drawn to be analyzed? In industry, companies often make claims about the longevity of their products. For instance, GE might make the claim that its light bulb has an average life of 400 hours or its batteries last an average of forty hours. How do they arrive at these figures? They simply test a sample of the given product. To do otherwise would require that all the units were used—such as a population of burned-out light bulbs—and this would leave the company no products to sell.

Then again, many of these same considerations for why samples are drawn are applicable to life in general. When you come across milk that you suspect has spoiled or foods that you think you might dislike, do you consume all of the given substance or simply take a *sample*? If you come to college without a selected major, should you take all the courses offered at the given school to make this decision or just a few introductory courses in field areas that potentially interest you? A sample is not only the most logical choice, but it is by far the most feasible way to answer any of the above questions. In other words, we are all already users of samples.

In sum, samples are not only a practical way to collect data, personally and scientifically, but sometimes they are the only way in which information from a large population can be collected. With this in mind, we are now ready to discuss what the math associated with samples (statistics) enables us to do: make *inferences* about population parameters and test hypotheses.

Statistics

Finally we arrive at a basic definition for *statistics*: quite simply, the math associated with samples. Statistics are obviously much more than this, but at their most basic level of meaning they are "sample math." The mathematical notation typically used to represent statistics uses upper-case Latin letters.

Before proceeding to a fuller discussion of statistics and what they enable us to do, two key assumptions concerning sample statistics must be discussed: *randomness* and *representativeness*. For the purpose of this text, randomness means that once a given population has been defined, typically in the form of a list, then every unit has an equal chance of being selected. This can be accomplished two basic ways: (1) We can systematically take every "*n*th" unit from a population list, or (2) we can randomly select the units with a table of random numbers or a calculator that randomly generates numbers. Either way, the underlying assumption of randomness is that each sampling unit has an equal chance of being selected. In Figure 1.2, a sample of 5 drawn from a population of 30 was drawn—the numbers selected—using a table of random numbers.

If a sample is randomly generated, then it is also usually thought to be representative. The assumption of representativeness simply means the sample drawn reflects—represents—the larger population. Although we can never absolutely prove it, randomly selected samples are always generated with the idea that they are representative of the larger population from which they were drawn. If a sample is not randomly generated then, statistically speaking, we cannot assume it to be representative of the larger population from which it was selected.

When a random sample is considered representative, resultant statistics are not only used to describe a sample but are also used to make inferences and hypothesis tests. *Inferences* quite simply are *estimates* of population parameters. Thus, a given sample average is the best and most logical estimate of the true parameter average. Comparisons of averages representing different groups within the sample are also often undertaken; this is a form of *testing hypotheses*. While both of these procedures are discussed in detail in subsequent chapters, estimating population parameters and hypothesis testing are the two basic ways that statistics are utilized.

Descriptive Versus Inferential Statistics

Many statisticians find it useful also to differentiate between descriptive and inferential statistics. The distinction between these two terms is really an expansion of our discussion so far and is further illustrated in Figure 1.3. As noted, all population parameters are descriptive. That is, parameters describe certain characteristics of a population. These descriptions can be averages, proportions, or numerous other mathematical calculations of a variable. They can also describe the relationship between two or more variables. However, the resulting findings cannot be generalized beyond the population from which they were generated. Thus, population parameters are always descriptive.

Statistics are also used in a similar manner. Correspondingly, they are called *descriptive statistics*. Identical to parameters, descriptive statistics are used to summarize a given variable. Also, like parameters, they simply summarize the values from which they are generated and are not used to make generalizations. The only difference between the two is that descriptive statistics are calculated using a sample while parameters are derived from a population of values. While this differentiation has important implications for how certain formulas are actually calculated, parameters and descriptive statistics are used to the exact same end: to *describe* a set of numbers.

Inferential statistics, however, are quite simply the previously outlined estimates of population parameters and hypothesis testing. As you probably have concluded, they are also extremely important to social and behavioral science research. Although there are other equally meaningful ways that scientists gather data, only inferential statistics enable us to make scientific generalizations about large groups of people. Using a random sample that is usually just a fraction of the larger population from which it was drawn, inferential statistics enable us to make relatively inexpensive and timely generalizations. Moreover, as noted, using a sample sometimes is the only way in which information about a population can be gathered.

In total, inferential statistics are important, powerful scientific tools available to anyone who hopes to better understand the social world we all reside in. We think that individuals who understand how statistics are calculated and what they represent, correspondingly, are often in a position to better understand our social world. While it is doubtful that we could convince Calvin of the value of understanding mathematics and statistics, especially considering that he is generally a strong proponent of an "ignorance-is-bliss" mentality (just ask Hobbes), we hope that you now have a preliminary indication as to why such knowledge might be worth having. Of course, this is only an "inference."

Figure 1.3 Descriptive Versus Inferential Statistics

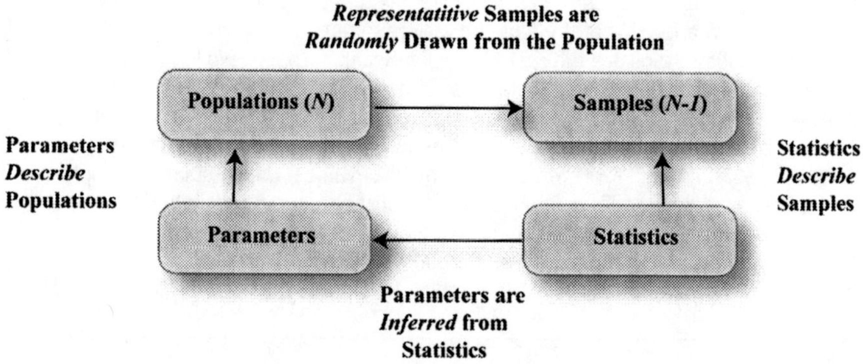

Chapter Summary and Conclusions

This chapter offered some basic definitions of what statistics are and are not. Although statistics are obviously not populations or parameters, they are directly related to these terms. Populations can be defined as nearly anything—every resident of your state or every student in your statistics class are both potential examples of populations. The math associated with populations are called parameters, and parameters are always descriptive.

Alternatively, statistics are quite simply the math associated with samples. Samples instead of populations are often utilized in the social and behavioral sciences because they are cost effective, timely, and practical. Statistics are either descriptive or inferential. Descriptive statistics are used to summarize variables and variable relationships. Inferential statistics, however, are used to scientifically estimate population parameters and test hypotheses. As such, inferential statistics are vital tools that social and behavioral scientists use.

Finally, this chapter offered some preliminary reasons why learning how to use and understand statistics might be of great value to you. It also was recognized that for students to make this realization, their math/statistics anxieties must be not only recognized but also dealt with in some meaningful manner. Your instructor, by selecting this textbook, must also think that this an important issue. Using cartoons, the rest of this textbook is devoted to alleviating student anxieties so that we can demonstrate how statistics can be used as a meaningful, sometimes funny way of better understanding social reality.

Box 1.2   Sports and Parameters

Often you will hear sports announcers say things like: "Kirby Puckett of the Minnesota Twins—on the way to winning the 1989 American League batting title—had career-high 'statistics'." Similarly, most newspapers and sports magazines also report the accomplishments of athletes as statistics: individual statistics, team statistics, pitching statistics, or quarterback statistics, to mention a few. What they are actually reporting are parameters.

Recall that statistics are the math associated with samples, while parameters are the math associated with populations. Thus, when a quarterback is reported as having a 55% pass-completion rate, this value is calculated by taking the number of all successful passes and dividing by the number of all attempted passes. Because "all attempts" represents a population of values, the calculated completion rate is a parameter. To actually create a statistic we would have to take a sample of all attempts.

Then again, which sounds better, the San Francisco 49ers team statistics or parameters? Perhaps this explains the continued misuse of the term "statistics."

Key Terms to Remember

- Descriptive Statistics
- Populations
- Parameters
- Estimates of Parameters
- Independent and Dependent Variables

- Hypothesis Testing
- Statistics
- Inferential Statistics
- Samples

Practice Exercises

1. If we talk about a baseball player's batting average and view it in terms of all trips to the plate, then this is a _____, not a _____.

2. Three reasons were offered in this chapter for why social scientists typically utilize a sample instead of a population. They are:
    1. _____
    2. _____
    3. _____

3. Characteristics measured in the social and behavioral sciences, such as age or income, that vary from person to person or unit to unit are called _____.

4. Variables in the social and behavioral sciences were proposed as occurring in one of three basic forms.
    These are:
    1. _____
    2. _____
    3. _____

5. Through research and personal observations, we have found that using humor, specifically cartoons, is an excellent way to reduce students' math/statistics anxiety. Thus, our two variables of research interest are humor and math/statistics anxiety. As such, _____ is seen as the independent variable, while _____ is seen as the dependent variable.

6. As evidenced in Cartoon 1.1, Calvin apparently experiences such high levels of math anxiety that he has become a math atheist. Correspondingly, he tries to avoid any mathematically oriented topics. In this instance, math avoidance is seen as the _____ variable, while math anxiety is seen as the _____ variable.

7. Statistics that are used to summarize a given variable are called _____ statistics.

8. Statistics that are used to estimate population parameters or to test hypotheses are called _____ statistics.

9. Conversely, inferential statistics enable us to do two basic things. These are
   1. _____
   2. _____

2

Basic Mathematical Concepts

The previous chapter offered an introduction to both the applicability and utility of statistics. Before proceeding to actual statistical analyses, however, we must present a basic discussion of mathematical concepts. Although those who are more mathematically versed may find this chapter to be an overly simplistic review, we suspect that most readers will find it to be quite useful.

Regardless of one's math background, the rest of the text simply builds upon the following presentation, so all students should thoroughly familiarize themselves with it. To assist you, this chapter is written in a manner that even those lacking math backgrounds should find quite simple to follow and understand. As the rest of the text is nothing more than variations of the mathematical concepts explored in this chapter, you should take this to be a quite promising sign—a strong indication that you will successfully survive this course.

This chapter ends with a discussion of levels of data measurement found in statistical analyses. Although this material is also quite easy to understand, it is imperative that you become familiar with it, too, because levels of measurement are determinants of what types of statistical analyses are subsequently utilized.

Math As a Recipe

All of us, at one time or another, have prepared and cooked food. In learning to do so, most of us followed a recipe. A recipe, offered by another person or found on a card/package, is quite simply the cooking directions for a given dish. Failure to follow such directions, as many of us can sadly attest, leads to ruined food and sometimes to an empty stomach.

To a certain extent, mathematical formulas can be likened to recipes. That is, the elements used to give instructions with a recipe are quite similar to those used with a mathematical formula. These elements are ingredients, amounts, operations, and order. Also, similar to when using a recipe, failure to follow the correct directions of a given formula, not surprisingly, causes the resultant answer to be wrong. This becomes exceedingly clear as we explore the following analogy.

Ingredients

The ingredients used in recipes are quite simply the materials to be prepared and cooked. These include things such as flour, sugar, yeast, and salt. There are also ingredients in statistical formulas and these, as discussed in Chapter 1, are *variables*. Recall that variables are any measurable social characteristics (e.g., age, gender, or a recent exam score). Mathematically, variables are often represented by letters; statisticians often use the letters *X, Y,* or *Z*. In a very real sense, variables measuring distinct elements are like the flavors of a meal, different variables are considered together and a whole new element/flavor often emerges.

Amounts

Recipes also include the amounts of the different ingredients to be used. For instance, a recipe might call for two cups of sugar, one teaspoon of baking soda, and eight ounces of milk. In other words, amounts are *numerical* values of different ingredients: *two* cups, *one* teaspoon, and *eight* ounces. This is also true in mathematical/statistical formulas. For example, a person can be 30 years old and make $30,000 a year. The values of 30 and 30,000 are, respectively, amounts of the variables of *age* and *yearly income*.

Operations

Recipes also require the completion of certain operations. For instance, in making a pizza crust from scratch, one must *knead* the dough and *spread* it on a pan. Specific operations are also required in math/statistical formulas; these are the familiar operations of *addition, subtraction, multiplication,* and *division*.

Order

To be a successful cook, one must not only use the specified ingredients in certain amounts and perform the right operations, but all of the operations must be done in a specific order. Using the pizza crust example again, one must (1) *knead* the dough before it can be (2) *spread* onto a pan to be subsequently (3) *baked.* If these operations are not completed in the correct order (for example, baking the dough before it is spread onto the pan), one ends up with a culinary disaster instead of a delight.

A certain order to the operations must also be followed on mathematical/statistical formulas. As many of you are aware, these are called the *rules of algebraic order.*

Table 2.1 summarizes the specific order in which mathematical operations must be completed. First, all operations in parentheses (e.g., $X - Y$) are completed. Second, are all operations of exponentiation (e.g., the number 3 squared). Third (after the first two operations are finished), and in this order all operations of multiplication and/or division are

Table 2.1   Rules of Algebraic Order

Algebraic Order
1. (   )
2. exponentiation
3. × and/or ÷
4. + and/or −

undertaken. The final mathematical operations completed are addition and/or subtraction.

The rules of algebraic order are not only applied to the material found on the remaining pages of this chapter but also to the rest of this text, so if you are not completely familiar with them, you are strongly urged to either mark this page or write the rules down somewhere prominently in your notes. After all, like recipes and cooking, when using mathematical formulas if one fails to follow all the operations in the specific order asked, then any results will be a disaster—*the wrong answer.*

Summation Notation

Recipe instructions often make use of abbreviations and special symbols such as cups (c.), tablespoons (Tbsp.), or teaspoons (tsp.). Mathematical formulas also use special symbols and abbreviations as instructions. While many of these are the familiar symbols used to represent basic mathematical operations (×, ÷, +, and -), some symbols used in statistical formulas may appear quite foreign. More specifically, most statistical formulas use specialized symbols to represent an additional mathematical operation called summation notation. Actually, this procedure is a variant of a mathematical operation you are already quite familiar with: addition. Regardless, to best demonstrate what this mathematical symbol instructs us to do, we finally must undertake some mathematical calculations.

To assist in this discussion, we offer Cartoon 2.1 and its corresponding data sets found in Table 2.2. The first *data set* (the group of numbers found under the X column heading) is measurements of the variable (level of desire for a "bush" in the White House) for ten different dogs. More specifically, on a scale of 1 (low) to 10 (high), this first set of scores represents ten dogs' self-reported levels of desire—*do not* to do—for a bush in the White House. The second set of numbers, found under the Y, represents the number of times one was used from 1989 to 1993. In other words, the second data set represents the

Cartoon 2.1   FRANK & ERNEST

FRANK & ERNEST reprinted by permission of Newspaper Enterprise Association, Inc.

Table 2.2   Bush-In-the-White House Data Set

Dog	Desire a "bush" in the White House (X) Independent Variable	Number of Times a "bush" was Used (Y) Dependent Variable
1	1	2
2	2	2
3	3	3
4	4	5
5	4	7
6	5	9
7	5	11
8	7	11
9	8	12
10	9	13

variable "number of times a bush was used" by the same ten dogs whose level of desire for a bush in the White House was also measured.

We can also view these two data sets as representing an independent and dependent variable. In fact, the letters X and Y are traditionally used by statisticians to present, respectively, independent (X) and dependent (Y) variables. (If the terms "independent variable" or "dependent variable" are at all confusing to you, please refer back to Chapter 1 for a more detailed discussion.)

Box 2.1   Real-Life Statistics

We should note that the above data sets and most of the data sets that follow in this text are simply made up as what we hope are fun examples. This is not to say, however, that the examples given are not applicable to real-life situations. To the contrary, every example found in this text is potentially applicable to some real-life circumstance.

While the present cartoon example may seem somewhat absurd (as we noted) for instance, math phobia (anxiety) really can adversely affect an individual's performance when answering a mathematical problem. Thus, alternatively viewing the values reported for the independent variable (X) in Table 2.2 as level of math/statistics anxiety and the dependent variable (Y) values as "incorrect answers" on a recent twenty-five-question statistics exam, the data sets would then potentially reflect a real-life situation; math/statistics anxiety adversely affects students' math exam scores.

So, although they often appear seemingly absurd, the examples found in this text are still realistic insofar as one's imagination makes them such. We believe that using one's imagination (and humor) not only makes the reasoning behind statistics easier to grasp, it also makes learning the material more fun.

For the present example, then, the independent variable is self-reported level of desire for a bush in the White House (X) whereas the dependent variable is number of times one was used (Y). As such, desire for a bush is conceptualized (seen) as a determinant (a cause) of the usage. When the two data sets are considered together, as desire for a bush levels increase, the number of times a dog uses a bush in the White House correspondingly increases. With this in mind, let's say we are given the following simple mathematical formula called the "sum of X." (As we will see, this is actually a sub-part of several larger statistical formulas. For this and the next few examples, however, more simply we will refer to these formula sub-parts as "formulas.")

Sum of X: ΣX

You are already familiar with the X in this formula, it informs us that we are dealing with an independent variable. The symbol that precedes X, Σ, is called sigma. Sigma, in mathematical terms, denotes summation. Or, stated slightly differently, sigma instructs us to sum a set of numbers. This is an example of summation notation. Applied to the "desire" data set (column 1 of Table 2.2), the sum of X instructs us to add together all observed X values. Done below, the sum of X is 48.

$$1 + 2 + 3 + 4 + 4 + 5 + 5 + 7 + 8 + 9 = 48$$

Alternatively, if the ΣY is asked for, it is calculated by simply taking all Y values and summing them together; with the above data set, this is:

$$2 + 2 + 3 + 5 + 7 + 9 + 11 + 11 + 12 + 13 = 75.$$

In slightly more complicated statistical formulas that involve the use of summation notation, the rules of algebraic order (discussed previously) must also be applied. Unfortunately, however, we have found that some students often become confused when summation notation is used simultaneously with the rules of algebraic order. As such, and considering that most statistical formulas use both of these statistical procedures, we suggest that you pay special attention to the discussion that follows.

Found below are two formulas that appear to be similar, but are mathematically quite different. That is, while both formulas instruct us to sum and square values of the independent variable (X), because of the rules of algebraic order these operations are completed in basically opposite sequences. As a result, when these two formulas are applied to the exact same set of numbers, two very different answers are obtained.

Sum of All Squared X Values	Sum of X Values Squared
ΣX^2	$(\Sigma X)^2$

Thus, the first formula, appropriately labeled "Sum of All Squared X Values," tells us to separately square each of the X values (each observed value is multiplied by itself, e.g., $2 \times 2 = 4$ or $8 \times 8 = 64$), and then add them together. The reason for this specific order is that, once again, *exponentiation* precedes *addition*. Applying this formula to the first bush-in-the-White-House data set, then, we first individually square each X value. This is accomplished below.

$$1 \times 1 = 1 \qquad 2 \times 2 = 4 \qquad 3 \times 3 = 9 \qquad 4 \times 4 = 16 \qquad 4 \times 4 = 16$$

$$5 \times 5 = 25 \qquad 5 \times 5 = 25 \qquad 7 \times 7 = 49 \qquad 8 \times 8 = 64 \qquad 9 \times 9 = 81$$

Next, as demonstrated below, to derive the final answer we simply add these ten separate answers together. Thus, the sum of all squared X values is 290.

$$1 + 4 + 9 + 16 + 16 + 25 + 25 + 49 + 64 + 81 = 290$$

Thus, the ΣX^2 equals $\boxed{290}$

In the second formula, labeled "Sum of X Values Squared," we are instructed to add together all the X values, and then square this single value to get the final answer. Once again, the reason for this, as dictated by the rules of algebraic order, is that mathematical operations *within parentheses* (even when adding) always precede *exponentiation*.

When this second formula is applied to the same data set, as expected, we get a very different answer. Calculated below, we find that the sum of X values squared equals 2304 (versus 290).

$$1 + 2 + 3 + 4 + 4 + 5 + 5 + 7 + 8 + 9 = 48. \text{ And then } (48)^2 = 2304.$$

Thus, the $(\Sigma X)^2$ equals $\boxed{2304}$

As you might think, there are numerous other ways that the rules of algebraic order and summation notation can be applied in different statistical formulas. While the calculation of the sum of all squared X values and/or the sum of X squared values are required in many statistical formulas, there are other applications that are also widely used. As such, and to assist in later presentations, we briefly review a few of the more commonly used applications.

The following two (sub)formulas (or variants of them) are used in several statistical formulas. While both of these formulas instruct us to multiply the X value by the Y value, when this operation is actually completed it is once again wholly dependent upon the rules of algebraic order. (Unless otherwise specified, when values are found directly next to each other, this mathematically denotes multiplication.)

$$(\Sigma X)(\Sigma Y) = (\Sigma X) \times (\Sigma Y)$$
$$(\Sigma X)^2 (\Sigma Y)^2 = (\Sigma X)^2 \times (\Sigma Y)^2$$

Specifically, the first formula tells us to add together the X values, to add together all the Y values, and then to multiply these two values together to obtain the final answer: *parentheses*, then *multiplication*. Conversely, the second formula also tells us to add together the X values and to add together the Y values; but before the resultant answers are multiplied together, each sum must be individually squared: *parentheses*, *exponentiation*, and then *multiplication*.

Applied to bush-in-the-White House data sets (Table 2.2), each of these formulas, respectively, is mathematically summarized below. Thus, the sum of X multiplied by the sum of Y equals 3600:

$$(\textstyle\sum X) = 1 + 2 + 3 + 4 + 4 + 5 + 5 + 7 + 8 + 9 = \boxed{48}$$

and then

$$(\textstyle\sum Y) = 2 + 2 + 3 + 5 + 7 + 9 + 11 + 11 + 12 + 13 = \boxed{75}$$

$$(48)\,(75) = \boxed{3600} = (\textstyle\sum X)\,(\textstyle\sum Y)$$

However, the sum of X squared multiplied by the sum of Y squared equals 12,960,000:

$$(\textstyle\sum X) = 1 + 2 + 3 + 4 + 4 + 5 + 5 + 7 + 8 + 9 = \boxed{48}$$

and then

$$(\textstyle\sum Y) = 2 + 2 + 3 + 5 + 7 + 9 + 11 + 11 + 12 + 13 = \boxed{75}$$

$$(48)^2 = 2304 \; ; \; (75)^2 = \boxed{5625}$$

and then

$$(2304)\,(5625) = \boxed{12{,}960{,}000} = (\textstyle\sum X)^2(\textstyle\sum Y)^2$$

While all of the statistical formulas found in this text are composed of the above subparts (or slight variants of them), to summarize the discussion of algebraic order and summation notation we offer the following formula. This formula is an actual statistical measure of what is called sample variance (applied to a dependent variable [Y] in this example) and is discussed in detail in a subsequent chapter. For now, let's just focus on the order of the mathematical operations called for in this formula:

$$\underline{\text{Sample Variance}} = \frac{\sum Y^2 - \dfrac{(\sum Y)^2}{n}}{n-1}$$

Note that this formula has two dividing points in its presentation. As most of you probably know, this tells us to divide the numerator portion of the formula (symbols above the line) by the denominator (symbols below the line). Moreover, these dividing points—lines—also serve as a variant form of parentheses; that is, the operations above and below these lines must be completed before this type of division is done.

To this end, we obviously have to determine three different values represented in this formula; the sum of all squared Y values ΣY^2, the sum of Y values squared $(\Sigma Y)^2$, and the newly introduced letter n that appears twice in this formula. Recall that the first two sub-formulas, now applied to a dependent variable (Y), were previously calculated using the "desire" (X) data set. The lower-case letter n represents the size of a given sample data set (versus an upper-case N that represents the size of a population of numbers). With this in mind, and using the previously offered "usage" data set (Table 2.2), let's actually do the calculations required for this formula (sample variance).

Working from left to right on the formula, we first determine the sum of all squared Y values; each of the Y values is squared and then added together.

$$2 \times 2 = 4 \qquad 2 \times 2 = 4 \qquad 3 \times 3 = 9 \qquad 5 \times 5 = 25 \qquad 7 \times 7 = 49$$

$$9 \times 9 = 81 \qquad 11 \times 11 = 121 \qquad 12 \times 12 = 144 \qquad 13 \times 13 = 169$$

and thus

$$\Sigma Y^2 = 4 + 4 + 9 + 25 + 49 + 81 + 121 + 121 + 144 + 169 = \boxed{727}$$

Next, we calculate the sum of Y values squared; all the Y values are added together, and then squared as shown below.

$$(\Sigma Y)^2 = (2 + 2 + 3 + 5 + 7 + 9 + 11 + 11 + 12 + 13)^2 = (75)^2 = \boxed{5625}$$

The n or sample size, again, is the number of research subjects measured. In the present case, there are 10 research subjects/dogs (measurements of Y); thus, $n = 10$. Because we now know each of the values called for in the formula, we simply plug them into it.

$$\frac{727 - \dfrac{(75)^2}{10}}{10 - 1} = \frac{727 - \dfrac{5625}{10}}{9} = \frac{727 - 562.5}{9} = \frac{164.5}{9} = \boxed{18.2777}$$

Thus, the final answer is $18.277\overline{7}$.

Before proceeding, three brief observations are warranted concerning the above calculations. First, instead of giving confusing rules of when to round up or down when fractions are encountered, in this text we simply carry all calculations to the fourth decimal point and report final answers exactly as they are found on the calculator's register. Thus, we report the above answer to be 18.2777. This brings us to our second noteworthy observation: The bar above the very last value found in this answer, as many of you know, tells us that the 7 repeats infinitely.

Finally, and perhaps most importantly, if you can do the above operations correctly, you should take this to be a very promising sign. After all, the rest of the text is simple variations of the above calculations. If, however, any of the above material is confusing, please review it before proceeding.

More Practice with Summation Notation

The preceding summation formulas are all quite common and are used extensively throughout this text. We next turn to some less common notation formulas that illustrate some useful strategies for interpreting new formulas when you encounter them. Some of these formulas are used in later chapters, while other formulas are purely illustrative.

A common procedure in statistics requires combining information from both the independent (X) and dependent (Y) variables. For example, ΣXY (the sum of X times Y) says to first multiply each X value by its corresponding Y value and then sum the resulting values (products): *multiplication* then *addition*. This could also be expressed as $\Sigma(XY)$: *parentheses* then *addition*. This type of summation procedure is used extensively in chapters 10, 11, and 12.

Applied to the bush-in-the-White House data, this formula is summarized below. The sum of X times Y equals 453:

$$\Sigma XY =$$
$$(1)(2) + (2)(2) + (3)(3) + (4)(5) + (4)(7) + (5)(9) + (5)(11) + (7)(11) + (8)(12) + (9)(13) = ?$$
$$2 + 4 + 9 + 20 + 28 + 45 + 55 + 77 + 96 + 117 = \boxed{453}$$

New students of statistics often find it difficult to distinguish between $\Sigma X - 1$ and $\Sigma(X-1)$. $\Sigma X - 1$ instructs us to subtract 1 from the sum of X. In contrast, $\Sigma(X-1)$ instructs us to subtract 1 from every value of X (*parentheses* first) then sum the resulting values (*addition*). These summations further illustrate an important rule about using summation notation in formulas: In cases of addition/subtraction where there are no parentheses to guide you, do the summation first, then perform the addition/subtraction operations requested.

Using the White House data, these formulas are summarized below. Subtracting 1 from the sum of X is equal to 47.

$$\Sigma X = \boxed{48}$$
$$\Sigma X - 1 = 48 - 1 = \boxed{47}$$

Alternately, the sum of X minus 1 is equal to 38.

$$\Sigma(X-1) = (1-1) + (2-1) + (3-1) + (4-1) + (4-1) + (5-1) + (5-1) + (7-1) + (8-1) + (9-1) = \boxed{38}$$

As a final example, we offer ΣX^2-1 vs. $\Sigma(X-1)^2$. ΣX^2-1 asks us to square each X, then sum the resulting values, then subtract 1 from the resulting sum. Remember that the rules of algebraic order tell us to calculate exponents before we perform addition/subtraction, and when there are no parentheses, do the summation before any other addition or subtraction procedures. Alternately, $\Sigma(X-1)^2$ tells us to subtract 1 from each X, square that result, and then sum all the squared values. Algebraic order tells us to do what is in the parentheses first, then do the exponents, then do the summation.

Again returning to the bush-in-the-White House data, we summarize the formulas below. Subtracting 1 from the sum of X squared is equal to 289.

$$\Sigma X^2 = \boxed{290}$$

$$\Sigma X^2-1 = 290 - 1 = \boxed{289}$$

However, the sum of X minus 1, squared, is equal to 204.

$$\Sigma(X-1)^2 = (1-1)^2 + (2-1)^2 + (3-1)^2 + (4-1)^2 + (4-1)^2 + (5-1)^2 + (5-1)^2 + (7-1)^2 + (8-1)^2 + (9-1)^2 =$$

$$= (0)^2 + (1)^2 + (2)^2 + (3)^2 + (3)^2 + (4)^2 + (4)^2 + (6)^2 + (7)^2 + (8)^2 =$$

$$= 0 + 1 + 4 + 9 + 9 + 16 + 16 + 36 + 49 + 64 = \boxed{204}$$

Levels of Measurement

Summation notation and the rules of algebraic order can be applied to any set of numbers. When these procedures are found in a given formula, however, there are often limitations on the types of data sets that can be used. More specifically, some formulas require that certain types of variables be used in their calculation. While one way in which variables are distinguished in a given formula is in the use of letters such as X and Y (representing, respectively, an independent and dependent variable), what are called "levels of measurement" often must also be considered.

As previously noted, social scientists set out to measure different characteristics. Characteristics can be measured as constants or variables (this observation and those that follow concerning levels of measurement are summarized in Figure 2.1). An example of a constant in the physical sciences is the temperature at which water freezes: 32 degrees Fahrenheit or 0 degrees Celsius. That is, under normal circumstances, water always—constantly—freezes at this temperature.

Box 2.2   Additional Summation Notation Procedure

Some statistical formulas require use of a further summation notation procedure. Using the letters i and N, this additional type of notation tells where to begin and end summing numbers from a given data set. More specifically, i represents an observation (or set of observations) of a given variable. When a numerical value is placed next to an i with an equal sign in between (such as in the formula below with $i=3$), this says to begin summing the given set of numbers at the third observation. Conversely, the N (as you might guess) indicates which observation to end the summing with. Thus, also found in the formula below, an $N = 7$ says to stop summing at the seventh observation. The formula below says to sum the X of i's from 3 to 7.

Sum of the X of i's from 3 to 7: $\Sigma Xi_{i=3}^{N=7}$

To put this into plain English, we reintroduce the desire/usage data sets (Table 2.3) to assist in this discussion. Additionally, some of the intermediate determinations for the formula above and the one that follows are also found in this table.

To sum the X of i's from 3 to 7 in this data set, as graphically represented above, the third through the seventh observations simply are added together. So, we add $3 + 4 + 4 + 5 + 5$ to obtain the final answer of 21.

Alternatively, as the formula below instructs us, let's say that we want to know the sum of Y of i's from 4 to 9 for the "usage" data set.

Sum of the Y of i's from 4 to 9: $\Sigma Yi_{i=3}^{N=9}$

As shown above, the sum of the fourth through the ninth observations of the above Y data set, $5 + 7 + 9 + 11 + 11 + 12$, equals 55.

Although this additional summation notation procedure is not found in any further presentations in this textbook, many instructors and other texts assume that you are familiar with it.

Table 2.3   Additional Summation Notation Procedures Applied to Bush-in-the-White House Data Sets

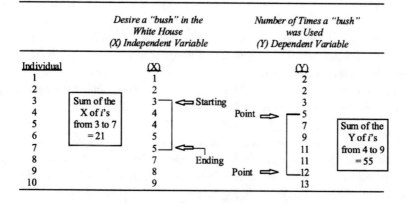

Figure 2.1   Levels of Measurement

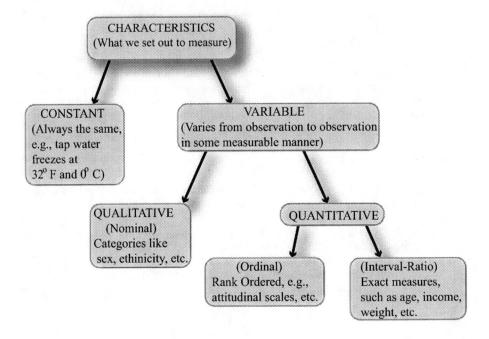

In the social and behavioral sciences, however, there are no real constants. Thus, researchers are almost exclusively interested in measuring variables. Remember that a variable is any characteristic that changes from element to element in some measurable manner. While the range of possible variables that can be measured in the social and behavioral sciences is limited only by the given researcher's imagination, the manner in which characteristics are measured always assumes one of three basic forms: nominal, ordinal, and interval-ratio. The abbreviation NOIR is an easy way of remembering these three terms in the order they occur. These types of variables, discussed in turn below, are also referred to as level of measurement.

Nominal variables, also referred to as *qualitative* variables, are social characteristics that have no real numerical meaning. For instance, things such as hair or eye color, gender, religious orientation, country or state of birth, and skin color are all variables measured in terms of non-numerical qualities. And, although numerical values can be placed on these characteristics so that different groups can be numerically compared, they still have no real mathematical meaning. Thus, while a researcher might be interested in comparing differences between men and women in terms of the number of times they used a bush in the White House or scores on a recent exam, neither gender can have a numerical value placed upon it in any meaningful sense. In sum, the nominal level of measurement simply differentiates people by using non-numerical characteristics.

Ordinal and interval-ratio variables not only differentiate individual characteristics, they also assign numerical ranks to any measurable differences that are found between observations. In other words, while nominal variables use qualitative forms of measurement, ordinal and interval-ratio variables use quantitative (numerically ranked) forms of measurement. As such, they are also referred to as *quantitative* variables.

Ordinal variables, as the term implies, are concerned with individual characteristics that can be *ordered* in some meaningful manner. That is, an ordinal level of measurement numerically scales (rank orders) observations associated with a given individual characteristic.

Many surveys include ordinal questions in terms of respondents' expressed attitudes about a given subject. For instance, we could administer a questionnaire that includes an item that asks subjects to respond to the statement, "All colleges and universities should require students to take a statistics course to graduate." While there are many responses we might receive, questionnaires typically offer a set of standardized responses that are ranked. Standardized responses, also referred to as closed-ended questions, simply mean that possible subjects' responses are predetermined.

One widely used set of standardized answers measures respondents' reported level of agreement or disagreement on a given topic using a five-point scale: strongly agree = 1, agree = 2, neutral = 3, disagree = 4, and strongly disagree = 5. Although none of these responses in itself has any numerical meaning, when they are rank ordered, each value relative to the others does take on a numerical meaning. Thus, we can numerically differentiate between a respondent who strongly agrees (1 point) with the above statement (probably someone who has already passed the statistics class you are currently enrolled in) versus someone who strongly disagrees (5 five points) with it (possibly most students prior to taking this class).

While ordinal variables measure different rank-ordered responses, they do not tell us the degree of difference between observations. That is, while there is a measurable difference between a respondent who strongly agrees on a given topic versus one who disagrees, the magnitude of this difference is unknown and cannot be determined. Thus, we would have no way of knowing if someone who strongly agrees with the above statement is two, three, or four times more supportive of such a requirement for graduation versus someone who simply disagrees with it.

To measure meaningfully the magnitude of difference between various observations we must use what are called *interval-ratio* variables. This level of measurement uses exact measurement intervals to differentiate potential observations. Income, age, weight, and number of times a bush was used in the White House are all examples of interval-ratio variables. Each one of these variables can be measured using equal measurement intervals: dollars, years, pounds, and number of times used.

Moreover, the measurement units for each of these examples, the intervals, do have meaning themselves, whereas those associated with ordinal variables are entirely constructed by the given researcher. Thus, it makes sense to conclude that someone who makes $20,000 a year makes exactly twice as much as someone who makes $10,000 a year. Alternatively, the dog who used a bush twelve times used it four times as much as the dog who only used it three times. Once again, however, we cannot make these same sorts of precise conclusions concerning ordinal or nominal levels of measurement.

Several summary observations are warranted concerning levels of measurement. This section began by noting that levels of measurement often determine which statistical procedures can be used. The importance of this observation is that some statistical procedures are seen as more powerful than others. Specifically, statistical procedures developed for interval-ratio measurement are seen as most powerful. Next, ordinal statistical procedures are seen as less powerful than nominal procedures. Thus, nominal, ordinal, and interval-ratio variables are respectively seen as having different "levels" of measurement power: from lower to higher.

A related observation is that the three levels of measurement, considered together, constitute an actual ordinal scale. That is, while a nominal variable is seen as a rather inexact way of measuring a given social characteristic, interval-ratio variables are seen as a more precise, definitive form of measurement, and ordinal variables are seen as falling somewhere in between. Accordingly, and at the risk of sounding redundant, these three type variables are referred to as *levels*—rank ordered—of measurement.

Box 2.3   Discrete and Continuous Variables

Statisticians often find it helpful to classify variables in terms of whether they are discrete or continuous. *Discrete variables* can occur as either qualitative or quantitative characteristics. Mathematically speaking, discrete variables are separate, distinct measurements of a given characteristic. As a result, there are inherent gaps between each observation that cannot be measured. Gender, degree of agreement or disagreement on a given topic, number of children a woman gives birth to, or level of desire for a bush-in-the-White House are all discrete measurements. That is, each of these variables is measured in non-overlapping categories that numerically cannot be further broken down. Thus, while it is common practice to report such concepts as that women have an average of 2.2 children, it is literally impossible to have 2.2 children. In other words, although a given woman can logically have 2 or 3 children, she cannot have a fraction (.2) of a child.

Continuous variables, on the other hand, can take on literally any value within a predetermined range of numbers. Weight, temperature, or time it takes to use a bush are all examples of continuous variables. Each of these variables can be meaningfully broken down into ever finer measurement units. For instance, the amount of time it takes a dog to use a bush can be measured in terms of years, days, hours, minutes, seconds, fractions of a second, and so forth. Unlike discrete variables, then, continuous variables can be expressed logically in even finer measurement units.

In sum, all nominal and ordinal levels of measurement are also discrete variables. An internal-ratio level of measurement, however, can occur as either a discrete or continuous variable.

Further, because interval-ratio variables are more powerful, for analysis purposes this level of measurement is the most desired. Unfortunately, however, many if not most measurable characteristics available to social and behavioral scientists are nominal and ordinal. As a result, researchers regularly (and somewhat inappropriately) use statistical techniques developed for interval-ratio variables on lower levels of measurement. For instance, it is common practice to analyze an ordinal attitudinal scale as interval-ratio data. While some researchers see no problems in doing this, most correctly recognize that using upper-level statistical procedures on lower-level data increases the likelihood that inaccurate and incorrect conclusions may be drawn.

Finally, there are instances in which social scientists redefine higher levels of measurement into lower ones to make it easier to interpret the results of the given statistical test. For example, years of education, an interval-ratio measure, is often collapsed into an ordinal scale of primary, secondary, undergraduate, and graduate levels of education. Although these four basic categories are not equal, resultant findings from them are sometimes easier to interpret. In most instances, however, because of the increased risk of obtaining invalid results with lower levels of measurement, one should avoid redefining upper levels of measurement whenever possible.

Chapter Summary and Conclusions

This chapter likened statistics to a recipe. More specifically, both recipes and statistics use ordered operations applied to predetermined amounts of ingredients. If the operations found in a recipe or a formula are not correctly used in the right order, however, erroneous results will be obtained—such as burnt food or a wrong answer. An additional discussion of levels of measurement concerning types of ingredients—nominal, ordinal, interval-ratio variables—was also offered in this chapter. Special attention is given to issues of measurement in many of the chapters that follow, and one must always carefully follow the instructions given with any formula to obtain a correct answer, so please carefully review the definitions for any of the following terms that are at all unfamiliar to you. This will significantly reduce the possibility of having a "math atheist's nightmare" on the next exam.

Key Terms to Remember

- Ingredients
- Amounts
- Operations
- Algebraic Order
- Summation Notation
- Constants
- Qualitative Versus Quantitative Variables
- Levels of Measurement—Nominal, Ordinal, and Interval-Ratio
- Discrete Versus Continuous Variables

Practice Exercises

1. In your own words, what are ingredients, amounts, operations, and order in reference to statistical formulas?

2. The data set (X) found in Table 2.4 represents the number of school terms that 10 social science majors have put off taking a required statistics class. The second data set, Y, is each student's measured level of math/statistics anxiety. Use these data sets to complete the following exercises on algebraic order and summation notation.

a. ΣX b. ΣY

c. $(\Sigma X)^2$ d. $(\Sigma Y)^2$

e. ΣX^2 f. ΣY^2

g. $\Sigma X^2 - 1$ h. $(\Sigma Y)^2 - 1$

i. $\Sigma(X-1)$ j. $\Sigma(Y-1)^2$

k. $(\Sigma X)(\Sigma Y)$ l. $\Sigma X i_{i=3}^{N=7}$

m. $\Sigma Y i_{i=2}^{N=5}$ n. $\Sigma Y i_{i=3}^{N=9}$

Table 2.4   Postponement and Math/Statistics Anxiety

(X) Number of Terms Taking Statistics Has Been Postponed	(Y) Level of Math/Statistics Anxiety
1	3
2	3
2	3
3	2
3	4
2	4
3	5
3	5
4	5
4	7

3. For each of the following variables, define what level of measurement they are: nominal, ordinal, interval-ratio.
   a. age
   b. hair color
   c. an attitudinal scale
   d. height
   e. IQ
   f. religion
   g. your name
   h. gender
   i. income

4. Now determine if these same variables are discrete or continuous.

Frequency Distributions, Graphs, and Charts

As noted in Chapter 1, one of the foremost uses of statistics in the social and behavioral sciences is to describe phenomena in terms of variables and the relationships between them. One simple and highly effective way to do this is visually using graphs and charts—summary illustrations of quantitative and qualitative variables. Such pictorial displays are not simply aesthetically pleasant ways to summarize sets of numbers, they also enable us to visualize things about variables that we might miss by looking at just the numbers. Graphs and charts allow us to view variables and variable relationships in a manner that is often more meaningful and easier to understand. Perhaps this explains their widespread use in magazines, textbooks, and on television.

This chapter explores graphs and charts in terms of how they are constructed and what they represent. Both graphs and charts ultimately represent and are constructed using what are called frequency distributions: predetermined organizational categories that group and summarize observations of a given variable(s). Quantitative versus qualitative variables, however, call for different types of histograms, frequency polygons, bar charts, and pie charts. As such, we first discuss quantitative and qualitative frequency distributions in terms of what they represent and how they are constructed. These four types of graphic representations then are discussed individually.

Quantitative Frequency Distributions

At the most basic level, frequency distributions take raw data, also referred to as *ungrouped* data, and *group* (place) them into predetermined categories. Moreover, for any data set to be grouped in a meaningful manner, it must utilize what are called *mutually exclusive* and *exhaustive* categories. "Mutually exclusive" means that no one observation can be placed into more than one category at a time. Alternatively, "exhaustive" means that there is an available category for each observation. What a frequency distribution does is describe the rates (frequency) of occurrence of variable observations in mutually exclusive and exhaustive categories.

When dealing with quantitative variables (ordinal and interval-ratio levels of measurement), the grouping of data is accomplished using numerical categories representing a

Cartoon 3.1   FOX TROT

range of numbers. A quantitative frequency distribution, then, is made up of predetermined numerical categories that are mutually exclusive and exhaustive. Thus, if we had ten numerical observations of a given variable, to construct a frequency distribution of it, every observation must be grouped into a predetermined numerical category. Moreover, there must be an available category for each observation.

What we have said thus far is pretty abstract, so let's use the following example to better explain the above terms. Cartoon 3.1 and its accompanying data set (see Table 3.1) represent the number of times an adolescent child has to go "huh" and/or "heh" before his or her parents become angry. The data set tells very little other than that there are 25 observations in this sample ($n = 25$) and that the least number of huh/heh's it took to make a parent angry was 2 while the most was 29. Although we have rank ordered the observations from least to most, it is nearly impossible to describe efficiently and summarize 25 separate observations. Constructing a frequency distribution, however, enables us to arrange this data set into a potentially far more meaningful format. To this end, the first step we must undertake is to determine what sort of numerical categories to use. These are referred to as class intervals.

Class Intervals

A class interval is a predetermined numerical category that can contain more than one possible observation in its range. Theoretically, the size of a given class interval and its

Table 3.1   Huh and/or Heh Data Set

Number of "Huh" and/or "Heh" Required to Anger Parents

2	8	14	17	22	
4	10	14	18	23	
7	12	15	19	24	($n = 25$)
7	12	17	19	28	
8	13	17	20	29	

range are arbitrary and literally can be any conceivable values. If, however, we choose an interval that is too large or too small, the resulting frequency distribution will be meaningless.

For example, if we select an interval of 30 covering the range of 1 to 30 for the huh/heh data set, all of the observations would fall into one category. Conversely, if we select an interval of 2 covering the ranges of 1 to 2, 3 to 4, and so forth, the resulting frequency distribution would look nearly identical to the actual observations in the raw data set. Either way, the resultant frequency distribution does not organize the data set in a manner that increases our understanding of it.

Most of the presentations of quantitative frequency distributions in social and behavioral science literature use an interval size that results in somewhere between 5 to 15 total intervals being used. In the huh/heh data set, with its observations ranging from 2 to 29, using an interval size of 5 enables us to place all of the observations into just six categories. While this will be clearly demonstrated in a moment, grouping this data set into six categories (versus 30 observations) will obviously give a very different picture of it.

Where to start the first class interval is also somewhat arbitrary. The beginning interval, however, must always include the first observation(s). Once a starting point is selected, it determines the placement of each subsequent interval. The last interval must always include the final observation(s).

The first observation in the huh/heh data set is 2, so we have set the starting point of the first interval at the numerical value of one. Unless your data set includes a value of zero or a negative value, the starting point of the first interval should always be above the value of zero. Whenever possible, use the value of one as a starting point to make it easier to determine the placement of subsequent intervals.

Using a starting point of one and a class interval of five, the first grouping (interval) is 1 through 5. Any observations of 1, 2, 3, 4, and 5 are placed into this category. The next interval of five contains the values of 6 through 10, the third interval contains 11 through 15, the fourth contains 16 through 20, the fifth contains 21 through 25, and the sixth and last interval contains 26 through 30. The resultant class intervals are found in Table 3.2.

Using six intervals allows us to have a category in which each of our observations will fit. Thus, the intervals used in this frequency distribution are exhaustive. Moreover,

Table 3.2   Class Intervals

Intervals of Five	AF	CF	RF	CRF	
1 - 5	2	2	2/25 = .08 8%	.08	(8%)
6 - 10	5	7	5/25 = 0.2 20%	0.26	(26%)
11 - 15	6	13	6/25 = 0.24 24%	0.52	(52%)
16 - 20	7	20	7/25 0.26 28%	0.8	(8%)
21 - 25	3	23	3/25 0.12 = 12%	0.92	(92%)
26 - 30	2	25	2/25 = .08 8%	1	(100%)

because no observation can fit into more than one of these intervals (demonstrated more clearly below), the categories are also mutually exclusive. Next, we must determine the absolute and relative frequencies of occurrence of observations for each of these intervals.

Absolute and Cumulative Frequencies

We are now ready to start organizing the data into a potentially more meaningful representation. To this end, the first thing we must do is determine the number of observations that occur in each of the class intervals.

The rate in which observations occur in any given class interval is referred to as the *absolute frequency* (af). Thus, in the huh/heh data set, because there are two observations in the first interval of 1 through 5, a 2 and a 4, its absolute frequency is 2. For the interval of 6 through 10, there are five observations that fit: 7, 7, 8, 8, and 10; thus its absolute frequency is 5. Table 3.3 is a summary of the absolute frequencies for all the class intervals in our distribution.

The *cumulative frequency* (cf) of occurrence refers to the number of observations that have accumulated to a given class interval. In other words, cumulative frequencies are determined by incrementally adding the absolute frequencies together. For instance, the cumulative frequency up to the second interval is determined by simply adding the first and second absolute frequencies together.

In our frequency distribution, the class interval of 1 through 5 has a cumulative frequency of 2 (the same as its absolute frequency) because we are only interested in observations that occur up to, and including, the first interval. The cumulative frequency for the second class interval is determined, as already noted, by adding the absolute frequencies of the first (1 through 5) and second (6 through 10) intervals; 2 af +5 af = 7 cf. To calculate the next cumulative frequency, then, the value of 7 is added to the absolute frequency of the next interval (11 through 15); thus, 7 + 6 = 13. The remaining cumulative frequencies are simply determined by adding each subsequent absolute frequency to the previous cumulative frequency: 13 + 7 = 20, 20 + 3 = 23, and 23 + 2 = 25. All of these cumulative values are summarized in Table 3.4; the corresponding absolute frequency values that were used in their calculation are also shown.

Organizing our data set in this format enables us to start to draw some meaningful conclusions about it. For example, slightly more than half of the adolescents (13 out of

Table 3.3   Absolute Frequencies

Class Interval	Absolute Frequency (af)
1 - 5	2
6 - 10	5
11 - 15	6
16 - 20	7
21 - 25	3
26 - 30	2

Table 3.4 Absolute and Cumulative Frequencies

Class Interval	Absolute Frequency (af)	Cumulative Frequency (cf)
1 - 5	2	2
6 - 10	5	7
11 - 15	6	13
16 - 20	7	20
21 - 25	3	23
26 - 30	2	25

25) were able to anger their parents using between 1 and 15 huh/heh's. Alternatively, only 7 of the 25 adolescents were able to anger their parents when 1 to 10 huh/heh's were utilized. Moreover, as one might expect, none of the 25 adolescents required more than 30 huh/heh's to anger his or her parents. (Please note: The cumulative frequency of the last interval must always equal the number of observations in the given data set. If it does not, something has been done wrong and the calculations must be rechecked.) In other words, we are starting to get an idea of just how many huh/heh's are required to get most adolescents' parents angry.

Relative and Cumulative Relative Frequencies

Even more can be learned about a given data set by calculating the relative and cumulative relative frequencies. Mathematically, a *relative frequency* (rf) is any absolute frequency divided by the total number of observations. In other words, this type of measurement is concerned with the rate of occurrence found in any given interval relative to all of the occurrences (observations). The easiest way to express this is as a percentage.

Thus, in our example, for the first class interval of 1 through 5, we take the corresponding absolute frequency value of 2 and divide by the overall number of observations in this data set to get 2/25 = .08 or 8%. The value of .08 or 8% tells us that 8% of all the observations occur in the class interval of 1 through 5. For the next class interval of 6 through 10, the absolute frequency of 5 is divided by 25 to get 5/25 = .20 or 20%.

The remaining relative frequencies, summarized with the first two in Table 3.5, are obtained as follows: class interval 11 through 15 gives 6/25 = .24 or 24%; class interval 16 through 20 gives 7/25 = .28 or 28%; class interval 21 through 25 gives us 3/25 = .12 or 12%; and the class interval of 26 through 30 gives us 2/25 = .08 or 8%.

Expressing frequencies of occurrence in relative (percentage) terms allows us to make even more refined observations about our data set. For instance, we can note that for nearly one quarter (24%) of our adolescents it took 11 to 15 huh/heh's to anger their parents. Alternatively, 8% of the adolescents angered their parents with just 1 to 5 huh/heh's.

The final component of our frequency distribution that we must define and construct is the *cumulative relative frequency* (crf). In a manner similar to constructing cumulative frequency, the cumulative relative frequency is calculated by taking each relative frequency

Table 3.5　Relative Frequencies

Class Interval	Absolute Frequency (af)	Relative Frequency (rf)
1 - 5	2	2/25 = .08 (8%)
6 - 10	5	5/25 = .20 (20%)
11 - 15	6	6/25 = .24 (24%)
16 - 20	7	7/25 = .28 (28%)
21 - 25	3	3/25 = .12 (12%)
26 - 30	2	2/25 = .08 (8%)

value and adding it to each preceding cumulative relative value. Thus, the cumulative relative frequency for the class interval of 1 through 5 is simply .08 (8%). The cumulative relative frequency of the next class interval of 6 through 10 is determined by adding .08 + .20 = .28 (28%). Next we take this answer, .28, and add to .24 (for the class interval of 11 through 15) and get .52 (52%), we continue in this fashion until we reach the final class interval. As reflected in Table 3.6, the final cumulative relative frequency should always equal 1.00 or 100%.

(Please note: Sometimes this final answer will be slightly larger or smaller than 1.00. This is due to a rounding error. Assuming that previous calculations have been done correctly, we will rightfully treat it as 1.00. After all, the total cumulative frequencies relative to the number of observations in the data set, 25/25, equals 100%. If, however, the total crf is drastically different than the value of 1.00 (*e.g.*, .95 or 1.1), then an error has been made and calculations must be rechecked.)

All of the calculations made to this point (af, cf, rf, and crf) are summarized as a complete frequency distribution in Table 3.7. Compared to the original data set, grouping each data set into class intervals of 5 makes it much easier to describe. This, in turn, often makes it easier to draw meaningful conclusions about the given data set. For instance, since 80% of the adolescents were able to anger their parents using 1 to 20 huh/heh's, it is apparently quite an efficient strategy for eliciting such a response. Alternatively, 1 to 5 huh/heh's do not appear to work very well; only 2 (8%) of the adolescents were able to

Table 3.6　Relative and Cumulative Frequencies

Class Interval	Relative Frequency (rf)	Cumulative Relative Frequency (crf)
1 - 5	2/25 = .08 (8%)	.08 = .08 (8%)
6 - 10	5/25 = .20 (20%)	.08 + .20 = .28 (28%)
11 - 15	6/25 = .24 (24%)	.28 + .24 = .52 (52%)
16 - 20	7/25 = .28 (28%)	.52 + .28 = .80 (80%)
21 - 25	3/25 = .12 (12%)	.80 + .12 = .92 (92%)
26 - 30	2/25 = .08 (8%)	.92 + .08 = 1.00 (100%)

Table 3.7 Complete Frequency Distribution of Huh/Heh Data Set

Class Interval	af	cf	rf	crf
1 - 5	2	2	.08	.08
6 - 10	5	7	.20	.28
11 - 15	6	13	.24	.52
16 - 20	7	20	.28	.80
21 - 25	3	23	.12	.92
26 - 30	2	25	.08	1.00

anger their parents using this number of huh/heh's. In sum, constructing a frequency distribution is a very simple but effective first step in analyzing any data set.

Qualitative Frequency Distributions

As noted, frequency distributions can also be constructed using qualitative variables. Let's say that we are also interested in the types of families our 25 different adolescents come from. Unlike the number of huh/heh's data set, however, family type is a qualitative variable: a nominal level of measurement. As such, numerical values cannot be placed upon observations of this variable in any meaningful manner. This, obviously, eliminates the usage of class intervals as categories to group the data. Thus we simply use groupings of types of families. To demonstrate this more clearly, we offer the data set found in Table 3.8; it represents the rate of occurrence (absolute frequency) for the variable of family type.

Several observations are warranted. First, for each of the family types (categories), the absolute frequency is simply noted. Using these non-numerical groupings, these values reflect the given category's absolute frequency (e.g., seven children come from families where both natural parents are present). Second, the categories we have utilized to group our data set (five family types) are mutually exclusive and exhaustive. That is, there is an available category for every observation to be grouped into, and each observation can fit into only one category.

Table 3.8 Absolute Frequencies for Five Family Types Data Set

Family Type	Number of Adolescents
1. Both Stepparents	1
2. One Natural Parent and One Stepparent	9
3. Father Only	2
4. Mother Only	6
5. Both Natural Parents	7
	25 Total

Table 3.9   Absolute and Cumulative Frequencies for Five Family Types Data Set

Family Type	Absolute Frequency (af)	Cumulative Frequencies (cf)
1. Both Stepparents	1	1
2. One Natural Parent and One Stepparent	9	10
3. Father Only	2	12
4. Mother Only	6	18
5. Both Natural Parents	7	25

Finally, although numbered 1 through 5, the order in which these categories is presented is quite arbitrary. For example, instead of using "Both Stepparents" as the first category, any of the family types could be in its place. Moreover, the presentation order of any of the above categories is entirely arbitrary.

Consequently, the above and any subsequent presentation of a qualitative variable are less systematic than that of a qualitative variable and its corresponding class intervals. Mathematically, this limits the depth of any descriptions and conclusions we might make. Nevertheless, we can still calculate the cumulative, relative, and cumulative relative frequencies for this distribution.

Following the same steps as used before, because the absolute frequencies are already given, we first calculate the cumulative frequencies. Once again, the first cumulative frequency is simply the first category's (Both Stepparents) absolute frequency of occurrence: 1. The next cumulative frequency is determined by adding the first category (Both Stepparents) to the second category (One Natural Parent and One Stepparent) to give us 9 + 1 = 10. This process continues (see Table 3.9) until we add the last category and get the expected value of 25 (equal to the total number of observations).

The next task is to determine the relative frequency of occurrence for each category. As before, this is accomplished by taking the absolute frequency of occurrence for each category and dividing it by the overall number of observations in the data set: 25. For the category of "Both Stepparents" we take 1/25 = .04 (4%); this is the relative frequency for this category. Then we take 9/25 = .36 (36%); 2/25 = .08 (8%); 6/25 = .24 (24%); and 7/25 = .28 (28%). All of these operations are summarized in Table 3.10.

The final step is to calculate the cumulative relative frequencies. This is accomplished in Table 3.11 in the same manner as with the first data set; each cumulative relative frequency is added to the next relative frequency to get the next category's cumulative relative frequency.

Putting all this information together gives us the complete frequency distribution of family type found in Table 3.12.

Grouping the data in this format once again enables us to make meaningful conclusions about them. For example, the largest category of children comes from reconstituted

Table 3.10   Absolute and Relative Frequencies for Five Family Types Data Set

Family Type	Absolute Frequency (af)	Relative Frequencies (rf)
1. Both Stepparents	1	1/25 = .04 (4%)
2. One Natural Parent and One Stepparent	9	9/25 = .36 (36%)
3. Father Only	2	2/25 = .08 (8%)
4. Mother Only	6	6/25 = .24 (24%)
5. Both Natural Parents	7	7/25 = .28 (28%)

Table 3.11   Relative and Cumulative Relative Frequencies for Five Family Types Data Set

Family Type	Relative Frequency (rf)	Cumulative Relative Frequencies (crf)
1. Both Stepparents	.04 (4%)	.04 = .04 (4%)
2. One Natural Parent and One Stepparent	.36 (36%)	.04 + .36 = .40 (40%)
3. Father Only	.08 (8%)	.40 + .08 = .48 (48%)
4. Mother Only	.24 (24%)	.48 + .24 = .72 (72%)
5. Both Natural Parents	.28 (28%)	.72 + .28 = 1.00 (100%)

Table 3.12   Complete Frequency Distribution for Five Family Types Data Set

Family Type	af	cf	rf	crf
1. Both Stepparents	1	1	.04	.04
2. One Natural Parent and One Stepparent	9	10	.36	.40
3. Father Only	2	12	.08	.48
4. Mother Only	6	18	.24	.72
5. Both Natural Parents	7	25	.28	1.00

families; more than one-third of the children (36%) come from families where one of the present parents had divorced and remarried. Because the order in which the categories are listed is entirely arbitrary, categories can be simultaneously considered together. For instance, we can easily determine that 96% of the children come from families having at least one natural parent, whereas 40% come from families with at least one stepparent.

Graphing Techniques

Another meaningful way to present data that builds upon what has been discussed thus far is using pictorial displays in the form of histograms, frequency polygons, bar charts, and pie charts. The old cliché that a picture is worth a thousand words is also true in statistics. (Then again, a cartoon is worth scores of statistics examples!) Each of these techniques, now explored in turn, literally presents a given data set as a picture.

Histograms

One way to graphically present data is by using a histogram. While all of you have seen histograms in magazines, newspapers, textbooks, and on television, you probably did not know that the graphic was called this or how it was constructed. Histograms can only be constructed using quantitative data, so we simply reuse the huh/heh data set and its corresponding frequency distribution in the following discussion.

Histograms are constructed using contiguous vertical bars that represent the absolute frequencies of observations found in predetermined class intervals (categories). In other words, histograms are simply graphic presentations of the number of observations found in each class interval of a frequency distribution. For these bars to touch and be contiguous, however, we must take mutually exclusive categories and make them connect in some meaningful format. To accomplish this, we need to calculate what are called *upper* and *lower real limits*.

Our task is to make the interval boundaries touch, so we must identify a common boundary that two intervals can share. The easiest way to do this is to use the point that occurs exactly between two intervals' boundaries. Mathematically, this is determined by taking one class interval's upper limit (top of its range) and adding it to the next interval's lower limit (bottom of its range); this total is then divided by two. The resultant answer is one interval's upper real limit and the other interval's lower real limit.

Applied to the huh/heh frequency distribution, the upper real limit for the first interval is determined by taking the upper limit of this class interval and adding to the second class interval's lower limit, and then dividing this value by 2: (5 + 6 = 11)/2= 5.5. The resultant answer of 5.5 is both the first interval's upper real limit and the next class interval's real lower limit. Incrementally repeating this procedure, we add the upper limit of the second interval (10) to the lower limit of the third interval (11), divide this answer (21) by 2, and find the shared boundary of 10.5.

These and all the remaining calculations are summarized in Table 3.13, but there are two values whose calculation warrants further explanation: the smallest lower real limit of .5 and the largest upper real limit of 30.5. In each of these cases, two class intervals are not listed, so a hypothetical one is used. Thus the limits of 31 (for the interval of 31 through 35) and 0 (for the interval of –4 to 0) are used to give (0 + 1 = 1)/ 2 = .5 and (30 + 31 = 61)/2 = 30.5.

Table 3.13   Upper and Lower Real Limits

Class Interval	Upper and Lower Real Limits	Absolute Frequency (af)
1 - 5	.5 - 5.5	2
6 - 10	5.5 - 10.5	5
11 - 15	10.5 - 15.5	6
16 - 20	15.5 - 20.5	7
21 - 25	20.5 - 25.5	3
26 - 30	25.5 - 30.5	2

We now have all the information needed to construct a histogram. Before doing this, however, two more terms must be introduced: the X and Y axes. The X axis (also referred to as the *abscissa*) is the horizontal axis on a graph. With a histogram, the X axis is typically used to represent the upper and lower real limit values. Conversely, the Y axis (also referred to as the *ordinate*) is the vertical axis; with a histogram it is typically used to represent the absolute frequency (af) values. With this in mind and using the previously determined upper and lower real limits, we constructed a histogram for the huh/heh data (see Figure 3.1).

Although the actual construction of this histogram is largely self-explanatory, several important observations are still needed. First, the width of the intervals and the height of the bars for histograms are graphically always represented in equal units. The above intervals, represented using upper and lower real limits, are all in equal units of 5 whereas the given interval's absolute frequency is in units of 1. Thus, the third interval covers the distance of 5 (10.5 to 15.5) and goes up six equal spaces (af = 6). Finally, because the intersection of the X and Y axes is portrayed as being 0 (which is often done), for aesthetic purposes the starting point for the first histogram bar on the X axis starts just to the right of this intersection.

Frequency Polygons

Frequency polygons also represent class intervals; instead of using bars with two points (upper and lower real limits) to do this, they utilize single points called *midpoints*. More specifically, these single points represent the exact center—middle—of any given interval. Mathematically, we accomplish this by adding together the upper and lower limits of a given interval and then dividing this answer by 2; *(upper limit + lower limit)/2 = interval midpoint*. Applying this, then, to the huh/heh frequency distribution and its first class interval yields (1 + 5 = 6)/2 = 3. Thus, the first interval's midpoint is 3.

Figure 3.1   Histogram for Huh/Heh Data

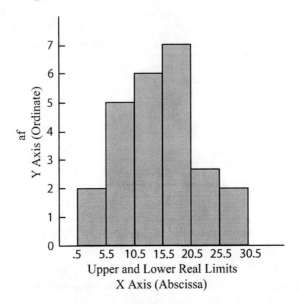

Table 3.14   Class Interval (CI) Midpoints

Class Interval	CI Midpoints	Absolute Frequency (af)
1 - 5	3	2
6 - 10	8	5
11 - 15	13	6
16 - 20	18	7
21 - 25	23	3
26 - 30	28	2

Repeating this procedure with the remaining intervals finds the midpoints of (6 + 10 = 16)/2 = 8; (11 + 15 = 26)/2 = 13; (16 + 20 = 36)/2 = 18; (21 + 25 = 46)/2 = 23; and finally (26 + 30 = 56/2 = 28. All of these midpoint values and the absolute frequencies they represent are summarized in Table 3.14.

(Please note: The difference between each of these midpoint values (i.e., 3, 8, 13, 18, 23, and 28) is exactly the same as the interval size: 5. If, incrementally, the differences between all the midpoint values are not exactly the same, the calculations have been done incorrectly. In such instances, obviously, one must go back and correct the error.)

The construction of the frequency polygon is very similar to that of a histogram. The absolute frequencies are once again found on the Y axis. The class intervals on the X axis

Figure 3.2   Frequency Polygon for Huh/Heh Data

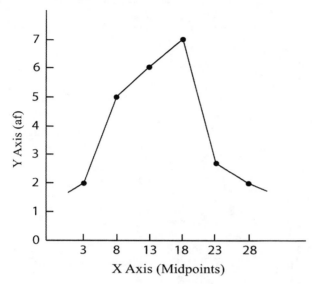

are designated by their midpoints, however, rather than the upper and lower real limits. A simple dot is placed on the graph where the absolute frequency and midpoint intersect. Once all the dots are plotted, simply connect them with straight lines. Finally, at the beginning and ending midpoints the lines are flared to show that the data set does not extend beyond these intervals. Applied to the "huh/heh" data, all of this is found in Figure 3.2.

Bar Charts

We can also construct graphic representations using qualitative instead of quantitative data. One technique that does this with qualitative variables is called a *bar chart*. Although this graphic technique appears to be similar to a histogram, it is plotted very differently. While both represent absolute frequencies on the *Y* axis, because a bar chart represents qualitative characteristics, the *X* axis cannot be labeled in any systematic manner. Thus, the resultant bars represent frequencies of occurrence applied to non-numerical categories. To demonstrate the construction of a bar chart, we have recreated the family type data (a qualitative variable) in Table 3.15.

Because the bar chart's *X* axis represents qualitative characteristics instead of actual numerical values, each family type must be represented by a single bar. In other words, each family type is represented with a labeled category that also indicates its absolute frequency by the bar's height. Figure 3.3 is a bar chart constructed with the family type data.

Three things are worth noting about this bar chart and about bar charts in general. First, this technique, unlike that of a histogram, is plotted so that the bars do not touch. That is, unlike ordinal and interval-ratio levels of measurement, since qualitative characteristics

Table 3.15   Absolute Frequencies for Five Family Types Data Set

Family Type	*Number of Adolescents*
1. Both Stepparents	1
2. One Natural Parent and One Stepparent	9
3. Father Only	2
4. Mother Only	6
5. Both Natural Parents	7
	25 Total

Figure 3.3   Bar Chart for Family Type Data

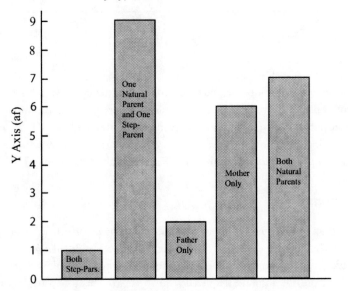

(e.g., family type) cannot be scaled, there is no way to display in any meaningful manner categories as touching. This leads to the second point: the order in which the categories appear on a bar chart is largely arbitrary. To be consistent, however, most researchers will label the bars in the same order they appear in the original data set. Finally, for aesthetic and ethical reasons (see discussion in Box 3.1), it is preferable for the width of the bars and the distances between them to be equal.

Box 3.1   Emphasizing Differences Visually

While histograms, frequency polygons, and bar charts should all use equal measurement units in their presentation, the actual width and height of the units used is arbitrary and can give very different impressions about a given data set.

If one was trying to promote the idea that to anger an adolescent's parents requires numerous, very different amounts of huh/heh's, for example, one would lengthen the distances to portray the absolute frequency and/or shorten the distances used to portray the upper and lower real limits.

On the other hand, if trying to minimize the differences, one would do the opposite and shorten the absolute frequency distances and/or lengthen the upper and lower real limits that represent the class interval distances. Using a histogram, both of these portrayals are presented in Figures 3.4 and 3.5.

A real-life example of this deceptive ploy is how fluctuations of the unemployment rate are reported in newspapers or on television. If a given reporter or editor is trying to show a drastic increase or decrease in the unemployment rate, the lengths of the bars are increased while the widths of the bars are decreased. Alternatively, if someone is trying to minimize changes in the unemployment rate, then just the opposite is done and the lengths of the bars are decreased dramatically while the widths are increased. Pictorially, this is one way that people can lie with statistics.

Figure 3.4   Accentuating Differences

Figure 3.5   Minimizing Differences

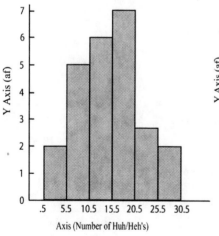

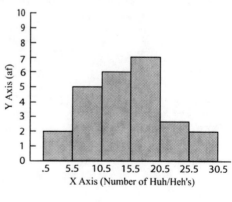

Pie Charts

Pie charts can be used with either qualitative or quantitative data. A pie chart represents the percentage of occurrence for variable measurements (their relative frequencies), with proportional slices of a circle (pie). To determine the size of the slices used, we take the total number of degrees found in a circle (360°) and multiply this value by the given category's relative frequency. For instance, if the relative frequency of a category is 25%, we multiply this value times 360 (.25 X 360) and get 90. In other words, a 90° angle is required to represent 25% of a category on a pie chart. All angles are calculated from the very center of the circle.

Replicated in Table 3.16 is the huh/heh data with the corresponding class intervals, absolute frequencies, relative frequencies, and calculated degrees of coverage—slice size—required for each interval.

Each category, determined by degrees in an angle, is plotted on an actual circle slice size (see Figure 3.6). Each category is also labeled with both a percentage value and in terms of the class interval it represents. Note that, when all categories have been plotted, the total number of degrees used always equals 360; 100% of all the categories are represented.

As noted, pie charts can also be constructed with qualitative data. Table 3.17 reports the absolute frequencies, relative frequencies, and calculated slice sizes for the previously used family type data—a qualitative variable.

Following the same procedures used for the huh/heh data and using the same calculations as used above results in the pie chart depicted in Figure 3.7. Instead of numerical intervals as pie labels, however, actual parent types are used.

Table 3.16   Slice Size of Class Intervals

Class Interval	Absolute Frequency (af)	Relative Frequency (rf)	Slice Size in Degrees
1 - 5	2	.08 (8%)	.08 x 360 = 28.8
6 - 10	5	.20 (20%)	.20 x 360 = 72.0
11 - 15	6	.24 (24%)	.24 x 360 = 86.4
16 - 20	7	.28 (28%)	.28 x 360 = 100.8
21 - 25	3	.12 (12%)	.12 x 360 = 43.2
26 - 30	2	.08 (8%)	.08 x 360 = 28.8
			Total = 360.0 Degrees

Figure 3.6   Pie Chart for Huh/Heh Data

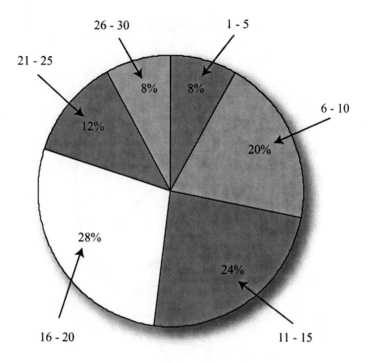

Table 3.17   Slice Size of Family Types

Family Type	Absolute Frequency (af)	Relative Frequencies (rf)	Slice Size in Degrees
1. Both Stepparents	1	.04 (4%)	.04 x 360 = 14.4
2. One Natural Parent and One Stepparent	9	.36 (36%)	.36 x 360 = 129.6
3. Father Only	2	.08 (8%)	.08 x 360 = 28.8
4. Mother Only	6	.24 (24%)	.24 x 360 = 86.4
5. Both Natural Parents	7	.28 (28%)	.28 x 360 = 100.8
			Total = 360.0 Degrees

Figure 3.7   Pie Chart for Family Type Data

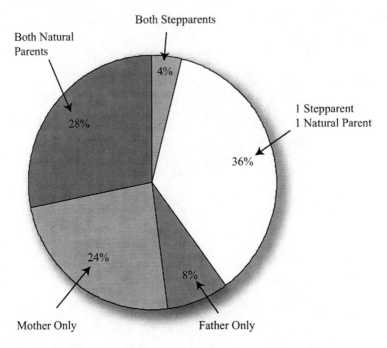

Chapter Summary and Conclusions

Instead of the summary that has been offered at the end of previous chapters, we review the materials in this chapter using Cartoon 3.2. The homework is also based upon this cartoon.

Let's say our current interests are the number of beers that 15 sampled cartoon characters (such as Hagar, Zonker, Frank and Ernest, etc.) consume in a week's period. The data set in Table 3.18 represents the findings. Note: To assist in subsequent calculations, the data are presented in ascending order from lowest to highest.

For review purposes, the task is to construct a frequency distribution containing absolute, cumulative, relative, and cumulative relative frequencies using class intervals of three (3). These class intervals with corresponding absolute and cumulative frequencies are found in Table 3.19. (Please note: The intervals start at the suggested value of 1; are mutually exclusive and exhaustive; and when considered together their cumulative frequency equals the sample size.)

A complete frequency distribution also contains the relative and cumulative relative frequencies. Recall that relative frequencies are calculated by dividing the absolute frequency of each class interval by the sample size (15 in this example). Then the cumulative frequencies for the intervals are determined by adding each interval's relative frequency to the preceding cumulative relative frequency. All of these calculations combined with the absolute and cumulative frequencies are summarized in Table 3.20.

Cartoon 3.2   HAGAR THE HORRIBLE

© Reprinted with special permission of King Features Syndicate.

(Please note: Each relative frequency is carried out to the fourth decimal point exactly as found on the calculator; thus, when the relative frequencies are summed together to determine the last cumulative relative frequency, the final answer equals .9998, instead of the expected value of .00. While this is due to rounding errors, observe that when the cumulative frequency of the last category, 15, is divided by the sample size, 15, the correct final answer of 100% is given.)

Now that the frequency distribution is complete, we can construct a histogram and frequency polygon for the data. Remember that, to do this, we need to calculate upper and lower real limits and midpoints for the class intervals. All of these calculations are summarized in Table 3.21 with the absolute frequencies they represent.

Recall that the upper and lower real limits are calculated by taking one class interval's upper limit and adding it to the next class interval's lower limit, and then dividing this answer by 2 (e.g., (6 + 7 = 13)/2 = 6.5). The lower real limit of the first interval is calculated by taking its lower limit and adding it to the upper limit of the interval that would precede it (0 in this case), and then dividing this answer by 2. With the case in hand, we take 0 + 1 = 1, divide this answer by 2 to get .5: the lower real limit for the first class interval. Conversely, the upper real limit for the final class interval is calculated by adding 1 to 16 (the lower limit of the next class interval that is not presented) and dividing this value by 2: (15 + 16 = 31)/ 2 = 15.5. Midpoints are derived by adding the upper and lower limits of any class interval, and then dividing by 2 (e.g., (7 + 9 = 16)/2 =8).

Table 3.18   Cartoon Characters' Weekly Beer Consumption Data Set

Number of Beers Consumed Weekly by Cartoon Characters			
	1	6	11
	2	7	12
	4	7	12
	4	9	12
(*n* = 15)	5	10	15 (Hagar's Answer)

Table 3.19   Class Intervals and Absolute and Cumulative Frequencies

Class Interval	Absolute Frequency (af)	Cumulative Frequency (cf)
1 - 3	2	2
4 - 6	4	6
7 - 9	3	9
10 - 12	5	14
13 - 15	1	15

Table 3.20   Complete Frequency Distribution of Beer Consumption Data Set

Class Interval	af	cf	rf	crf
1 - 3	2	2	.1333	.1333
4 - 6	4	6	.2666	.3999
7 - 9	3	9	.2000	.5999
10 - 12	5	14	.3333	.9332
13 - 15	1	15	.0666	.9998 (1.00)

This is all the information required to construct a histogram and frequency polygon for this data set (see Figures 3.8 and 3.9). Remember that, for our purposes, we have used the Y axis to represent absolute frequencies and the X axis to represent the upper and lower real limits and midpoints. Also, for our histogram, the beginning point of our first upper and lower real limit starts at .5, so it is placed just to the right of where the X and Y axes intersect.

To construct a bar chart we must have a qualitative data set. As such, we further "asked" our 15 cartoon characters which types of beer they usually drink. Table 3.22 represents a data set of the findings.

A bar chart (Figure 3.10) was constructed using this information. (Please note: The Y axis once again represents the absolute frequencies, whereas the X axis simply represents labeled categories in the same order found in Table 3.22.)

As with all of the previous graphics discussed in this chapter, Figure 3.10 gives a representative picture of what the data looks like. While numbers can speak for themselves, pictures often say things clearer and more forcibly, which is why they can also be used deceptively. This ploy is often undertaken by advertisers and the media in general, so being conversant in statistics and knowing about such practices makes it more difficult for one to be deceived.

Table 3.21   Class Interval Upper and Lower Real Limits/CI Midpoints

Class Interval	Upper and Lower Real Limits	CI Midpoints	Absolute Frequency
1 - 3	.5 - 3.5	2	2
4 - 6	3.5 - 6.5	5	4
7 - 9	6.5 - 9.5	6	3
10 - 12	9.5 - 12.5	11	5
13 - 15	12.5 - 15.5	14	1

Figure 3.8   Histogram for Beer Consumption Data

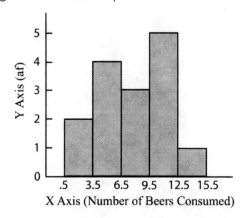

Figure 3.9   Frequency Polygon for Beer Consumption Data

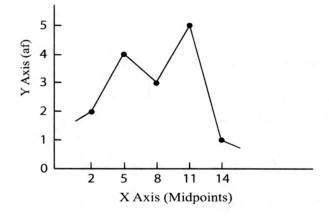

Table 3.22   Brand of Beer Data Set

Brand of Beer	Number of Characters Who Consume That Brand of Beer
Bongo Beer	1
Swiller Light	2
Lights-Out-Lager	5
Budget Brew	3
Belcher's Pride	1
Cirrhosis Light	3
	15 Total

Figure 3.10   Bar Chart for Type of Beer Consumed

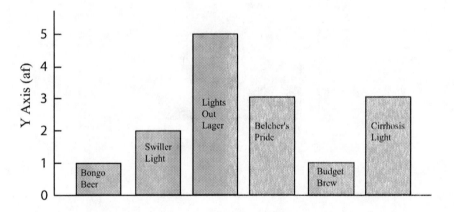

Key Terms to Remember

- Quantitative Frequency Distribution
- Qualitative Frequency Distribution
- Class Intervals
- Absolute Frequencies
- Cumulative Frequencies
- Relative Frequencies
- Cumulative Relative Frequencies
- Midpoints
- Upper and Lower Real Limits
- X Axis and Y Axis
- Histograms
- Frequency Polygons
- Bar Charts
- Pie Chart

Practice Exercises

1. Using the data found in Table 3.23 (below), construct a frequency distribution using class intervals of five minutes; calculate the absolute, cumulative, relative, and cumulative relative frequencies. Present your findings in a table format.
   a. Using the frequency distribution just constructed, calculate (1) the upper and lower real limits, and (2) the midpoints for each interval.
   b. Using the above information, construct (1) a frequency polygon, (2) a histogram, and (3) a pie chart.

Table 3.23   Time Required to Drink Beer Data Set

Number of Minutes Taken to Drink One Can of Beer in the Summertime for 12 Cartoon Characters		
2	8	
2	11	
3	12	
6	14	$(n = 12)$
7	15	
7	17	

2. Using the data found in Table 3.23 (above), construct a frequency distribution using class intervals of three minutes; calculate the absolute, cumulative, relative, and cumulative relative frequencies. Present your findings in a table format.
   a. Using the frequency distribution just constructed, calculate (1) the upper and lower real limits, and (2) the midpoints for each interval.
   b. Using the above information, construct (1) a frequency polygon, (2) a histogram, and (3) a pie chart.

3. Using the data found in Table 3.24 (page 56), construct a frequency distribution using class intervals of ten minutes, calculate the absolute, cumulative, relative and cumulative relative frequencies. Present your findings in a table format. (Hint: your first class interval should start at 20.)
   a. Using the frequency distribution just constructed, calculate (1) the upper and lower real limits, and (2) the midpoints for each interval.
   b. Using the above information, construct (1) a frequency polygon, (2) a histogram, and (3) a pie chart.

Table 3.24   Beer and Visits to the Bathroom Data Set

Number of Minutes Until a Visit to the Bathroom is Required After Drinking the First Can of Beer for Our 12 Cartoon Characters

20	47	
22	53	
27	54	
31	57	($n = 12$)
38	59	
45	62	

4. Using the data found in Table 3.24 (above), construct a frequency distribution using class intervals of fifteen minutes, calculate the absolute, cumulative, relative, and cumulative relative frequencies. Present your findings in a table format.
   a. Using the frequency distribution just constructed, calculate (1) the upper and lower real limits, and (2) the midpoints for each interval.
   b. Using the above information, construct (1) a frequency polygon, (2) a histogram, and (3) a pie chart.

5. Say we are interested in the brand of beers consumed by the twelve cartoon characters in Table 3.25. Instead of the Midwest (perhaps St. Louis), where the previous data were apparently collected (found in the chapter summary), the above cartoon characters lived in the Pacific Northwest. We find the data listed in Table 3.25 (below).
   a. Construct a frequency distribution for this qualitative data test.
   b. Using the above information, construct (1) a bar chart and (2) a pie chart.

6. The histogram in Figure 3.11 (opposite page) presents the time required to drink a beer for students attending Bacchus University (so named for the Greek god of wine and merriment). Using this graph construct a frequency distribution that includes the class intervals and midpoints and the absolute, cumulative, relative, and cumulative relative frequencies.

7. The frequency polygon in Figure 3.12 (opposite page) presents the time required to drink a beer for students at Temperance State College. Using this graph, construct a frequency distribution that includes the class intervals and midpoints and the absolute, cumulative, relative, and cumulative relative frequencies.

Table 3.25 Pacific Northwest Brand of Beer Data Set

Brand of Beer	Number of Characters Who Consume That Brand of Beer
Party Time Pilsner	1
Schacht Pale Ale	2
Marathon Malt Liquor	5
Dud's Suds	3
Aspelmut's Premium Porter	3
	14 Total

Figure 3.11 Histogram for Time Required to Drink a Beer for Students at Bacchus University

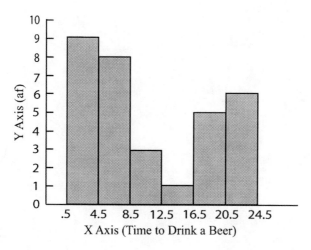

Figure 3.12 Frequency Polygon for Time Required to Drink a Beer for Students at Temperance State U.

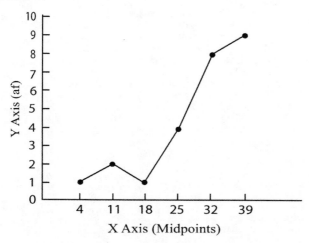

4

Measures of Central Tendency

Chapter 3 demonstrated various ways of grouping raw data into frequency distributions and creating corresponding graphic representations of the distributions. While these transformations gave us some preliminary ideas about what frequency distributions look like, they also involved several values to make these summaries (e.g., upper and lower real limits and histograms).

This chapter explores several techniques that allow us to summarize a whole data set using just one value. Moreover, while there are actually several ways a data set can be summarized with a single measure, this chapter describes four measures of central tendency: mode, median, mean, and weighed mean. As shown in Chapter 3, levels of measurements have a direct bearing on which techniques we can use. These measures are also presented using grouped data. Before turning to each term introduced, a brief introduction concerning measures of central tendency is warranted.

Measures of Central Tendency

When analyzing a given data set it is often quite helpful to identify the most typical score it contains. Mathematically, the most typical location within a data set is usually defined in terms of the average score most commonly found in the center of a set of numbers. That is, a *measure of central tendency* identifies what is seen as a middle point of data set. While there are several ways to make this determination, each of the following measures is ultimately concerned with describing and summarizing an entire data set of numbers with one single score seen as located in or near the center of the distribution.

Mode

The mode is the value that occurs most often or frequently in a data set. A good way to remember this term is to equate the "o" in *mode* with the value that occurs most "often." In terms of mathematical notation, we differentiate between a sample mode (a statistic) and population mode (a parameter), as shown below. (Remember that parameters describe a given data set that represents a whole population. Sample statistics, on the other hand, both describe a set of numbers and imply what its true value (the

Cartoon 4.1   CALVIN AND HOBBES

corresponding parameter) is in the population from which it is drawn. Thus, when any of the following measures are considered as statistics, they are also crude estimates of population parameters.)

$Mo_{\bar{x}}$ = Sample Mode

Mo_{μ} = Population Mode

The mode can be used with all levels of measurement. Using Cartoon 4.1 as a backdrop, let's say we are interested in the nominal characteristic of hair color of students in a statistics class that Calvin is presently enrolled in (N =50). The findings are reported in Table 4.1.

The modal category of this nominal distribution is brown hair. Twenty-two of Calvin's classmates have this hair color, which is more than any other color. Because we are treating the above data set as a population of values, designed by a capital N, the final answer with correct corresponding notation is Mo_{μ} = Brown Hair (22).

Instead of hair color, let's say we are interested in the attitudes toward taking statistics of those students who have successfully taken this class. From past statistics classes, we randomly sample 25 such students (n = 25) and ask them whether they strongly agree, agree, are neutral, disagree, or strongly disagree with the statement, "Taking a statistics class should be a requirement for all students to graduate." Remember, attitudinal scales yield an ordinal level of measurement. Our findings are reported in Table 4.2.

The mode in this case, the answer that occurs most often, with a frequency of 14, is strongly agree or 1. Our data is a sample of students, so the final answer with correct nota-

Table 4.1   Hair Color of Calvin's Classmates

Color	Frequency
Red	3
Brown	22
Black	17
Blond	8
	50 Total

Table 4.2   Students' Responses to the Statement, "Taking Statistics Should Be a Requirement for Graduation"

Attitude	Frequency
1. Strongly Agree	14
2. Agree	6
3. Neutral	3
4. Disagree	1
5. Strongly Disagree	5

tion is $Mo_{\tilde{x}} = 1$ (strongly agree). Most students strongly disagree with the above statement prior to taking statistics, but successful completion of such a course apparently converts many "math atheists" (see Cartoon 1.1).

Finally, let's say we are also interested in determining the number of minutes per day our sample of 25 students spent studying statistics to be able to successfully complete this class. Our findings are reported in Table 4.3. With a frequency of 5, the mode for this sample data set is 20 minutes; $Mo_{\tilde{x}} = 20$.

Although the mode enables us to report the frequency that occurs most often (in a sense the most popular response), it also has some specific limitations, one being that a given data set may not have a mode. Let's say, for example, that the above measured seconds spent studying instead of minutes. This might result in none of the scores being the same. Thus, there would be no mode in this hypothetical example. Moreover, there are also situations in which data sets have more than one mode. For instance, in the above example, if we eliminated the scores of 20 and 33 minutes then the frequencies of 3 and

Table 4.3   Absolute Frequencies for Time Spent Studying Statistics

Number or Minutes Spent Studying Statistics	Absolute Frequency
20	5
22	2
25	3
30	3
33	4
36	3
37	2
40	2
41	1
Total = 25	

their corresponding measurements (25, 30, and 36) would be the mode. In situations such as this, the mode is pretty meaningless.

Finally, while the mode is the response that occurs more often, it is not necessarily the most representative value of a distribution of scores. The above data set had a mode of 20 minutes, but this single score does not tell much about the rest of the scores in the distribution. The measures of median and mean often give more accurate representations of a whole distribution of scores.

Median

The median in a data set is similar to a median on a highway. A highway median usually divides a roadway in half. Likewise, a statistical median is the value in a data set which divides a set of observations in half; one-half of the observations are located above the median and one-half are found below it.

Although a median cannot be calculated for a nominal distribution, it can be used for both ordinal and interval-ratio distributions. And, while medians are often calculated for ordinal data sets, because such a level of measurement is discrete, answers that result in fractions are somewhat meaningless (e.g., an attitude of 2.5 on a given scale). Thus, continuous data are preferred in calculating medians (and means). If any of these terms are confusing, please refer back to Box 2.3 in Chapter 2 for a more detailed discussion.

To calculate the median, a date set must first be rank-ordered—arranged in ascending or descending order. The median, then, is simply the value located in the exact middle of a ranked distribution. The following notation is used to differentiate between a sample and population median.

$Mdn_{\bar{x}}$ = Sample Median

Mdn_{μ} = Population Median

Using Cartoon 4.2, let's say we are interested in the number of city blocks it takes a dog to "catch" a car. We sample 10 dogs and find the following values (expressed in blocks) 8, 2, 7, 4, 2, 0, 5, 4, and 2. To find the median, first rank-order the data set: 8, 7, 5, 4, 4, 3, 2, 2, 2, and 0. Once the data set is ranked, use the following formula to

Cartoon 4.2   MOTHER GOOSE & GRIMM

determine the exact middle of it. (Please note: Unlike the first three data sets presented in this chapter that were grouped into frequency distributions, this data set is comprised of ungrouped, raw data).

Formula to Determine the Middle of a Ranked Set of Numbers

$$\frac{N+1}{2} = \text{Middle of Data Set}$$

In this case at hand, the exact center of the data set is $(10 + 1)/2 = 5.5$. This tells us that the median is found at the 5.5 observation. Put another way, counting to 5.5 observations means the median falls between the 5th and 6th rank-ordered observations. The corresponding values of the 5th and 6th observations are 3 and 4. (Be careful not to confuse rank-ordered observations (e.g., 5th and 6th) with their actual corresponding values (e.g., 3 and 4). Although a median is determined using ranked observations, it is expressed as an actual data set value.) Thus, the final step is to take these two values, add them together, and divide by two: $(3 + 4)/2 = 3.5$. The median ($Mdn_{\bar{x}}$) for this data set is 3.5.

Note that one half of the scores is below the median and one half is above it: 8, 7, 5, 4, 4, (Median = 3.5), 3, 2, 2, 2, 0. Thus, half of our dogs took less than 3.5 blocks to catch a car, whereas the other half took more than 3.5 blocks to accomplish this feat.

The above example was calculated with an even-numbered data set ($n = 10$). This median is even easier to calculate with odd-numbered data sets. Let's add another value (0) to our data set on dogs chasing cars to make it odd numbered: 8, 7, 5, 4, 4, 3, 2, 2, 2, 0, and 0. Once again using the formula $(n + 1)/2$, we find that the center of this new data set is the sixth observation: $(11+1)/2=6$. Simply counting to the 6th rank-ordered observation finds ($Mdn_{\bar{x}}$) =3. In this data set it took the dogs a median of three blocks before they caught the car: 8, 7, 5, 4, 4, (Median = 3), 2, 2, 2, 0, 0.

Mean

The measure discussed thus far only indirectly considers all the values found in a data set, with the most typical observation relative to others or the middle of ranked observations. A mean, however, directly considers in its calculation each value—observation— found in a data set. This is accomplished by determining what is called the arithmetic average. Mathematically speaking then, a *mean* is literally the most "average" value in a data set. As such, it is also often seen as a more exact and representative measure of central tendency. Moreover, in various forms the mean is one of the most widely used measures in statistics.

To mathematically determine an average, simply sum all the numerical values found in a data set and then divide this value by the overall number of observations in the data set. Each numerical value is used in its calculation, so the resultant single measure—the mean—literally represents each value. (Conversely, if we take the mean value and multiply it by the sample size ($n\bar{X}$) we find it equals the sum of all the X values.) The formulas to accomplish this for a sample mean ($\bar{X}$) and a population mean (μ) are as follows:

<u>Sample Mean (Called "x bar")</u>

$$\bar{X} = \frac{\sum X}{n}$$

<u>Population Mean (Called "Mu")</u>

$$\mu = \frac{\sum X}{N}$$

Using the rules of algebraic order and summation notation, both of these formulas tell us to sum all of the X values and then divide by the total size of the sample or population. A mean cannot be used with nominal data and is predominantly used with interval-ratio data.

Referring back to our car-chasing data (8, 2, 7, 4, 3, 2, 0, 5, 4, and 2), to determine the mean for this set of observations, we first sum all these values (X of i's), $\sum X = 37$. (Note that a mean adds together all the values, so observations need not be rank-ordered.) The sum of the Xs is then divided by the number of observations in the data set; in the present case, 10. Thus, the final answer is $37/10 = 3.7$, or $\bar{X} = 3.7$. Our canines took an average of 3.7 blocks to catch the car.

While the mean is mathematically seen as the most representative value of a data set, there are instances where this conclusion is questionable. In instances where a data set contains an extreme score or scores, the resultant mean value may appear to be anything but a point of central location. (Data sets that include extreme values are also often skewed. More is said about this type of distribution later.)

To illustrate, say that we separately measured 5 additional dogs in terms of how many blocks it took each to catch a car and found the following: 2, 3, 5, 5, and 25. The mean for this data set is 8: $(2 + 3 + 5 + 5 + 25 = 40)/5 = 8$. The mean value of 8 is significantly larger than four of the five observations in this data set. As such, it doesn't appear to be very representative or centrally located, although mathematically it is.

Weighted Mean

Sometimes we are presented with situations where the mean must take into account another factor in its calculation. For example, let's say we are interested in the average number of seconds it took five different groups of dogs to catch a car. In other words, instead of one data set of dogs we are interested in the average times of five separately sampled sets of dogs. The findings for our speedy canines are reported in Table 4.4.

Table 4.4   Time Taken to Catch Car Data Sets

Group	Number of Dogs in Group	$\bar{X}$ Time in Seconds
One	15	40
Two	20	38
Three	25	35
Four	30	33
Five	35	30

Simply take the average from each group, sum these values, and divide the total by the number of groups: $(40 + 38 + 35 + 33 + 30)/5 = 35.2$ seconds. This is basically how we have calculated means thus far; 35.2 seconds is the simple arithmetic average for all five groups. The problem with calculating the average this way is that it does not take into account group size. As such, the value of 35.2 seconds does not accurately represent all five groups.

The easiest way to deal with this problem is to calculate the average by using what is called a weighted mean. A weighted mean compensates for the differing group sizes in its calculation. In other words, it is a more accurate measure in situations where the raw data have been summarized into nominal groups. The notation and formula for the weighted mean are as follows.

Weighted Mean

$$\bar{X}_w = \frac{\sum WX}{\sum W}$$

This formula is stated as the sum of the weights times X, divided by the sum of the weights. Many students have trouble determining which are the weights and which are the Xs. Quite simply, because X is the variable, it represents the characteristic of primary concern. On the other hand, W is the a factor that changes X.

The above case is concerned with the number of seconds required to catch a car; thus, it is X (e.g., 40, 38, 35, 33, and 30). Because group size potentially changes the overall value of the Xs, it then represents the weights (W = 15, 20, 25, 30, and 35). (Recall that the mean of any group multiplied by its corresponding size ($n\bar{X}$) equals the sum of all the X values. Thus, the resultant weighted-mean answer is the same that would be obtained if we used the raw data to make this determination.) To illustrate, let's calculate the weighted mean for the car-chasing data.

$$\bar{X}_w = \frac{(15)(40) + (20)(38) + (25)(35) + (30)(33) + (35)(30)}{15 + 20 + 25 + 30 + 35}$$

$$= \frac{4275}{125} = \boxed{34.2 \text{ seconds}}$$

Box 4.1   Dog's College Grades

Referring to the actual dog who caught the car in Cartoon 4.2, because he is obviously above average in his capacities, let's say he hates his day job (chasing cars) and has been attending night school to obtain a bachelor's degree in City Planning. Obtaining such a position would enable him to program traffic lights to make it easier to catch cars. His grade point averages and the number of credits taken for his four years of attending college are listed in Table 4.5. The school he is attending requires 135 credits with a 2.0 GPA. Will he receive his diploma at the end of this term?

Table 4.5   Dog's College Days

Year	Number of Credits	GPA
First Year	20	1.50
Sophomore	30	1.75
Junior	40	2.00
Senior	45	2.50
(A = 4, B = 3, C = 2, D = 1, F = 0)		

First, calculate a simple arithmetic mean by taking the sum of his GPAs and dividing by the number of school years:

(1.50 + 1.75 + 2.00 + 2.50)/4 = 7.75/4 = 1.9375.

A 1.9375 GPA, although close, falls short of the graduation requirement of a 2.0. A more accurate alternative would be to calculate his GPA using a weighted mean which would take into account the number of credit hours earned each year: (20 x 1.50) + (30 x 1.75) + (40 x 2.00) + (45 x 2.50)/(20 + 30 + 40 + 45) = 275/135 = 2.037.

The correct weighted GPA enables our fleet-of-foot and oh-so-bright canine to graduate. If your school offers courses for variable credit (e.g., biology 2 credits versus statistics 4 credits), it also calculates your overall GPA using a weighted mean.

By using a weighted mean, we find that for all five groups the average number of seconds it took the dogs to catch a car is actually 34.2 seconds. This is one whole second less than in the case in which we did not consider group size.

Locating the Mean, Median, and Mode in Skewed Distributions

While the level of measurement often decides which measure of centrality we use, the shape of a distribution may also affect this decision. If a distribution is symmetrical, we

Figure 4.1   A Symmetrical Distribution

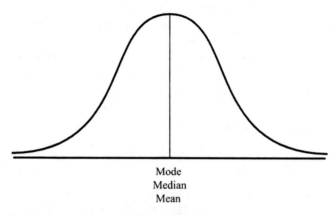

Mode
Median
Mean

Figure 4.2   Positively and Negatively Skewed Distributions

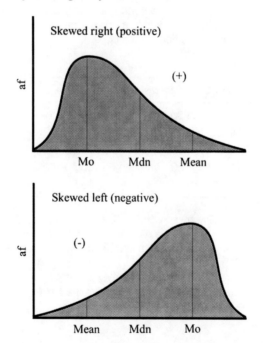

expect to find the mode, median, and mean all in the same location: equal or nearly equal. Figure 4.1 is a representation of a symmetrical distribution.

Often, however, due to extreme observations in a data set, we are presented with distributions that are skewed. When a distribution is skewed, the mode, median, and mean are found at different locations within it. Distributions that are skewed take two dichotomous shapes: skewed right (positive) and skewed left (negative). Figure 4.2 illustrates each of these distributions.

In both of these distributions the mean is found in what is called the tail region of the distribution. The far-left and far-right regions of a distribution are considered its tails. Moreover, because both of these figures indicate the presence of extreme scores, the mean is skewed in the direction of these scores.

An example of skewed, positive distribution in the United States is incomes. The average income in this country is always significantly higher than the median income. This indicates that there are a number of individuals (e.g., Donald Trump, Bill Gates) that have extremely large incomes, and as a result they skew the distribution of income in the United States. Perhaps this explains why the median income is most typically used in this

---

Box 4.2   Calvin's Allowance

Referring back to Cartoon 4.1, let's say Calvin thinks his weekly allowance of $2.50 is too small in comparison to the amount other kids get. To determine if this is, in fact, true, we ask the other 15 students in Miss Wormwood's class what their weekly allowances are. Treating this as a population, we obtain the ungrouped, raw data set reported in Table 4.6. Our task is to calculate the mode, median, and mean to determine if Calvin's assertion is correct.

Table 4.6   Weekly Allowances

Weekly Allowances of Calvin's Classmates					
Robin	$4.00	Lisa	$5.00	Tony	$5.00
Sam	$4.50	Paula	$5.00	Steve	$3.00
Allan	$6.00	Randi	$5.50	Susie	$7.00
Harry	$4.00	Jeff	$6.50	Anna	$6.50
Doris	$4.50	Duane	$5.00	Billy	$3.50

First, the mode weekly allowance is $5.00. Specifically, four of Calvin's classmates receive this amount—Lisa, Paula, Duane, and Tony—and this amount occurs more often than any other. To calculate the median first rank-order store prices: 3, 3.5, 4, 4, 4.5, 5, 5, 5, 5, 5.5, 6, 6.5, 6.5, 7. Using the formula $(N + 1)/2$ we get $(15 + 1)/2 = 8$. The eighth rank-ordered value has a corresponding value of 5; this is the median. To calculate the mean (μ), take the $\Sigma X/N = 75/15 = 5$. Considering all three values simultaneously finds:

$Mo_\mu = \$5.00$

$Mdn_\mu = \$5.00$

$\mu = \$5.00$

Because all of these values are the same, we apparently have a symmetrical distribution. More importantly, perhaps, from Calvin's point of view, we do have evidence that his weekly allowance is much less than other kids in Miss Wormwood's class. Given the amount of money his disruptive behavior probably costs his parents, however, he is probably lucky to receive any allowance at all!

Table 4.7   Absolute Frequencies for Time Required to Drink a Beer After Chasing a Car

Class Interval	af
1 - 5	2
6 - 10	5
11 - 15	6
16 - 20	7
21 - 25	3
26 - 30	1
	$n = 24$

country. Instead of having a significant majority of citizens making less than the average income, only one-half of the population ever makes less than the median income. Dependent upon one's ideological outlook, one measure is seen as superior to other.

Computing the Mode, Median, and Mean Using Grouped Data

Sometimes we are presented with data that have been grouped into frequency distributions using class intervals (as discussed in Chapter 3). When data are grouped in this manner and the original raw data are unavailable, we are forced to use variant formulas to calculate the mode, median, and mean.

Referring back to both Cartoons 3.2 and 4.2 as backdrops, let's say we are interested in the average amount of time (in minutes) it takes for a dog to drink—lap up—a beer after chasing a car. Our previous sample of 25 dogs resulted in the findings found in Table 4.7; the raw values used in its construction were unavailable. Our task is to determine the mode, median, and mean using the information found in this frequency distribution.

The simplest way to determine the mode is to find the interval that occurs most often, and then calculate this interval's midpoint. For the above data, the class interval that has the highest absolute frequency, an af of 7, is 16–20; (16 + 20 = 36)/2 = 18, which means the midpoint of that class interval is 18. Thus 18 minutes is the modal amount of time required to drink a can of beer. The raw data are unavailable, however, so this is an estimated modal value.

To calculate the median for group data we must first determine the cumulative frequencies for our distribution. This is done in Table 4.8. Remember that when we calculate the median we are looking for the middle observation in a ranked data set. To this end we take $(n + 1)/2$ or 25/2, which tells us that the 12.5th case is the median. This observation is found in the class interval of 11–15 ($cf = 13$). However, we do not know exactly where in this interval it would fall. To more accurately make this estimate we use the following formula.

Grouped Median Formula

$$Mdn_{group} = \text{Class Interval Lower Real Limit} + \left(\frac{\frac{n}{2} - cf_{below}}{af_{MdnCI}} \right) \text{ (Interval Size)}$$

Where:

cf_{below} :   Represents the cumulative frequency for the Class Interval that falls numerically below the Median Class Interval. When your class intervals are ranked in ascending order (smallest to largest) the cf_{below} will be physically located above the Median Class Interval.

$af_{Mdn\,CI}$:   Represents the absolute frequency for the Median Class Interval.

Applied to our example:

$$Mdn_{group} = 10.5 + \left(\frac{\frac{24}{2} - 7}{6} \right) 5 = 10.5 + (.833\overline{3})(5) = \boxed{14.6665}$$

Stated in the context of our example, the median time it took the dogs to lap up a can of beer was 14.6665 minutes.

The formula (below) for calculating the mean using grouped data is similar to that of the weighted mean. However, instead of weights and actual observations (X*is*) we use the absolute frequency for a given interval multiplied by its midpoint. Applied to the beer-drinking example once again, let's calculate this alternative mean. The intermediate steps for this calculation are reported in Table 4.9.

Formula for Mean Using Grouped Data

$$\overline{X}_{group} = \frac{\sum (afm)}{n}$$

Final Calculations of Mean for Grouped Data

$$\overline{X}_{group} = \frac{347}{24} = \boxed{14.458\overline{3}}$$

The 24 dogs took an average of 14.458$\overline{3}$ minutes to drink a can of beer after chasing a car. Apparently, car chasing is a strenuous activity that causes many of these dogs to become quite thirsty.

Chapter Summary and Conclusions

This chapter discussed several measures of central tendency that social scientists use to describe and summarize data distributions. All of these measures locate single points that are seen as most typical in a given distribution. While all of these measures make this

Table 4.8   Absolute and Cumulative Frequencies for Time Required to Drink a Beer After Chasing a Car

Class Interval	af	cf
1 - 5	2	2
6 - 10	5	7
11 - 15	6	1
16 - 20	7	20
21 - 25	3	23
26 - 30	1	24
	$n = 24$	

Table 4.9   Intermediate Steps for Calculating the Mean Using Grouped Data

Class Interval	af	CI Midpoint m	af m
1 - 5	2	3	6
6 - 10	5	8	40
11 - 15	6	13	78
16 - 20	7	18	126
21 - 25	3	23	69
26 - 30	1	28	28
	$n = 24$		$\Sigma(afm) = 347$

determination using different types of information, each has its advantages and disadvantages. Moreover, measures of central tendency are seen as starting points for analyzing data sets. The next analysis procedure usually undertaken is to determine the amount of variability found in a data set, the topic of the next chapter.

Key Terms to Remember

- Measures of Central Tendency
- Mode
- Median
- Mean
- Weighted Mean
- Skew

Practice Exercises

1. We are interested in examining the age of Calvin's friends. Yes (believe it or not), in addition to Hobbes, Calvin actually does have friends. Calvin's twenty friends' ($N = 20$) ages are reported in Table 4.10 (below).

    a. What are the *mode, median* (remember to rank-order the data), and *mean* for this data set?

Table 4.10   Calvin's Friends' Ages

		Age	
12	10	10	9
4	9	11	8
11	8	8	9
6	11	4	8
6	8	6	7

2. To find the speed, in miles per hour (mph), that our dogs traveled when chasing cars, we sample 15 dogs and found the following (reported in Table 4.11 [below]).

    a. What are the *mode, median* (remember to rank-order the data), and *mean* for this data set?

Table 4.11   Speed (m.p.h.) that Dogs Traveled When Chasing Cars

	Speed	
12	17	19
11	10	22
9	26	16
15	14	13
21	7	24

3. Table 4.12 (on opposite page) lists three variables: color, year, and make of the car that the 15 dogs in our example were chasing.

    a. Calculate all possible measures of central tendency—mode, median, and mean—for this data set.

    (Hint: Be very careful here; be sure to carefully consider the type of data [discrete vs. continuous] each variable represents.)

Table 4.12   Types of Cars Chased by Fifteen Dogs

Color, Year, and Make of Car Chased								
Yellow	1969	Ford	Green	2003	Nissan	Turquoise	1993	Toyota
Blue	1991	Chevy	Black	2003	Dodge	Green	1995	Honda
Red	1995	Ford	Blue	1994	Honda	Rust	1992	Chrysler
Purple	1995	BMW	Blue	2003	Ford	Orange	1994	Honda
Green	1999	Honda	Green	1999	Honda	Silver	2003	AMC

4. We are interested in the overall average speed of dogs who chase cars in rural, suburban, and inner-city settings, and we find the following (reported in Table 4.13 [below]).

   a. Calculate the weighted and unweighted means for this data set.

   b. Which is more accurate?

Table 4.13   Average Speeds for Different Groups of Dogs

Group	Number of Dogs in Group	$\bar{X}$ Speed (mph)
Rural	10	17
Suburban	15	15
Inner City	20	12

5. We are interested in last semester's grades of the dog who caught the car, so we obtain his grades from the registrar's office (reported in Table 4.14 [below]).

   a. Calculate the weighted and unweighted means for this data set.

   b. Which is more accurate?

   c. If these were your grades, which GPA would you rather have?

Table 4.14   Grades of the Dog Who Caught the Car

Course	Dog's College Grades Last Semester Number of Credits	GPA
Statistics	4	4
Biology	2	2
Criminology	3	3
English	4	4
Chemistry	3	2
Bowling	1	2
(A = 4, B = 3, C = 2, D = 1, F = 0)		

6. Table 4.15 (below) presents the data from exercise 2 grouped into 7 class intervals.
   a. Using this grouped data set, find the grouped mode, median, and mean.
   b. How do these results compare with the result obtained in exercise 2? Why might these results be different?

7. For each of the following problems you are given the mean, median, and mode for a data set. Using these values determine whether the data set is likely to be skewed or symmetrical. For skewed data sets, report whether they are skewed left (positive) or right (negative).
   a. Mean = 10, Median = 5, Mode = 2
   b. Mean = 4.8, Median = 5.2, Mode = 5
   c. Mean = 90, Median = 87, Mode = 86
   d. Mean = 5, Median = 8, Mode = 10
   e. Mean = 110, Median 15, Mode = 117
   f. Mean = 10, Median = 10, Mode = 10
   g. Of the skewed distributions presented above, which one is probably the most skewed.

Table 4.15   Speed that Dogs Traveled When Chasing Cars: Grouped Data

Class Interval	af
1 - 4	0
5 - 8	1
9 - 12	4
13 - 16	4
17 - 20	2
21 - 24	3
25 - 28	1

Measures of Variability

Chapter 4 discussed different measures of central tendency used by social scientists. While the mode, median, and mean locate important single points within distributions that are most typical and average, they tell us little else. Thus, to get a more complete and accurate picture of a given distribution, we must consider additional summary measures.

This chapter discusses several measures of variability, also referred to as measures of dispersion. To this end, the measures of range, variance, and standard deviation are explored in terms of what they represent and how they are calculated. These three measures are also summarized with single values. A more complete and accurate description of a data set results when both measures of central tendency and variability are used. Moreover, like measures of central tendency, measures of variability are used regularly as sub-parts of numerous statistical techniques (discussed in the second half of this text). Before turning to any of these new techniques, however, we need a brief introduction to variability and why it is an important measure.

Measures of Variability

As the term suggests, measures of variability tell us how much the observations in a data set *vary*, how they are *dispersed* within a distribution. Although measures of central tendency indirectly take into account the amount of variability in their calculation, they cannot

Cartoon 5.1   NON SEQUITUR

Non Sequitur

By Wiley

assess how a set of observations is dispersed within a distribution. Using Cartoon 5.1 as a backdrop, for instance, we want to determine the number of miles a penguin must waddle in the desert before its traveling companion appears to be human. We take eight penguins from a zoo and eight penguins from the South Pole and drop them off in the middle of a desert. Expressed in terms of number of miles it took before its companion appeared to be human, we find the following (reported in Table 5.1). Calculate the mode, median, and mean for each of the data sets.

Not only are both groups the same size ($N = 8$), but the resultant mode, median, and mean are exactly the same for both groups: 5. If we were using just measures of central tendency to summarize these two data sets, we would conclude that the two distributions are apparently identical. This, however, is obviously not true. That is, while zoo penguins appear inevitably to have hallucinations that their traveling companion is human after five miles, there is a great deal of fluctuation (variability) as to when penguins from the South Pole have such illusory images. Thus, to get a more complete picture of a data set, we must know both its measures of central tendency and variability. Also, as we will see in later chapters, only when both values are simultaneously considered can meaningful comparisons of different data sets be made.

Range

One of the easiest ways to describe the amount of variation in a data set is to note its smallest and biggest values. Statisticians often refer to these values as *X maximum* and *X minimum*; literally, these are the largest and smallest values found in the data set. The values of X maximum and X minimum are also used to calculate the *range*: a simple measure of the distance between the largest and smallest observations in a data set. Mathematically, this is accomplished by subtracting the smallest value, X minimum, from the largest value, X maximum: *X maximum − X minimum = range*.

We will reuse Cartoon 5.1 as a backdrop to demonstrate this, and introduce its accompanying data set (Table 5.2). This data set represents a population of 15 humans in terms

Table 5.1   Number of Miles Traveled Before Traveling Companion Appeared to Be Human

Zoo Penguins	South Pole Penguins
5	2
5	8
5	4
5	7
5	5
5	6
5	5
5	3

Table 5.2   Miles Crawled Before Traveling Companion Appeared to Be a Penguin

Number of Miles		
2	7	13
4	9	14
4	10	15
4	11	19
5	13	20

of the number of miles each crawled across the desert before his or her traveling companion appeared to be a penguin. The data set is also rank-ordered to make subsequent calculations easier.

With the observations ranked, it is quite easy to see that the largest value, X maximum, is 20, while the smallest value, X minimum, is 2. To calculate the range, X minimum is subtracted from X maximum $(20 - 2)$, to find that this data set has a range of 18 miles in terms of how long it took before the given crawling person's partner appeared to be a penguin.

Often it is helpful to know the highest and lowest scores in a distribution, such as on a recent exam you took. Beyond noting the most extreme scores in a distribution and the distance between them, however, the range has no other value and is not used in any subsequent statistical procedures. As such, it is a very crude measure of the amount of variability in a data set.

Variance and Standard Deviation

While the range tells the width of a data set, it does not take into consideration all of the variability present in a data set. In fact, the only variability it does measure is two extreme values: the largest and smallest. Thus, while the above data set has a range of 18 miles, it gives no idea how the other observations are dispersed within it. As a result, we have no idea if most of the observations occur at the extremes of the distribution (by the 2 and 20) or if they tend to occur towards its center. Two closely related measures that make this determination are variance and standard deviation. Before describing how to calculate these measures, however, we must define more clearly what they represent.

For a measure to mathematically assess the total amount of variability in data set, it must consider the value of every observation in the set. Furthermore, such a measure requires a point from which the observations in the data set can be compared to assess the amount they fluctuate. A mathematical mean uses every observation in its calculation and gives us a single point, and so it is an excellent value to make this determination. That is,

Table 5.3   Mean Deviations for Penguin Hallucinations

$\Sigma(X - \mu)$ = Mean Deviation Applied to the Hallucination Data Set		
2 - 10 = -8	7 - 10 = -3	13 - 10 = +3
4 - 10 = -6	9 - 10 = -1	14 - 10 = +4
4 - 10 = -6	10 - 10 = 0	15 - 10 = +5
4 - 10 = -6	11 - 10 = +1	19 - 10 = +9
5 - 10 = -5	13 - 10 = +3	20 - 10 = +10

one way we can measure the amount of variability in a data set is to use its mean as a point from which each observation is compared.

The easiest way to make this determination mathematically is to subtract the mean from each observation, and then sum these answers into one final μ. The formula that does this, referred to as the *mean deviation*, along with the appropriate calculations applied to the hallucination data set (Table 5.2) are: N = 15 and μ = 10 ($\mu = \Sigma X/N$ = 150/15 = 10). Table 5.3 presents the resulting mean deviations for this data set.

Thus,

$$\Sigma(X-\mu) = -8 + -6 + -6 + -6 + -5 + -3 + -1 + 0 + 1 + 3 + 3 + 4 + 5 + 9 + 10 = 0$$

As you probably have noted, the problem with this approach is that the sum of the deviations equals 0. In fact, the sum of the mean deviation for symmetrical data sets is always zero (*0*). While this is an interesting outcome, a value of zero is a meaningless measure of dispersion. As such, an alternative method must be employed to measure the amount of variability in a data set.

One simple way to deal with this is to separately square each of the deviation values (e.g., –8 and –6), so that each negative value is canceled out (any negative value squared becomes a positive value). These squared values are then summed and subsequently divided by the number of observations to give us what is considered an average variation value. These operations are all found in the following *definitional formula* of variance.

$$\frac{\Sigma(X - \bar{X})^2}{N}$$

While definitional formulas give a clearer idea of the operations in the formula, they are also cumbersome to use (especially with larger data sets). As a result, what are called *computational formulas* are usually used. Notwithstanding the above definitional formula that is presented to demonstrate the operations used in calculating the variance (the sum of each observation minus the mean), this text exclusively uses computational formulas. This formula format is much easier to calculate and, although beyond the scope of this text, it is the algebraic equivalent of the definitional formula. (Regardless of which formula is used, the same answer is obtained.)

Listed below are two computational formulas for calculating variance. The first formula, represented by a σ^2 (sigma squared), is for population distributions, and the second formula, represented with an s^2, is for sample distributions.

$$\text{Population Variance} = \sigma^2 = \frac{\Sigma X^2 - \frac{(\Sigma X)^2}{N}}{N}$$

$$\text{Sample Variance} = s^2 = \frac{\Sigma X^2 - \frac{(\Sigma X)^2}{n}}{n-1}$$

The reason for the difference between the formulas (N versus $n-1$) is that the sample is an estimate. The implications of this are discussed in detail in later chapters on inferential statistics. Nevertheless, since a sample variance always has a smaller denominator ($n-1$ versus N), it will always result in an answer larger than the equivalent found using the population variance formula. Although it is important to note that these formulas yield different answers, to demonstrate this and how to make the calculations in general, we reuse the hallucination data (Table 5.2). That is, although this data set is noted to be a population ($N = 15$), we also treat it as a hypothetical sample ($n = 15$) for demonstration purposes.

Using the rules of algebraic order and summation notation (please refer back to Chapter 2 if any of the following calculations are confusing), both formulas ask for three initial and identical determinations: (1) What is N or n? (2) What is the sum of all squared X values? (3) What is the sum of the X values? The group size, N or n, of this data set is simply 15. The next determination, the sum of all squared X values, requires that each observation be squared and then these values are summed. Alternatively, the last determination, the sum of the X values, requires all the X values simply to be added together. With the column headings of X representing the raw data and X^2 representing each of the observations squared, each of these determinations is summarized below. The intermediate steps are presented in Table 5.4.

Thus,

$\underline{\Sigma X = \text{Sum of } X}$

$\Sigma X = 2 + 4 + 4 + 4 + 5 + 7 + 9 + 10 + 11 + 13 + 13 + 14 + 15 + 19 + 20 = \boxed{150}$

and

$\underline{\Sigma X^2 = \text{Sum of All Squared } X \text{ Values}}$

$\Sigma X^2 = 4 + 16 + 16 + 16 + 25 + 49 + 81 + 100 + 121 + 169 + 169 + 196 + 225 + 361$

$+ 400 = \boxed{1948}$

Table 5.4   Intermediate Steps for Finding Variance

X	X^2	X	X^2	X	X^2	
2	4	7	49	13	169	
4	16	9	81	14	196	
4	16	10	100	15	225	$N(n) = 15$
4	16	11	121	19	361	
5	25	13	169	20	400	

Having made these initial determinations, we plug them into their appropriate places on the given formula and find the following.

<u>Population Variance</u>

$$\sigma^2 = \frac{1948 - \dfrac{(150)^2}{15}}{15} = \frac{1948 - \dfrac{(22,500)}{15}}{15} = \frac{1948 - 1500}{15} = \frac{448}{15} = \boxed{29.86\overline{6}}$$

<u>Sample Variance</u>

$$s^2 = \frac{1948 - \dfrac{(150)^2}{15}}{15 - 1} = \frac{1948 - \dfrac{(22,500)}{15}}{14} = \frac{1948 - 1500}{14} = \frac{448}{14} = \boxed{32.0}$$

As expected, the sample variance using the smaller denominator value (14 versus 15) results in a larger final answer: 32.0 versus 29.8666.

Although the variance is used as a sub-part in many statistical formulas that are explored in the remaining chapters of this text, as a single summary measure it has very little meaning until it is converted into a standardized score called a *standard deviation*. This is accomplished mathematically by calculating the square root of the obtained variance value. In other words, to calculate a standard deviation value we automatically calculate the variance value. Because a variance involves the squaring of values in its calculation to determine the total amount that all observations deviate from the mean, calculating the square root converts it back into the original units of measurement. The formulas for population and sample standard deviations appear below with the remaining calculations applied to the hallucination data set (Table 5.2).

Several observations are necessary at this point. Recall that the σ and the s indicate whether we are calculating a parameter or a statistic. Remember, Greek letters are used to

Population Standard Deviation

$$\sigma^2 = \sqrt{\frac{\Sigma X^2 - \dfrac{(\Sigma X)^2}{N}}{N}} = \sqrt{\frac{1948 - 1500}{15}} = \sqrt{\frac{448}{15}} = \sqrt{29.8666} = \boxed{5.4650}$$

Sample Standard Deviation

$$s^2 = \sqrt{\frac{\Sigma X^2 - \dfrac{(\Sigma X)^2}{n}}{n-1}} = \sqrt{\frac{1948 - 1500}{15-1}} = \sqrt{\frac{448}{14}} = \sqrt{32.0} = \boxed{5.6568}$$

signify population parameters, while lower-case Latin letters are used to denote statistics. Moreover, because we are taking the square root of a value that is seen as squared, the previous square symbols used to denote variance formulas have been dropped. These symbols (i.e., σ and s), however, are not to be confused with any actual calculations. Rather, like previous formulas (and many to follow), these symbols are summaries of formulas that specify what calculations are undertaken.

Referring to the data set from which these calculations were made, we now know that these people not only took an average of 10 miles crawling on the desert floor before they had a penguin hallucination, but they also had a standard deviation of 5.465 miles. As will become clearer in the next chapter, this value (expressed in miles) enables us to infer what percentage of desert crawlers are this distance from the mean.

For now, however, variance and standard deviation values still allow us to make one important preliminary conclusion about any data set. Quite simply, the larger variance and standard deviation values, relative to the numerical values of the observations in the data set, the greater the amount of variability that is present in the data set. Conversely, smaller variance and standard deviation values indicate less variability.

Thus, the first hallucination data set (Table 5.1), where all of the observations equaled 5, has no variability; both variance and standard deviation values equal 0. The above data set, relatively speaking, however, has a great deal of variability in it and this is reflected in its large variance and standard deviation values.

Additional Example for Range, Variance, and Standard Deviation

Before summarizing this chapter, we now create one more data set around another cartoon example to review each of the formulas. To this end, we offer Cartoon 5.2 (to be used again for the Practice Exercises) and its corresponding data set found in Table 5.5.

(Note: It is not rank-ordered.) The data set represents a sample of 20 children who are six years old in terms of the number of times daily they question their parents' authority (e.g., I don't want to: go to bed, stop picking my nose, change my underwear, take a bath, take a math class, etc.).

Following the same order of presentation used at the beginning of this chapter, we first calculate the range. Again, this is accomplished by taking X maximum (23) and subtracting X minimum (1) from it: $23 - 1 = 22$. Thus, the range for this data set is 22.

This is a sample ($n = 20$) so we must calculate a sample variance and standard deviation. The computational formulas needed to do this are replicated below. Remember that these are virtually the same formulas except that the formula for standard deviation involves one more step: calculating the square root of the variance.

<u>Sample Variance</u>

$$s^2 = \frac{\Sigma X^2 - \dfrac{(\Sigma X)^2}{n}}{n-1}$$

<u>Sample Standard Deviation</u>

$$s^2 = \sqrt{\frac{\Sigma X^2 - \dfrac{(\Sigma X)^2}{n}}{n-1}}$$

Table 5.5   Number of Times 20 Sampled Children Question Their Parents' Authority in a Day's Period

Number of Times Authority is Questioned				
4	2	5	7	
11	9	16	6	
1	4	3	14	($n = 20$)
21	18	12	8	
7	23	11	10	

Cartoon 5.2   CALVIN AND HOBBES

Again, these formulas instruct us to calculate the sum of the Xs and the sum of all squared X values. The intermediate steps for this are presented in Table 5.6. We already know that the n (sample size) is equal to 20. (All of the calculations for these formulas are summarized below; please review them and make sure you understand how each one is made.)

Thus,

$\underline{\Sigma X = \text{Sum of } X}$

$\Sigma X = 4 + 11 + 1 + 21 + 7 + 2 + 9 + 4 + 18 + 23 + 5 + 16 + 3 + 12 + 11 + 7 + 6 + 14$

$\quad + 8 + 10 = \boxed{192}$

$\underline{\Sigma X^2 = \text{Sum of All Squared } X \text{ Values}}$

$\Sigma X^2 = 16 + 121 + 1 + 441 + 49 + 4 + 81 + 16 + 324 + 529 + 25 + 256 + 9$

$\quad + 144 + 121 + 49 + 36 + 196 + 64 + 100 = \boxed{2582}$

$\underline{\text{Sample Variance}}$

$$s^2 = \frac{2582 - \dfrac{(192)^2}{20}}{20 - 1} = \frac{2582 - \dfrac{(36,864)}{20}}{19} = \frac{2582 - 1843.2}{19} = \frac{738.8}{19} = \boxed{38.8842}$$

$\underline{\text{Sample Standard Deviation}}$

$$\sigma^2 = \sqrt{\frac{2582 - 1843.2}{20 - 1}} = \sqrt{38.8842} = \boxed{6.2357}$$

Table 5.6   Intermediate Steps for Finding Sample Variance and Standard Deviation

X	X^2	X	X^2	X	X^2	X	X^2
4	16	2	4	5	25	7	49
11	121	9	81	16	256	6	36
1	1	4	16	3	9	14	196
21	441	18	324	12	144	8	64
7	49	23	529	11	121	10	100

The final answers show that the number of times these 20 six-year-olds questioned their parents' authority has a variance of 38.8842 and corresponding standard deviation of 6.2357. The mean for this data set is 9.6 (192/20 = 9.6) and the standard deviation is 6.2357, so we can infer that most of the children questioned their parents' authority between 3 and 15 times a day. The last conclusion is based on the idea of a normal distribution and how scores are dispersed within it—which is the topic of the next chapter.

Chapter Summary and Conclusions

This chapter began by noting that, although measures of central tendency provide important information about a data set, they give no idea about how the observations are dispersed. It then discussed three techniques that measure the variability present in a distribution: the range, the variance, and the standard deviation. The range tells how much variation is in a data set in terms of two extreme values (the largest minus the smallest), but it does not take into consideration the rest of the values in the data set.

Variances and standard deviations give a much better measure of how much variability is in a data set by considering all the observations in their calculation. The larger the obtained values are for each of these measures, relative to the numbers being considered, the more variability there is in the data set. Conversely, small variance and standard deviation values indicate that there is very little variability in the data set. Finally, as will become apparent in the following chapters, variances and standard deviations are important sub-parts for numerous other statistical procedures.

Key Terms to Remember

- Measures of Variability
- X Maximum
- X Minimum
- Range
- Variance
- Standard Deviation

Practice Exercises

1. Assume that we collect information on the number of authoritarian orders ("you will do it because I say so" or "you will do it or else") the children's parents make daily. Findings are reported in Table 5.7 (below).
   a. Calculate the range.
   b. Treat this as a sample and calculate the variance and standard deviation using the appropriate formula ($n = 20$).
   c. Treat this as a population and use the appropriate formulas to calculate the variance and standard deviation.
   d. Which is larger, the sample standard deviation or the population variance? Why is one larger than the other?

Table 5.7   Daily Number of Authoritarian Orders Parents Give Their Children

Number of Orders			
6	3	2	3
12	1	11	7
4	4	2	14 ($n = 20$)
11	9	6	7
7	10	3	9

2. Instead of studying six-year-olds, assume we are now interested in the number of times thirteen-year-olds question parental authority in a day's period. Using 25 research subjects, we find the following as reported in Table 5.8 (below).
   a. Calculate the range.
   b. Treat this as a population and calculate the variance and standard deviation using the appropriate formulas ($N = 25$).
   c. Treat this as a sample and use the appropriate formulas to calculate the variance and standard deviation.
   d. Are these answers different than those found for the six-year-olds? If so, why?

Table 5.8   Number of Times 25 Thirteen-Year-Olds Question Their Parents' Authority In a Day's Period

Number of Times Authority Is Questioned by Thirteen-Year Olds				
8	23	5	7	15
11	29	16	6	27
10	14	3	14	18 ($n = 25$)
21	18	12	8	9
17	23	11	10	22

3. Referring back to Cartoon 5.1, say that our present research interests are the number of penguins a given person sees once he or she starts to hallucinate. We sample 15 people and find the following, expressed in terms of number of penguins seen during desert crawler's hallucination (see Table 5.9 below).
   a. Calculate the range.
   b. Treat this as a sample and calculate the variance and standard deviation using the appropriate formulas ($n = 15$).
   c. Treat this as a population and use the appropriate formulas to calculate the variance and standard deviation.

Table 5.9   Number of Penguins Seen During Hallucination

Number of Penguins		
6	3	2
12	1	11
4	4	2 ($n = 15$)
11	9	6
7	10	3

4. A statistics professor notices that her students often complain during class about having hallucinations involving penguins. She decides to assess the frequency of penguin hallucinations for students during statistics class and for students during introductory English class. The data for each class is presented in Table 5.10 (on opposite page).
   a. Find the sample variance and sample standard deviation for the statistics students.
   b. Find the sample variance and sample standard deviation for the English students.
   c. What conclusions can you draw about the frequency of students' penguin hallucinations in these two courses?

Table 5.10 Frequency of Hallucinations for Statistics and English Students

Number of Penguins Hallucinated by Each Student			
Statistics (n = 22)		English (n = 22)	
10	20	1	20
11	21	1	21
13	21	5	24
14	22	6	27
15	22	9	29
17	23	11	29
18	25	11	31
18	26	13	34
19	27	16	35
19	29	19	39
20	30	20	39

6

Locating Points Within a Distribution

Chapters 4 and 5 explored techniques for locating and describing points of centrality and variability in distributions. This chapter takes these ideas a step further and uses them to locate and summarize any given observation relative to all observations in a distribution.

Specifically, this chapter explores techniques to calculate what are called percentile scores and standardized scores derived from a normal distribution, also called a Z distribution. Standardized scores are also explored in terms of how they can be used to calculate percentile rankings. The measures discussed in this chapter ultimately allow us to compare and summarize where any given observation is located relative to all the observations in a data set from which it was drawn.

Although we have just introduced several foreign but similar-sounding terms—percentiles, standardized scores, and normal/Z distribution—don't panic. As with previous presentations, in turn, each of these rather simple but also difficult-sounding concepts is explored in detail.

Percentile Ranks and Percentiles

At one time or another, nearly everyone in our society has been assigned a percentile ranking. Often percentile rankings are applied to us without our knowledge. A few examples of percentile rankings that may have been applied to you include SAT scores, IQ scores,

Cartoon 6.1   ADAM

GRE (Graduate Record Exam) scores, grades, your class ranking in your high school class, income level, and so forth. In each of these examples, a percentile ranking designates where your score occurs—is located—relative to the rest of the scores in the distribution. A person can obtain a score on the GRE in the 98th percentile, but—if still in graduate school—have a personal income that places him or her in the 10th percentile of this latter measure. While most people have an intuitive feeling that being ranked in the upper percentiles is typically good and appearing in the bottom percentiles is often bad, many people probably have no idea how this measure is actually calculated.

To demonstrate what has been stated abstractly thus far, we offer Cartoon 6.1 and its accompanying data set (Table 6.1). The data set reflects our current research interests: video-game scores for 20 ten-year-olds. More specifically, this data set gives video-game scores for 20 children on a scale of 0 to 50. A score of 0 means virtually no knowledge of video games, whereas a score of 50 means comprehensive knowledge of such games. Thus, Bob with a score of 50 is seen as having perfect knowledge of video games. Alternatively, Steve's score of 14 means that he has very little knowledge of these types of games.

Say we want to know how Alex's score compares to those of the other kids. In other words, we want to know Alex's percentile ranking. The formula used to make this determination is provided below. The notation to the left of the equal sign (Pr) simply indicates the formula being used. The two symbols to the right of the equal sign (*B* and *N*), however, do call for specific computations. The *B* represents the number of observations found "below" the score for which we are calculating a percentile ranking. The *N* should look familiar, it represents the total number of observations in the data set. The capital *N* signifies that all data sets used to calculate percentile ranks are viewed as populations rather than samples. The resultant answers of *B* / *N* is then multiplied by 100 to give an actual percentile ranking.

$$P_r = \frac{B}{N} \times 100 = \text{percentile ranking of } X_i$$

Before we can calculate Alex's percentile ranking, however, we must first rank-order the raw data in either ascending or descending order. This is the only meaningful way the number of scores below (*B*), the score of interest, can be determined. The order in which a data set is ranked largely depends on whether a high or a low score is seen as more desir-

Table 6.1   Video Game Scores for 20 Ten-Year-Olds

Video Scores							
Janice	46	Anna	38	Allan	15	Pina	32
Harry	49	Randi	28	Alex	43	Katie	17
John	27	Dan	24	Nicole	47	Billy	29
Jenny	34	Jeff	22	Roby	41	Steve	14
Jim	23	Chris	42	Helen	31	Bob	50

Table 6.2   Ranked Video Game Scores

			Ranked Scores		
1.	Bob	50	11.	Helen	31
2.	Harry	49	12.	Billy	29
3.	Nicole	47	13.	Randi	28
4.	Janice	46	14.	John	27
5.	Alex	43	15.	Dan	24
6.	Chris	42	16.	Jim	23
7.	Roby	41	17.	Jeff	22
8.	Anna	38	18.	Katie	17
9.	Jenny	34	19.	Allan	15
10.	Pina	32	20.	Steve	14

able in the given context. We jokingly think knowledge of video games is a positive characteristic, so the original scores have been ranked from highest to lowest. Finally, to assist in subsequent calculations, the scores also are numbered. Table 6.2 represents the reformatted data set.

We are now ready to calculate Alex's percentile ranking. Applying this data set to the above formula, first note that it contains 20 observations, so $N = 20$. To determine B, count the number of rank-ordered scores that occur below the score of interest. For Alex, then, there are 15 scores that occur below his (6–20), so $B = 15$.

Plugging these values into the formula below informs us that Alex's score ranks in the 75th percentile of video game scores. Stated slightly differently, we are saying that 75% of the other kids' scores fall below Alex's score. Reflected by his score, Alex is obviously pretty knowledgeable about video games.

$$P_r = \frac{15}{20} = .75 \times 100 = \boxed{75^{\text{th}} \text{ percentile}}$$

Starting with Harry's score, let's calculate a few more percentile rankings with this data set. Once again, N equals 20, while B in this case equals 18 (the number of scores occurring below Harry's). We plug these values into the formula below to find that Harry's score is in the 90th percentile. With a corresponding score of 49, he is obviously quite knowledgeable about video games.

$$P_r = \frac{18}{20} = .90 \times 100 = \boxed{90^{\text{th}} \text{ percentile}}$$

Finally, let's say we are interested in Dan's percentile ranking. There are five scores below Dan's, so divide the B (5) by the N (20) to find that he is ranked in the 25th percentile. All of this is mathematically summarized below. With a score of 24, Dan would appear fairly knowledgeable about video games. In comparison to the other kids, however, Dan's score is relatively low; only 25% of the kids had a score less than his.

$$P_r = \frac{5}{20} = .25 \times 100 = \boxed{25^{th} \text{ percentile}}$$

As another example, let's say we are interested in the exam scores of 10 students who are presently using this textbook. The statistics exam administered to these students was worth 100 possible points. To assist with subsequent calculations, their scores (reported in Table 6.3) are already rank-ordered from highest to lowest.

Summarized below are the calculations for Tony's, Tammy's, and Josh's percentile rankings.

$$P_r = \frac{B}{N} \times 100$$

As you can see, Tony is ranked in the 80th percentile, Tammy is ranked in the 50th percentile, and Josh is in the 20th percentile. As with the previous video-game example, these students' scores of 93, 82, and 74, respectively, have been converted into rankings.

While ranking scores is often a helpful way to organize and interpret findings, the original scores and the context from which they are derived should not be forgotten. For instance, let's say that on the last quiz in this class your score was ranked in the 10th percentile. That is, only 10% of the students had a score lower than yours. On the other hand, you had 94% right on the next quiz which earned you a solid A. In this example, we imagine you will take the A, and who cares how you compare to the other students in the class? In other words, although percentile rankings can help us make important comparisons, we still must take into account the original scores and the context from which they were drawn.

Standardized Scores and Distributions: Z Scores

Another way to rank scores is to use standardized scores combined with a normal distribution. A normal distribution is the theoretical shape in which we expect frequencies of

Table 6.3   Exam Scores for 10 Statistics Students

	Exam Scores				
1.	Kendra	96	6.	Robin	78
2.	Tony	93	7.	Chris	77
3.	Collin	89	8.	Josh	74
4.	Lisa	86	9.	Sarah	71
5.	Tammy	82	10.	Michael	70

observations to be distributed in a data set. A normal curve is also referred to as the bell-shaped curve, a *Z*-score distribution, and a Gaussian distribution.

Describing where observations are located in a normal distribution involves using two measures explored earlier—the mean and the standard deviation. Recall that a mean is the mathematical average and a measure of centrality for a distribution, and the standard deviation measures the average amount of variability present. (If any of these terms or concepts are unfamiliar to you, please refer to Chapters 4 and 5.)

Using these measures in concert, we can calculate what is called a *Z* score for every actual and hypothetical observation in a data set. Chapter 9 demonstrates how *Z* scores also allow us to compare the distributions of two or more data sets to discover if there are differences between them. For now, however, we explore how *Z* scores enable us to determine where a given observation is located in a data set, in terms of its probability of occurrence relative to the whole distribution. The formula for calculating *Z* scores is as follows:

$$\frac{X - \mu}{\sigma} = Z \text{ Score or } Z \text{ of } X$$

Remember, the μ in the formula represents a population mean, the σ represents a population standard deviation, and the X represents a given observation. Mathematically, the formula instructs us to subtract the population mean (μ) from the observation (X) of interest, and then divide this answer by the data set's population standard deviation. The

Cartoon 6.2   CALVIN AND HOBBES

resultant answer is a *Z score* (also referred to as the *Z* of X), which is the number of standard deviations that the score is from the mean.

(Please note: Theoretically, *Z* scores always represent a population of observations. Often, however, because a sample theoretically takes on the shape of a normal distribution in samples larger than 120, many statistics textbooks use a sample mean and sample standard deviation to calculate *Z* scores. Either way, assume that a rather large data set is being used whenever *Z* scores are being calculated.)

Before discussing *Z* scores any further, it would be helpful to first practice calculating them. To this end, we offer Cartoon 6.2 and the findings that accompany it; $\mu = 100$ and $\sigma = 15$. These findings represent the IQs of fourth-grade children who are *not* "willfully stupid" enough to drive their wagon over a cliff—poor Hobbes. (Please note: An average IQ of 100 with a standard deviation of 15 are the same values that researchers use to describe human IQs.)

Average IQ Score for Fourth-grade Children: $\mu = 100$
Standard Deviation for Fourth-grade Children: $\sigma = 15$

With this in mind, what is the *Z* score for a child with an IQ of 85? 130? 105? 100? (Each of the calculations is reported below.)

$$\frac{X - \mu}{\sigma} = Z \ ; \qquad \frac{85 - 100}{15} = \boxed{-1} \ ; \qquad \frac{130 - 100}{15} = \boxed{+2} \ ;$$

$$\mu = 100, \sigma = 15 \ ; \qquad \frac{105 - 100}{15} = \boxed{+.3333} \ ; \qquad \frac{100 - 100}{15} = \boxed{0}$$

One should quickly note that the average of a *Z* distribution always equals 0 in *Z* score units: $(100-100)/15 = 0$. That is, an observation that equals the mean obviously does not deviate from it. Further, when an *X* (observation) larger than the mean is considered, we always obtain a positive *Z*, while an *X* (observation) smaller than the mean results in a negative *Z*. It will be important to differentiate between negative and positive *Z* scores in later applications, so please make careful note of this in all your calculations. Thus, a child with an IQ of 85 is one whole standard deviation below (–1) the mean, whereas a child with an IQ of 130 is two whole standard deviations above the mean (+ 2). Alternatively, a child with an IQ of 105 is one-third of a standard deviation above the mean (.3333).

In addition to telling how many standard deviations an observation is from the mean in a data set, *Z* scores are also used to predict the likelihood of a certain value in a data set being observed. This is accomplished by locating the observation, expressed as a *Z* score, on a normal distribution—also known as a bell-shaped curve (see Figure 6.1). This figure of a normal distribution, like histograms and frequency polygons, represents a frequency distribution. Unlike most histograms and frequency polygons, however, it is perfectly symmetrical in shape. Theoretically, 50% of the observations in a normal distribution are found to the right of the mean (also conceived of as the mode and median) and 50% are found to the left.

The bell-shaped curve represents the frequencies of occurrence in a distribution; the higher the line is in relation to the Y axis, the more likely this value is to occur in the data set. Thus, as reflected in Figure 6.1, observations on a normal distribution are more likely to occur around the mean, while the further one gets from the mean the less likely a given observation is to occur.

With this figure in mind, let's reevaluate one of the *Z*-score determinations we made. Now we not only determine how many standard deviations a child with an IQ of 85 is from the mean, but also how many children in general have an IQ of *85 or less*. (The example is based upon humans' IQ scores, so one could also think of it in terms of the probability that the next person you meet—perhaps on a blind date—will have an IQ of 85 or less.)

For example, when the *Z* score of –1 (85–100/15 = –1) is located on the X axis of the above figure, we find only a small percentage of children with an IQ less than 85. More specifically, a *Z* score of –1 applied to the above figure tells us that 15.87% of the children have an IQ of 85 or less. We determined this value by noting that part of the distribution to the left of the mean equals 50% and the distance from the mean to –1 is 34.13%; thus, 50% – 34.13% = 15.87%.

Alternatively, we might want to know how many children have an IQ between 100 and 115. Using Figure 6.1, we find that 34.13% of the children have an IQ of 100 to 115. Because 50% of the children have an IQ of 100 or less, we can further conclude that 84.13% of the children have an IQ of 115 or less; 50% + 34.13% = 84.13%.

Many of you may find what just was abstractly stated to make intuitive sense, but from past experience we would guess that just as many of you are somewhat lost at this point. Moreover, what do we do when we have *Z* scores that are not whole numbers (e.g., .3333 or –1.35)? A more systematic and simpler way to make all of these determinations is to

Figure 6.1   Shape of the Normal Distribution

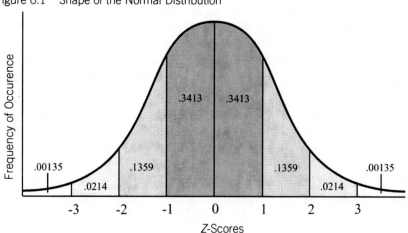

use Appendix 1, which contains a summary table of Z scores applied to the normal distribution. Each listed Z value in this table (found in column 1) also offers three corresponding probability values (columns 2–4). We can also use the probability values listed in this table to determine corresponding actual values (X).

To demonstrate more clearly this table's usage, we offer the following mean and standard deviation for women's heights in the United States:

Average for Women's Height in the United States: $\mu = 64$ inches
Standard Deviation for Women's Height in the United States: $\sigma = 2.4$ inches

We are interested in the percentage of women who measure 70 inches tall or taller. Although there are several different ways of determining this, we suggest that you use the following four steps. We have found that students who consistently follow these simple steps significantly reduce the number of errors they make.

Step 1

Take the score of interest, X = 70, and plug it into the Z-score formula. The result is also called the *Z of X*. As reported below, a woman who is at least 70 inches tall has a corresponding Z score of 2.5.

$$\frac{70 - 64}{2.4} = \boxed{2.5} = \text{Z of X or Z Score for 70 inches}$$

Step 2

Make a graphic representation of where the Z score of interest appears on the normal distribution. This determines which of the four columns in Appendix 1 are used. These columns represent different portions of the normal distribution. The mean of a distribution always equals zero and is the distribution's center, so all scores to the right of the mean are larger than the mean value and all corresponding Z scores are positive. All observations on the left-hand side of the distribution are smaller than the mean and corresponding Z scores are negative.

In the present example, the value of 70 inches is larger than the mean of 64 inches. Thus, this value in our pictorial representation is to the right of the mean. A large Z score like this one (2.5) indicates that this observation is located well into the far-right tail region of the distribution. (Recall that the tail regions are the areas to the far right or far left of the distribution.) Figure 6.2 shows what this looks like graphically. Because we are concerned with women who are 70 inches or taller, the region of the distribution to the right of our score, X = 70 or Z = 2.5, has been shaded.

Figure 6.2   70 Inches Tall or Taller

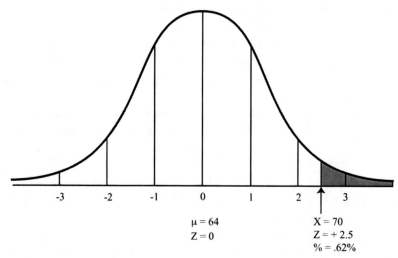

$$\mu = 64 \qquad\qquad X = 70$$
$$Z = 0 \qquad\qquad Z = +2.5$$
$$\% = .62\%$$

Step 3

Now that we have a visual idea of where our Z score is positioned on the normal distribution, we locate it in Appendix 1. As previously noted, the first column on each page of the table contains Z scores. The Z scores are ranked in ascending order of 0 to 3.70, so the Z score of 2.5 is located toward the end of the table. (Please note that Z scores in this table are carried to only two decimal points. Thus, instead of rounding up or down with Z scores that are carried to numerous decimal points (e.g., 1.9578), use the Z score exactly as it appears on the calculator to two decimal places (e.g., 1.95). Using Z scores in this manner still results in very accurate final answers and eliminates the need to memorize additional rounding rules.

Step 4

The final step is to determine which of the three remaining columns in Appendix 1 contains the correct probability value we are seeking, given a Z value of 2.5. This is where our graphic is helpful; it tells us that we are concerned with the tail region of the distribution. This region is less than 50% of the distribution, so we simply refer to it as "the Small Part."

In Appendix 1, column 2 is entitled "Z to the Mean." To use this column in the present example, we would have to be interested in the area from the mean, 64 inches, to our score of interest, 70 inches. Obviously, we are not interested in this column. Column 3 is entitled "the Big Part." This column represents areas of the distribution that are greater than 50% of it. In other words, if we were interested in the percentage of women who are 70 inches or shorter we would use this column. As a result, we are also not interested in this score.

Finally, we have column 4, entitled "the Small Part." This column represents the tail regions of the distribution, the shaded portion of Figure 6.2. Thus, the answer for Step 4—the final answer—found in column 4 is .0062. This indicates that of every 10,000 women in the United States, only 62 are 70 inches tall or taller. This can also be expressed as a probability; there is a .62% (less than 1%) chance that the next woman you randomly meet (perhaps on a blind date) will be five-foot-ten or taller. In other words, few women in the United States are 70 inches tall or taller.

To assist with the following examples, the four steps just used are summarized below. (Note that these are general steps that somewhat more complicated examples will build upon.)

Step 1: Calculate the Z score.
Step 2: Make a graphic representation of the Z of X in terms of what area of the normal curve you are examining.
Step 3: Locate your Z score in Appendix 1.
Step 4: Determine the appropriate column (columns 2 to 4) and report the final answer.

Turning to some further examples, say that we are now interested in how many women in the United States are 5 feet tall (60 inches) or shorter. Once again, we first calculate a Z score (Step 1), as presented below.

$$\frac{60-64}{2.4} = \boxed{-1.666\overline{6}} = Z \text{ of X or } Z \text{ Score for 60 inches}$$

Step 2 says to make a graphic representation of the Z of X. That is, we must draw the normal curve and locate the part of the distribution of interest. Because 60 inches is less than the mean score of 64 inches and the corresponding Z score of −1.6666 is a negative Z value, we obviously are interested in the area to the left of the mean. Further, since we are concerned with the area of 60 inches or less, we shade the tail region to the left of this score. Both of these steps are presented in Figure 6.3.

Step 3 calls for us to locate the Z score in Appendix 1, which is found in column 1. Recognizing that a Z score is negative is helpful in graphically locating its position on a distribution, and is required in later calculations. At this point, however, when utilizing Appendix 1 we disregard the sign (+ or −) and treat the Z score as an absolute value. In the present example, −1.6666 appears in the appendix as simply 1.66 (recall that we take the Z score exactly as it is found on the calculator register to two decimal places.) As in the previous example, because we are interested in a tail region of the distribution, the final answer (Step 4) is located in "the Small Part," column 4. Thus, the final answer is .0485, so we can conclude that 4.85% of women in the United States are 60 inches tall or shorter. We can also conclude that the probability that the next woman you will randomly meet will be five feet tall or shorter is 4.85%, a relatively rare outcome. Moreover,

Figure 6.3   60 Inches Tall or Shorter

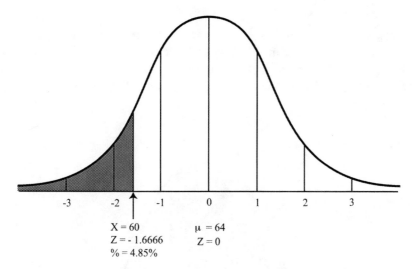

from the previous two examples we can also conclude that almost all U.S. women are between 60 and 70 inches in height.

The next example utilizes one of the other columns in Appendix 1. Here, we want to find out what percentage of women in the United States are 66 inches tall or shorter. First we calculate a *Z* score.

$$\frac{66 - 64}{2.4} = \boxed{.8333} = \text{Z of X or Z Score for 66 inches}$$

Our X of interest is larger than the mean and has a positive *Z* score. Thus, we know it is located on the right-hand side of the distribution. We are interested in the region of the distribution below this point (shorter), so we shade the area below it. All of these determinations (Step 2) appear in Figure 6.4.

One should immediately note that the shaded region covers more than 50% of the distribution. Thus, we utilize column 3 in Appendix 1, "the Big Part," but first we must complete Step 3, and locate the *Z* score of .8333 (actually .83) in column 1. The final answer (found in column 3) is .7967, which says that 79.67% of all women in the United States are 66 inches tall or shorter.

Next let's say we are interested in finding the percentage of women who are 61 inches tall and taller. First we calculate the *Z* score and find that the *Z* of X is a –1.25. A negative score combined with a score that is less than the mean (61 < 64) indicates that the graphic representation of this location point is to the left of the mean. We are concerned with the region to the right (61 inches tall and taller), so we shade it. Both this *Z*-score calculation and its graphic representation (Figure 6.5) are as follows:

$$\frac{61-64}{2.4} = \boxed{-1.25} = Z \text{ of } X \text{ or } Z \text{ Score for } 61 \text{ inches}$$

Having completed Steps 1 and 2, we now locate the Z score of –1.25 (1.25) in Appendix 1. Once this is accomplished, we find that the final answer (Step 4) in column 3 is .8944. That is, 89.44% of all women in the United States are 61 inches tall or taller.

So far we have used only columns 3 and 4 in Appendix 1. Now, however, we want to know what percentage of women in the United States are between 62 and 64 inches in

Figure 6.4   66 Inches Tall or Shorter

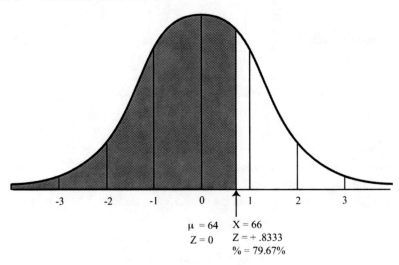

μ = 64   X = 66
Z = 0   Z = + .8333
           % = 79.67%

Figure 6.5   61 Inches Tall or Taller

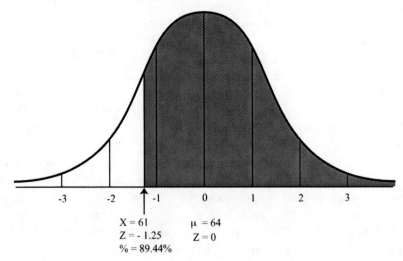

X = 61   μ = 64
Z = - 1.25   Z = 0
% = 89.44%

height (64 inches is the mean). Again, we start by calculating a *Z* score, just for 62 inches in this case, and then make a graphic representation of it (see Figure 6.6).

$$\frac{62-64}{2.4} = \boxed{-.8333} = Z \text{ of X or Z Score for 62 inches}$$

Instead of shading a complete area of the distribution below or above a point of interest, in this example we shade the region from our point of interest of 62 inches to the mean (64 inches). This also indicates that the answer to Step 4 is found in column 2, "The Mean to *Z*." First, however, we must locate this *Z* score in column 1 of Appendix 1. Having done this (using the absolute *Z* score of .83), we find that the final answer in column 2 is .2967. Thus, we conclude that 29.67% of women in the United States are 62 to 64 inches in height.

Here's a similar example with a twist. Let's say we are now interested in the percentage of women who are 63 inches to 67 inches in height. This problem is the same as the above, except that it is concerned with an area of *Z* to the mean from both sides of the mean. Thus, we calculate two separate *Z* scores (Step 1) and then sum their two corresponding probability values. These two *Z*-score calculations are as follows, and their graphic representation appears in Figure 6.7.

$$\frac{63-64}{2.4} = \boxed{-.416\overline{6}} = Z \text{ of X or Z Score for 63 inches}$$

$$\frac{67-64}{2.4} = \boxed{+1.25} = Z \text{ of X or Z Score for 67 inches}$$

Figure 6.6   62 to 64 Inches Tall (the Mean)

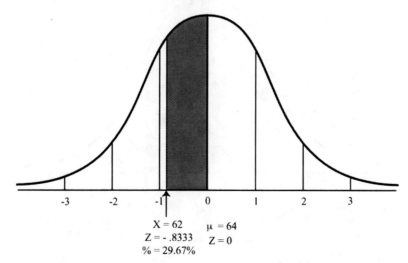

X = 62   μ = 64
Z = -.8333   Z = 0
% = 29.67%

Next locate both of these Z scores in Appendix 1: 0.41 and 1.25. Their corresponding probability values in column 2 (The Mean to Z) are then summed together to get .3944 + .1591 = .5535. (In a sense, with the extra operation of summing these two values together, we have added a Step 5.) From this result we conclude that roughly 55.35% of women in the United States are between 63 and 67 inches tall.

Building upon this example, we now examine the percentage of women whose heights are between 65 and 70 inches. Here, again, we are interested in an area between two points on the normal distribution; however, this area falls on only the right-hand side of the distribution. Fortunately, the procedure to make this determination is very similar to the previous example.

Thus, as we did above, we first calculate two separate Z scores and then locate them on a graphic representation (Figure 6.8). Note that, on this representation, a sizeable portion of the tail region on the right-hand side of the distribution is appropriately shaded.

$$\frac{65-64}{2.4} = \boxed{+.416\overline{6}} = Z \text{ of } X \text{ or } Z \text{ Score for 65 inches}$$

$$\frac{70-64}{2.4} = \boxed{+2.50} = Z \text{ of } X \text{ or } Z \text{ Score for 70 inches}$$

Next, we determine the probability values for both of these Z scores in terms of their distance from the mean (column 2). The corresponding probability values for the Z scores of .41 (65 inches) and 2.5 (70 inches), respectively, are .1591 and .4938. Instead of adding these values together, as above, we subtract the smaller value from the larger (to do otherwise would result in a negative probability value, which is logically impossible). In other words, we are subtracting the probability value of the unshaded area, 64 to 65

Figure 6.7   63 to 67 Inches Tall

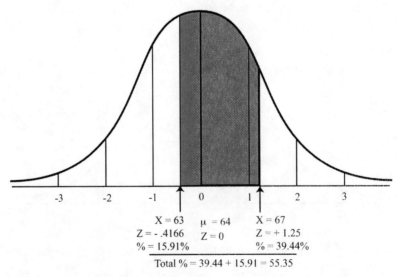

X = 63   μ = 64   X = 67
Z = -.4166   Z = 0   Z = +1.25
% = 15.91%   % = 39.44%

Total % = 39.44 + 15.91 = 55.35

Figure 6.8   65 to 70 Inches Tall

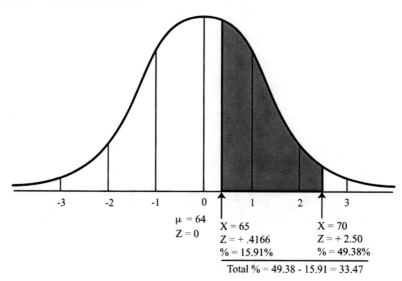

inches tall, from the probability area of the mean to the second score, 64 and 70 inches in height: .4938 − .1591 = .3347.

(Please note: Sometimes our students make the *mistake* of subtracting 65 inches from 70, or the Z score of .41 from 2.5, to make the determination. Because the area under the normal curve, expressed as a probability value, is unequal, *actual probability values always must be used to make this determination.* Otherwise, as you might expect, an incorrect answer will result.)

Thus far, we have used Z scores to discover the percentage of the distribution above or below a given X (observation) or between two Xs. Sometimes, however, it is useful to do this the opposite way, and discover what the X value is for a given probability score. The formula to accomplish this, an algebraic derivative of the original Z-score formula, appears below.

$$X = Z\sigma + \mu$$

To use this new formula we basically use the steps for the original Z formula in reverse. Moreover, to make its usage easier, we treat the observation in the data set as rank-ordered. That is, the percentages to the left of the mean are seen as less than 50% while those to the right are seen as greater than 50%. Thus, the furthest point to the left of the distribution is seen as 0%, whereas the furthest right point is seen as 100%.

To clarify the discussion thus far, it is helpful to use an actual example. Say we want to know the height that 25% of all women are equal to or shorter than. Utilizing the above formula, we already know the mean is 64 inches and the standard deviation is 2.4 inches. As such, the only missing piece of information in this formula is the Z score. To make this determination, it is helpful to once again visualize the problem applied to the

Figure 6.9   25% Equal To or Shorter Than

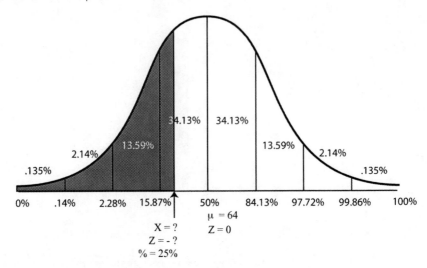

normal curve—this is Step 1. Because 25% is less than 50%, it is placed to the left of the mean and the corresponding area below it is shaded (see Figure 6.9).

Next, we determine which of the three columns of probability scores to use. We are concerned with the shaded region, which is "the Small Part" of the distribution, so we look to column 4 and select the probability score that is closest to 25% (.25). The value of .25 falls between two values: .2514 and .2483. Of these two values the value that is closer to .25 is .2514—this is Step 2. The corresponding Z score for this value is −.67— this is Step 3. (Remember that all Z values to the left of the mean are negative. This is very important because failure to take a Z score's sign into account with this formula results in an incorrect answer.) Finally, Step 4 is to plug this Z score into the formula and do the appropriate calculations. These are summarized step by step below.

$$X = (-.67)2.4 + 64 = -1.608 + 64 = \boxed{62.392 \text{ inches}} = X$$

The final answer shows that 25% of all women in the United States are 62.392 inches tall or shorter. (Alternatively, we can also conclude that 75% of women in the United States are 62.392 inches tall or taller.)

Following is a summary of the four steps used to make this determination:

Step 1: Make a graphic representation using the information given and shade the appropriate area under the normal distribution.

Step 2: Using this information, locate the percentage value in the appropriate column (always column 3 or 4) in Appendix 1.

Step 3: Take the corresponding Z score from Step 2 and plug it into the formula with the other given information.

Step 4: Calculate the final score, which is the X of interest.

Figure 6.10   90% Equal To or Shorter Than

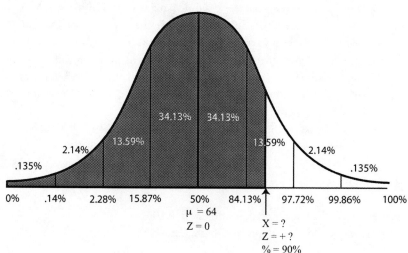

Here's another example: We now want to know what height 90% of U.S. women are equal to or less than. Following the steps outlined above, start by constructing a graphical representation of this information as it appears on the normal curve (Figure 6.10).

Then use this information to determine which column of Appendix 1 to use—this is obviously column 3, "The Big Part" column. The score closest to 90% (.90) is .8997. The corresponding *Z* score is +1.28 and, since 90% occurs on the right-hand side of the distribution, the corresponding *Z* score is positive. To calculate the final answer, take this *Z* score and plug it into the formula as shown below.

$$X = (1.28)2.4 + 64 = 3.072 + 64 = \boxed{67.072 \text{ inches}} = X$$

The final answer tells us that 90% of women in the United States are 67.072 inches tall or shorter. So the vast majority of women in our society are five-foot-seven or shorter.

Figure 6.11 shows an excellent way to visually summarize both of these operations (determining a probability value from an X value or determining the X value for a probability value). Until you become comfortable with making these determinations, we suggest that you refer to this figure.

Percentiles and *Z* Scores

As mentioned, *Z* scores can be employed to calculate percentile rankings. A *Z* distribution by design ranks scores from lowest to highest, so we can also use it to determine any observation's percentile ranking. And, although the manner of calculating rankings is different than the previously discussed percentile-ranking formula, we still express percentile rankings exactly as we did before (e.g., 22nd or 78th percentile ranking). Moreover, the *Z* distribution also enables the determination of any percentile ranking's actual score (X).

To do this, we must view the Z distribution in the same manner as we did when calculating Xs from percentages. That is, percentile rankings on a Z distribution are conceptualized in ascending order from lowest to highest (left to right) on the distribution. Thus, observations with the lowest percentile rankings (e.g., 2nd, 3rd, and 7th) are found in the far-left tail region of the distribution; observations in the middle rankings (e.g., 47th, 50th, and 52nd) are found very near or on the mean of the distribution; and observations in the highest percentile rankings (e.g., 94th, 96th, and 99th) are found in the far-right tail region of the distribution.

To clarify the discussion thus far and outline the steps involved in this application, let's go ahead and calculate some percentile rankings using Z scores. Instead of using heights, we have replicated the information on IQ scores below for the following example. (Note: heights can just as easily be ranked.)

Average IQ Score for Fourth-grade Children: $\mu = 100$
Standard Deviation for Fourth-grade Children: $\sigma = 15$

To start, let's say that we want to know the percentile ranking of a child that has an IQ of 80 (obviously a child with this low of an IQ has probably been over a cliff with Calvin one too many times). As before, the first step is to calculate a Z score. This is done below.

$$\frac{80-100}{15} = \boxed{-1.333\overline{3}} = \text{Z of X or Z Score for an IQ of 80}$$

The next step, also exactly as before, is to make a graphic representation of this information applied to the normal distribution (see Figure 6.12). (Please note: When calculating a percentile ranking using Z scores, we always shade the area below the Z of X regardless of whether it is located above or below the mean. The reason for this [as was for the previously discussed formula used to determine percentile rankings] is that we are always concerned with the number of scores that fall below the X of interest relative to all the scores in the distribution.)

Figure 6.11   Summary of Steps Used to Determine Probability Values and Actual Scores Using a Normal Distribution

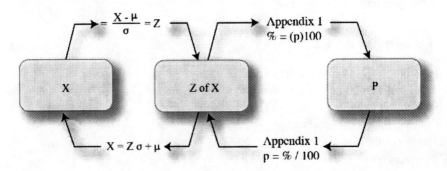

Figure 6.12   Percentile Ranking for an IQ Score of 80

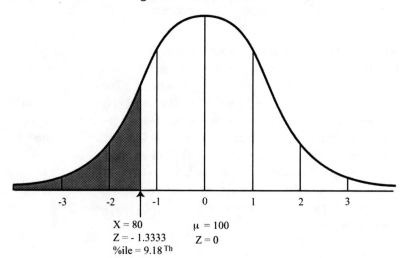

$$X = 80$$
$$Z = -1.3333$$
%ile = 9.18 Th

$$\mu = 100$$
$$Z = 0$$

The next step is to locate the calculated Z score (1.33) in Appendix 1. Having done this, next determine which column to utilize. At this point, there are three rules that should always be followed when determining percentile rankings: (1) Never use column 2; (2) always use column 3 when the Z score is positive (the X of interest is greater than the mean); and (3) always use column 4 when the Z score is negative (the X of interest is less than the mean). We never use column 2 because the area from the mean to the Z score is not of interest when we calculate percentile rankings.

Applying the above rules to this example shows that we use column 4, and results in an answer of .0918. The final step is simply to move the decimal point over two places to the right and then to express the answer as a percentile ranking. Thus, a child with an IQ of 80 is found in the 9.18th percentile. The five steps used in this application are summarized below:

Step 1: Calculate the Z score.
Step 2: Make a graphic representation of the Z of X in terms of where it is located on the normal curve and always shade the area below—to the left—of the score.
Step 3: Locate your Z score in Appendix 1.
Step 4: Using the above information, determine the appropriate column (3 or 4) and record the answer.
Step 5: Take the answer from Step 4 and move the decimal point over two places to the right. Expressed as a percentile ranking, this is your final answer.

In another example, we are now interested in the percentile ranking of a child with an IQ of 125. First we calculate a Z score (below).

$$\frac{125-100}{15} = \boxed{-1.666\overline{6}} = \text{Z of X or Z Score for an IQ of 125}$$

Following the steps, we next make a graphic representation of the normal distribution and shade the area below the X of interest (see Figure 6.13).

Next, we locate the Z score (1.66) in the appendix, and find that the corresponding answer in column 3 is .9515. Finally, we move the decimal point over two places to the right and our final answer is the 95.15th percentile. This tells us that a child with an IQ of 125 is ranked in the 95.15th percentile. In other words, this child is quite intelligent relative to other children, as very few children have a higher IQ.

Of course, we could also take percentile rankings and convert them into actual scores. To accomplish this we follow the same steps as presented above for converting probability scores into actual scores (Xs). Because we have already done these operations, they are not shown again here.

Chapter Summary and Conclusions

This chapter investigated various ways of locating scores in a distribution relative to all other scores in it. It first discussed percentile rankings, which are calculated using actual raw scores that are ranked. It next described how Z scores applied to a normal distribution enable one to determine the percentage of scores that occur above, below, or between Xs of interest. The steps in this procedure were reversed to determine actual scores (Xs) from percentages in the given distribution. Finally, the chapter discussed how Z scores are used to determine percentile rankings of any observation of interest.

Figure 6.13   Percentile Ranking for an IQ Score of 125

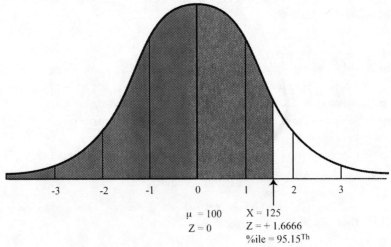

Key Terms to Remember

- Percentile Rankings
- Normal Distribution
- Z Scores
- "Z to the Mean" Column
- "The Small Part" Column
- "The Big Part" Column

Practice Exercises

1. Referring to Cartoon 6.1 and our video-game players, instead of being interested in the video-game scores of the ten-year-olds, we are now concerned with their parents' yearly incomes. Each child's parents' yearly income, expressed in thousands of dollars per year, is reported in Table 6.4. To simplify the presentation, we have continued to use the children's names to represent their parents' incomes.
   a. What is Nicole's percentile ranking?
   b. What is Harry's percentile ranking?
   c. What is Dan's percentile ranking?
   d. What is Helen's percentile ranking?
   e. What is Steve's percentile ranking?
   (Remember that the data set must be rank-ordered.)

2. Given the following information: IQ Scores: Mean (μ) = 100; Standard Deviation (σ) = 15. What is the probability that the next person you will meet will have an IQ of
   a. 115 or greater?
   b. 100 or less?
   c. between 90 and 105?
   d. 130 or greater?
   e. 90 or less?
   f. between 110 and 120?

3. Using the above IQ information, what IQ score is
   a. 90% of the population equal to or less than?
   b. 35% of the population equal to or less than?
   c. 50% of the population equal to or less than?
   d. 15% of the population equal to or less than?
   e. 73% of the population equal to or less than?

Table 6.4   Parents' Yearly Incomes*

				Incomes			
Janice	30	Anna	42	Allan	22	Pina	60
Harry	33	Randi	69	Alex	34	Katie	66
John	36	Dan	53	Nicole	29	Billy	46
Jenny	37	Jeff	49	Roby	57	Steve	38
Jim	25	Chris	43	Helen	41	Bob	23

* Remember that your data set needs to be ranked-ordered

Given the following information:

Heights of Women in the United States: Mean (μ) = 64; Standard Deviation (σ) = 2.4

4. What is the probability that the next woman you meet will be
   a. 60 inches tall or shorter?
   b. 70 inches tall or taller?
   c. Between 61 and 58 inches tall?
   d. 62 inches tall or taller?
   e. 58 inches tall or shorter?
   f. between 66 and 68 inches tall?

5. What height is it that
   a. 75% of all American women are equal to or shorter than?
   b. 86% of all American women are equal to or shorter than?
   c. 22% of all American women are equal to or shorter than?
   d. 37% of all American women are equal to or shorter than?
   e. 50% of all American women are equal to or shorter than?

6. Determine the percentile rankings of the following Z scores.
   a. −.75
   b. +1.5
   c. −1.5
   d. +3.0

7. Again using the above information on women's heights, what is the percentile ranking of a woman who is
   a. 61 inches tall?
   b. 64 inches tall?

c. 62.5 inches tall?
d. 67 inches tall?
e. 66.5 inches tall?
f. 69 inches tall?

8. With respect to the data on heights of U.S. women presented in problem 4, what would happen to the Z scores, the probabilities, and the percentile ranks for problems 4a to 4f if it was found that the population standard deviation was actually 2 and not 2.4?

a. Would each get larger, smaller, or stay the same?

b. What if the population standard deviation was really 3, instead of 2.4?

(Note: You should be able to answer these conceptually, but it may be helpful and good practice to work them out and confirm your estimates.)

7

Probability

The immediate reaction of many students to this chapter is, "I hate probabilities," and thus, "This is going to be one of the most difficult chapters." The authors also shared this adverse attitude about probabilities when we were presented with this material in our first undergraduate statistics courses. The following Bloom County cartoon perhaps best summarizes these attitudes.

Assuming that you have read the chapters in the order of their presentation, perhaps some readers thought there wasn't a very good chance ("probability") that they would make it this far into a statistics text. Isn't it amazing what Opus and a good instructor can accomplish?!

Having both personally survived presentations on probability as students and observed our own students "survive" and master the information found in this chapter, we have discovered over the years that it is no more difficult than any of the other presentations found in this text. Moreover, we have learned of its importance in theoretically understanding Chapter 6 and the chapters that follow. Further, we have included only the material that we see as vital to understanding basic probability theory. On a more practical level, those of you who have been contributors to games of chance ("chance" here being synonymous with probability) in Las Vegas and other gambling venues may be interested in potential techniques to increase your winnings or, more realistically, to decrease your losses.

To a certain extent, all of us are probability theorists because, daily, we ask ourselves such questions as:

- What is the probability that I can run this red light and not get a ticket or have an accident?
- What is the probability that I can pass the next quiz if I don't study for it?
- What is the probability that I can miss my date with Lee tonight and Lee will still speak to me tomorrow?

In other words, all of us constantly wonder about the probability of certain events occurring in our lives.

Cartoon 7.1   BLOOM COUNTY

On a more scientific level, our lives are even more directly influenced by probabilities. Weather forecasters tell us what type of weather we can expect tomorrow in terms of probabilities; a forecast of a 60% chance of rain tells us that we might want to have an umbrella with us on our travels. Actuaries, people who calculate insurance rates, use probabilities to dictate how much the monthly premiums are for our life, medical, and car insurance. The quality and safety of most consumer products are also determined using probabilities.

Furthermore, as is shown in the following chapters, there are many statistical techniques that enable social scientists to calculate the probability that they have arrived at a correct conclusion in their research. Some of these statistical techniques are the same ones that enable pollsters to infer political attitudes of the entire United States population and to predict the winners of the upcoming elections just using samples. In sum, although we may not recognize it, a great deal of the quality of our existence is determined by probabilities. As such, and like statistics in general, there is utility in having all of us understand probabilities.

This chapter begins with a discussion about basic rules of calculating probabilities for independent events, "and" statements, and "or" statements. Next is a discussion of how permutations and combinations are used to determine the probability of certain outcomes. The chapter ends with a demonstration of how combinations can be used to construct a frequency distribution of probabilities on which the normal curve (discussed in Chapter 6) is theoretically based.

Basic Probabilities: Independent Events, "And," and "Or" Statements

When asked simple questions, like "What is the probability of getting heads when flipping a balanced coin?" or "What is the probability of a child being born female?" we would guess that most people intuitively know what both answers are: 50%. As an aside, we should note that blemished, unbalanced coins can result in the coin's consistently coming up heads or tails, while the probability of a woman's giving birth to a female child is actually slightly less than 50%. The following examples will assume that one is using a balanced coin and that there actually is a 50/50 chance of having a female or male child.

We would also guess that, mathematically speaking, many people may not know how this outcome is determined. Quite simply, this is accomplished by dividing the number of *desired independent* outcomes, the numerator, by the number of *possible independent* outcomes, the denominator. In both these examples, and the ones that follow, an outcome is considered independent if it can occur only one way out of two or more possible ways (e.g., heads or tails, male or female). As such, it can also be referred to as a discrete or mutually exclusive outcome (event).

In the case of flipping a balanced coin and getting a head, it is mathematically expressed as:

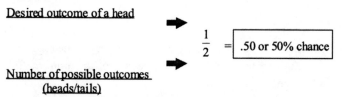

Desired outcome of a head

$$\frac{1}{2} = \boxed{.50 \text{ or } 50\% \text{ chance}}$$

Number of possible outcomes
(heads/tails)

Alternatively, and using Cartoon 7.2 as a backdrop, one can similarly calculate the probability of a woman's having a female child (with Calvin as an example, there are obviously more than enough male children running around already).

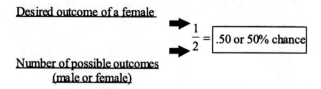

Desired outcome of a female

$$\frac{1}{2} = \boxed{.50 \text{ or } 50\% \text{ chance}}$$

Number of possible outcomes
(male or female)

Cartoon 7.2   CALVIN AND HOBBES

Applying this same logic to other events that have independent outcomes, we can ask questions such as "What is the probability of getting a five on one roll of a balanced die?"; "What is the probability of getting the number 27 on one spin of a roulette wheel?"; or "What is the probability of getting a red number on one spin of a roulette wheel?" Taking each of these in turn, the die question is answered by simply deducing that we are concerned with one outcome of an event that can occur six possible ways—the six sides/numbers on a die. This is mathematically expressed as follows.

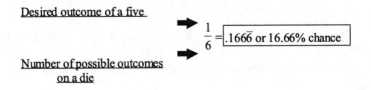

Desired outcome of a five

$$\frac{1}{6} = \boxed{.166\overline{6} \text{ or } 16.66\% \text{ chance}}$$

Number of possible outcomes
on a die

Thus we conclude that there is a 16.66% chance of getting a five on one roll of a die. Moreover, we can also conclude that the probability of any one of the numbers (sides) occurring is also a 16.66% chance.

Turning to the roulette wheel question, we must first determine the number of possible outcomes that can occur on one spin. Hypothetically, let's say the wheel under consideration has 100 numbers (1–100) on it of which one-half is black and one-half is red (50 black and 50 red). This information enables us to ascertain that the first question is concerned with one possible outcome, a 27, out of 100 possible outcomes. Or, as mathematically expressed below, there is a 1% chance of getting a 27 on one spin of a roulette wheel.

Desired outcome of a 27

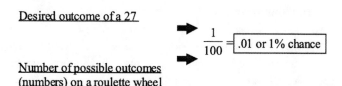

$$\frac{1}{100} = \boxed{.01 \text{ or } 1\% \text{ chance}}$$

Number of possible outcomes
(numbers) on a roulette wheel

Turning to the second roulette question, the probability of getting a red number, the answer is determined by dividing the number of red spaces on the wheel, 50, by the overall number of spaces found on it, 100. Thus, as expressed below, there is a 50% chance of a red number occurring with any one spin. In other words, the probability of getting a red number is much higher than that of getting any specific number on a single spin of the roulette wheel.

Desired outcome of a red number

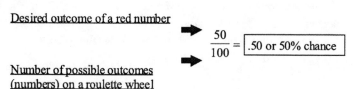

$$\frac{50}{100} = \boxed{.50 \text{ or } 50\% \text{ chance}}$$

Number of possible outcomes
(numbers) on a roulette wheel

Box 7.1   The Gambler's Fallacy

With events such as flips of a coin, the throws of a die, or spins of a roulette wheel, many people often falsely believe that the occurrence of one outcome diminishes the likelihood of its subsequent occurrence. For instance, if one flips a coin and desires heads, there is a 50% chance of this event's occurring. Assuming it does come up heads, using the above incorrect logic one might surmise that there is a decreased probability of its being heads on the next consecutive flip. This is simply not true.

Each time the coin is flipped it is still an independent event—and not contingent upon the occurrence of events that have preceded or that will potentially follow—so the probability of heads on the next flip is still 50%. The logic of inferring a decreased probability of occurrence in events such as a flip of a coin is known as *the gambler's fallacy*. As demonstrated later, however, we can calculate the probability of certain events, such as heads coming up on a coin toss, or a male child's being born, occurring in a certain order.

Another slightly more involved example utilizes a standard deck of cards. For you non–card players, let's briefly review what possibilities—types of cards—are found in a deck of cards. A deck is comprised of 52 cards: the overall number of possible outcomes. Further, each deck has four suits—hearts, diamonds, spades, and clubs—containing 13 cards each. Within each suit is an ace (4 aces in the deck); three face cards—a king, a queen, and a jack (12 face cards in a deck); and non-face cards that represent the values of two through ten (36 of these cards in a deck). (Please note: For simplicity, we do not consider the two joker cards here or in subsequent examples.)

Knowing the deck's composition, we can now ask simple questions such as, "What is the probability (how much of a chance is there) of drawing an ace from a deck of shuffled cards?" (For this and all of the following card examples to work, we must assume theoretically that the deck of cards has been shuffled several times, and that the cards are randomly located throughout the deck. As such, each card has an equal chance—possibility—of being selected.)

Following the same logic used to mathematically determine the likelihood of getting heads on a coin toss or of giving birth to a female child, there are two pieces of information that first must be determined: (1) the number of desired outcomes and (2) the number of possible outcomes. The number of desired outcomes (an ace) is 4, which is divided by the number of possible outcomes, in this case 52 (there are 52 cards in a deck that one could possibly select). This information is mathematically presented below. From this answer, we conclude that with one draw there is a 7.69% (almost an 8 in 100) chance of drawing an ace out of a deck of shuffled cards.

$$\frac{4}{52} = \frac{1}{13} = \boxed{.0769 \text{ or a } 7.69\% \text{ chance}}$$

Again using the same logic, we also can ask "What is the probability of drawing a face card from a deck of shuffled cards?" As we have already noted, there are 12 face cards, the number of desired outcomes, which is divided by the number of all possible outcomes, 52. As completed below, we find that there is a slightly greater than 23% chance (nearly 1 out of 4) of drawing a face card from a deck of shuffled cards. Conversely, however, there is still a greater chance of not drawing a face card (76.92%).

$$\frac{12}{52} = \frac{3}{13} = \boxed{.2308 \text{ or a } 23.08\% \text{ chance}}$$

All of the calculations performed so far have been fairly simple, and in all "probability" some of you may have already known how to do them. A slightly more difficult set of operations, however, is required to answer questions such as, "What is the probability of drawing a red ace *or* a black 5 from a deck of shuffled cards?" In a sense, we are now faced with two sets of desired outcomes connected with an "or" statement. As you may have guessed, an "or" statement, as found in the title of this section, involves additional mathematical operations. Specifically, when an "or" statement is encountered, we must add together different probability events.

To this end, we first calculate the probability of each separate outcome and then simply add them together. In other words, first calculate the probability of drawing a red ace out of a deck of shuffled cards (2/52). Then simply add these two values together to get the final answer. One way to add these values together is to use the separate probability values expressed as fractions. Because the present example has a common denominator of

52, however, the numerator values are simply added together to get the final answer. (Note: Whenever fractions are added together, they must have a common denominator. If they do not, the final answer will be incorrect.) All of this is shown mathematically below.

$$\frac{2}{52} + \frac{2}{52} = \frac{4}{52} = \frac{1}{13} = \boxed{.0769 \text{ or a } 7.69\% \text{ chance}}$$

Turning to another example, we now want to know, "What is the probability of drawing the Queen of Hearts *or* a 4 from a deck of shuffled cards?" Once again, independently determine the probability of each potential outcome and then simply add these values together to get the final answer (shown below).

$$\frac{1}{52} + \frac{4}{52} = \frac{5}{52} = \boxed{.0961 \text{ or a } 9.61\% \text{ chance}}$$

For another probability event say that we are now interested in a die. Once again using an "or" statement, we want to know, "What is the probability of rolling a 2 *or* a 5 on a balanced die?" As with previous examples, we first must determine the number of desired outcomes, and then divide by the overall number of possible outcomes. A die has six sides with six corresponding numbers; thus, there are six possible outcomes. Two of the outcomes are desired, a 2 *or* a 5, so individually express them and then add those values together to get the final answer. Thus, in mathematical terms we have a one-in-three chance (33.33%) of getting a 2 or a 3 on one shake of a die.

$$\frac{1}{6} + \frac{1}{6} = \frac{2}{6} = \boxed{.333\overline{3} \text{ or a } 33.33\% \text{ chance}}$$

To most of you, what has been presented thus far may seem quite simple. What if the last question was changed ever so slightly, however, and instead read, "What is the probability of rolling a 2 *and* then a 5 on a balanced die?" In other words, not only is the die thrown two separate times but, instead of an "or" statement, we are now presented with an "and" statement. This, of course, means that a different mathematical operation is used. Specifically, where an "or" statement tells us to *add*, an "and" statement tells us to *multiply*.

This restated question requires us to multiply two separate fractions together to obtain the final answer. The probability of independently rolling a 2 on a balanced die is 1 in 6, as is the probability of independently rolling a 5 (out of 6), so we multiply these two values together to get the final answer. Thus, the probability of rolling a 2 *and* then a 5 on a balanced die in this exact order is a rather unlikely outcome with a 2.77% chance of occurrence. This is mathematically demonstrated below.

$$\frac{1}{6} \times \frac{1}{6} = \frac{1}{36} = \boxed{.027\overline{7} \text{ or a } 2.77\% \text{ chance}}$$

To clarify, when fraction values are multiplied, we first multiply one numerator by the other numerator and, correspondingly, one denominator by the other denominator. To obtain the final answer we simply divide the resultant fraction's numerator by its denominator. This is how the above calculation was completed. (As an aside, an alternative solution to the above problem is to separately divide each fraction and then multiply the two values together to obtain the final answer. For the above illustration, this is .1666 x .1666 = .0277.)

Returning to our deck of cards, with its much larger number of possible outcomes, let's create another example of an "and" statement. We have two decks of shuffled cards and want to know the probability of drawing a king from the first deck *and* then a spade from the second deck. Using the proper procedural steps, first determine the probability of each separate event *and* then multiply these two values together to obtain the final answer. That is, there are four kings and thirteen spades, and thus, as expressed below, there is a 1.92% chance of drawing a king *and* then a spade from two separate decks of cards.

$$\frac{4}{52} \times \frac{13}{52} = \frac{52}{2704} = \boxed{.0192 \text{ or a } 1.92\% \text{ chance}}$$

For one last example of this type of operation, let's say we are interested in the probability of drawing a one-eyed jack *and* then an ace. There are two one-eyed jacks and four aces, so simply multiply these two values together and then divide the resultant numerator value by its corresponding denominator value. These steps and the final answer are presented below. In sum, there is less that a 1% chance (.29%) of drawing a one-eyed jack *and* then an ace. Some of you might keep this in mind the next time you are playing black-jack—where an ace and a jack are highly sought-after cards.

$$\frac{2}{52} \times \frac{4}{52} = \frac{8}{2704} = \boxed{.0029 \text{ or a } .29\% \text{ chance}}$$

In this last example using coins, we ask the following question, "What is the probability of getting three heads in a row out of the three consecutive flips of a coin?" To make this question more applicable in terms of operations we are presently reviewing, it can be restated more clearly as, "What is the probability of flipping a head *and* then a head *and* then a head?" The two "and" statements tell us to multiply the three separate probability values together. That is, since each of these outcomes has an independent 50% chance of occurring, we simply multiply $\frac{1}{2}$ (or .50) together three times. Both of these identical operations are done below, showing that there is a 12.5% chance of getting three heads in a row.

$$\frac{1}{2} \times \frac{1}{2} \times \frac{1}{2} = \frac{1}{8} = \boxed{.125 \text{ or a } 12.5\% \text{ chance}}$$

Or .5×.5×.5 = .125 or a 12.5% chance

As a noteworthy aside, this question reflects our previous discussion on the gambler's fallacy. That is, although there is only a 12.5% chance of getting three heads in a row, the probability of each independent event's (flipping a head) subsequent occurrence is still 50%.

Factorials, Permutations, and Combinations

While "and" and "or" statements are important operations in determining probability events, their application is limited to very simple examples. To consider more complex problems permutations and combinations are used. Before explaining what permutations and combinations are and how they are calculated, a brief discussion of factorials is warranted (this may be a review for some readers). The basic symbol that represents a factorial is an exclamation mark (!). Mathematically, this tells us to take whatever number is given and simply multiply it by every descending whole number found below it in the order of their occurrence to the value of 1. Applying this to an example, calculate 4! (stated four factorial). The final answer, 24, and the steps required to derive this answer are presented below.

$$4! = 4 \times 3 \times 2 \times 1 = \boxed{24}$$

or

$$(4 \times 3 = 12) \times 2 = 24 \times 1 = \boxed{24}$$

Alternatively, the required calculations and answers for 10!, 7!, 5!, and 3! are found below.

$$10! = 10 \times 9 \times 8 \times 7 \times 6 \times 5 \times 4 \times 3 \times 2 \times 1 = \boxed{3,628,800}$$

$$7! = 7 \times 6 \times 5 \times 4 \times 3 \times 2 \times 1 = \boxed{5,040}$$

$$5! = 5 \times 4 \times 3 \times 2 \times 1 = \boxed{120}$$

$$3! = 3 \times 2 \times 1 = \boxed{6}$$

(If you have a calculator with a factorial [!] button on it, then you simply press the desired number, press enter, and then press the factorial button.)

One quickly notices that factorials for even fairly small numbers (e.g., 10) result in rather large answers. Many calculators only go to eight or ten decimal places, which presents problems when calculating larger factorials. Because we are required to divide factorial values using both permutations and combinations, a simple way around the potential problem of large factorials is to write out each factorial. Then, simply cancel out all of the common numerator and denominator values.

Let's say that we must divide 12! by 10! As suggested above, calculations for this question can be done two different ways but still result in the same answer. Each of these ways is completed separately below. Students overwhelmingly have preferred the second approach of canceling out common values, so we use it in the remaining examples.

We must make note that when factorial values are canceled out, because we cannot have a zero (0) factorial, its value always becomes 1. Applying this rule to the above

$$\frac{12!}{10!} = \frac{12 \times 11 \times 10 \times 9 \times 8 \times 7 \times 6 \times 5 \times 4 \times 3 \times 2 \times 1}{10 \times 9 \times 8 \times 7 \times 6 \times 5 \times 4 \times 3 \times 2 \times 1} = \frac{479,001,600}{3,628,800} = \boxed{132}$$

versus

$$\frac{12!}{10!} = \frac{12 \times 11 \times \cancel{10 \times 9 \times 8 \times 7 \times 6 \times 5 \times 4 \times 3 \times 2 \times 1}}{\cancel{10 \times 9 \times 8 \times 7 \times 6 \times 5 \times 4 \times 3 \times 2 \times 1}} = \frac{12 \times 11}{1} = \frac{132}{1} = \boxed{132}$$

example, as demonstrated, canceling out all the numbers in the denominator leaves the value of 1. Moreover, even in the instances where an actual zero factorial (0!) is present-ed, because you cannot have a zero factorial, the value of 1 is still used. (The reason for this rule becomes more apparent shortly.)

Beginning with factorials applied to permutations, this type of operation, similar to an "and" statement, is always concerned with outcomes occurring in a specific order for a given event. Permutations are also calculated using the assumptions that once an element has occurred, it is no longer considered in future calculations; this is referred to as *without replacement.*

To demonstrate what "without replacement" means, we first must refer back to an "and" statement. We have four cards, with each card representing one of the four suits. Using this information, we want to determine, "What is the probability of drawing a heart *and* then a spade?" On the first draw, there is a one-out-of-four chance of getting a heart. For the sec-ond draw, there is a one-in-three chance of drawing a spade (note that we *have not replaced* the first card back into the deck). Finally, the two resultant fractions are simply multiplied together. This is presented mathematically below. Thus, we can conclude that there is a one-out-of-twelve (1/12) or 8.33% chance of drawing a heart and then a spade.

$$\frac{1}{4} \times \frac{1}{3} = \frac{1}{12} = \boxed{.083\overline{3} \text{ or a } 8.33\% \text{ chance}}$$

An alternative, perhaps easier, way to obtain this same answer is to use the following permutation formula. Four different symbols are found in this formula: (1) nPm simply represents the formula for permutations, (2) N is the total number of elements under con-sideration, (3) M is the number of elements considered in a specific order, and (4) "!" sim-ply means that the given numerical value is treated as a factorial.

$$nPm = \frac{N!}{(N - M)!} \qquad \begin{array}{l} N = \text{total number of elements considered} \\ M = \text{number of elements considered in a specific order} \end{array}$$

To apply the playing-card example to this formula, first determine that the total num-ber of elements (cards) is 4; thus, $N = 4$. Then we determine that the number of elements considered in a specific order is 2, a heart *and* then a spade; thus, $M = 2$. All of this is summarized below, with the resulting answer of 12. (Note: Because the $(N-M)$ is in parentheses, the rules of algebraic order dictate that we first must do the operation with-in parentheses (4–2) and then the factorial.)

$$nPm = \frac{4!}{(4-2)!} = \frac{4 \times 3 \times 2 \times 1}{2 \times 1} = \frac{4 \times 3}{1} = \boxed{12}$$

The final answer obviously is not 12; it only tells that there are twelve different ways that two cards out of four can occur in a specific order. Because we are only interested with one of these outcomes, a heart *and* then a spade, we simply divide 1 by 12 (1/12) to get the final answer of .0833 or an 8.33% chance (mathematically presented below):

$$\text{Probability} \quad = \frac{1}{P*} = \frac{1}{12} = \boxed{.0833} \quad = \text{Or there is a 8.33\% chance of this outcome in this specific order}$$

*P represents the answer obtained from the permutation formula.

The next example uses a 100-meter track race. We want to know, "What is the probability of picking the top three finishers, in the correct order of their completing the race, out of six runners competing in the race?" We assume that the racers are nearly identical in their individual capabilities. In reality, when races are run, whether by people or horses (as in the next example), seldom if ever are the participants equally matched. This notwithstanding, we use these examples of using permutations because most people are familiar with racing events. Referring back to the permutations formula, we discern that $N = 6$ (there are six runners in this race) and that $M = 3$ (the top three finishers of the race in the exact order of finishing—1st, 2nd, and 3rd).

Plugging these values into the permutation formula produces the value of 120. Once again, the obtained value (120) tells us that there are 120 different ways that the top three finishers of a race comprised of six runners can occur. We are only interested in one outcome—one race—so the value of one (1) is divided by 120 (1/120). The resultant answer shows that we have a .83% chance of picking the top three of six runners of a race.

$$nPm = \frac{6!}{(6-3)!} = \frac{6 \times 5 \times 4 \times 3 \times 2 \times 1}{3 \times 2 \times 1} = \frac{6 \times 5 \times 4}{1} = \boxed{120}$$

$$\text{Probability} \quad = \frac{1}{P} = \frac{1}{120} = \boxed{.0083} = \text{Or there is a .83\% chance of this outcome occurring in this specific order}$$

Next let's shift from track races to horse races and say that we are interested in the probability of picking the top two finishers of a race with ten horses in it. Using the permutation formula, we first determine that $N = 10$ (total number of horses in the race) and $M = 2$ (the number of horses considered in the exact order of their finishing first and second). These values are plugged into the formula and produce an answer of 90 (1/90), which gives us the final answer of .0111. In other words, we have a 1.11% chance of picking the top two finishers of a race comprised of ten horses.

$$nPm = \frac{10!}{(10-2)!} = \frac{10 \times 9 \times 8 \times 7 \times 6 \times 5 \times 4 \times 3 \times 2 \times 1}{8 \times 7 \times 6 \times 5 \times 4 \times 3 \times 2 \times 1} = \frac{10 \times 9}{1} = \boxed{90}$$

Probability $= \dfrac{1}{P} = \dfrac{1}{90} = \boxed{.011\overline{1}} =$ Or there is a 1.11% chance of this outcome's occurring in this specific order

The operations required to calculate permutations are fairly straightforward. While the answers produced by permutations are interesting, a related probability technique (called combinations) is far more valuable in understanding some of the underlying assumptions of statistics. Combinations enable us to answer questions such as, "Out of five consecutive births, what is the probability of two male children (hopefully not two children like Calvin) being born?" This question is far different from the ones asked using permutations.

Combinations are not concerned with a specific order of an outcome, but rather the probability of an outcome without concern for the order. Thus, in the question posed above, we are not concerned with the order in which the birth of two male children may occur, but rather with the probability that out of five consecutive births the birth of two male children will occur. Combining questions such as this with all other possible outcomes of the sex of a child (in the present case, out of five consecutive births) allows us to construct what is called a probability distribution (demonstrated shortly). This is where the real value of using combinations is found in understanding statistics.

Before examining the combination formula and its use, we first must determine the overall number of possibilities associated with five consecutive births. This is accomplished by using a simple formula that considers the number of possibilities for each event and the overall number of events. We use the numerical value of possible outcome for each independent event to the power of the overall number of consecutive events under consideration. In the present example, this is 2 (there are two possible outcomes for each event: a male or female child) to the fifth power (5 consecutive births) (this is shown below). The resultant answer tells us that there are 32 different ways—combinations—that male and/or female babies can occur out of 5 consecutive births (2 to the fifth power means that we take 2 x 2 = 4; 4 x 2 = 8; 8 x 2 = 16; 16 x 2 = 32).

$$2^5 = \boxed{32} \text{ (2 possible outcomes for 5 independent events-births)}$$

Next we determine the number of desired outcomes: 2 male children out of 5 consecutive births. To demonstrate the utility of the combination formula, however, we first take a more laborious approach to answering this question. This is accomplished deductively by writing out each possible way two male births out of five consecutive births can occur (see Table 7.1 opposite page). While we discover that there are 10 ways that two male children can occur out of 5 consecutive births, note that writing out each possibility is not only time consuming but also creates the distinct possibility for error. With a more complex question, such as the probability of 5 male children occurring out of 10 consecutive births, these conclusions are even more relevant.

Nevertheless, the final answer for the initial question is determined by dividing the value for the number of ways 2 male children can occur (10) by the total number of possible ways 5 consecutive births can occur (32); this equals .3125. Therefore, there is a 31.25% chance that a woman will have 2 male children in 5 consecutive births.

<u>Desired outcome of two male children</u>

$$\frac{10}{32} = \boxed{.3125 \text{ or a } 31.25\% \text{ chance}}$$

<u>Number of possible outcomes for five consecutive births</u>

Using the combination formula below, we can answer this same question in a far more expedient manner. Once again, the *nCm* symbolizes the formula for combinations; however, although the symbols of *N* and *M* are still in the formula, their meaning and application are slightly different—we now also consider an independent *M*! As noted, *N* represents the number of consecutive events considered while *M* is the number of elements of interest considered.

$$nCm = \frac{N!}{M!(N-M)!} \quad \begin{array}{l} N = \text{number of consecutive events considered} \\ M = \text{number of elements of interest considered} \end{array}$$

Thus, in our present example, $N = 5$ (5 consecutive births) while $M = 2$ (2 male births). These values are placed into their appropriate positions in the formula below to determine that out of 5 consecutive births there are 10 possible ways that 2 male children can occur. Divide the value of 10 by the value of 32—the number of possible ways 5 consecutive births can occur—results in the final answer being a 31.25% chance.

Table 7.1   Possible Combinations for Occurrence of Two Male Children Out of Five Consecutive Births

	Birth 1	*Birth 2*	*Birth 3*	*Birth 4*	*Birth 5*
1	M	M	F	F	F
2	M	F	M	F	F
3	M	F	F	M	F
4	M	F	F	F	M
5	F	M	M	F	F
6	F	M	F	M	F
7	F	M	F	F	M
8	F	F	M	M	F
9	F	F	M	F	M
10	F	F	F	M	M

$$nCm = \frac{5!}{2!(5-2)!} = \frac{5 \times 4 \times 3 \times 2 \times 1}{2 \times 1(3 \times 2 \times 1)} = \frac{5 \times 4}{2 \times 1} = \frac{20}{2} = \boxed{10}$$

Overall number of possible combinations is $2^5 = \boxed{10}$

<u>Desired outcome of two male children</u>

➤
➤ $\frac{10}{32} = \boxed{.3125 \text{ or a } 31.25\% \text{ chance}}$

<u>Number of possible outcomes for five consecutive births</u>

In the next example we want to know the probability (the chance) of a mother having 5 male children out of 7 consecutive births. Following the order of the steps used in the previous example, first calculate the overall number of possible combinations (outcomes) associated with 7 consecutive births. Recall that this is derived by taking the number of possible independent outcomes for each event to the power of the overall number of events under consideration. For the previous example, as completed below, we take 2 to the seventh power to get the obtained value of 128. In other words, there are 128 different ways (combinations) that 7 consecutive births can occur.

Overall number of possible combinations is $2^7 = \boxed{128}$

Next we must determine the number of possible ways that 5 male children out of 7 consecutive births can occur. Below we have entered the appropriate values into the combination formula to learn that there are 21 different combinations (ways) in which five male children out of seven consecutive births can occur. We divide the value of 21 (the number of desired outcomes) by the overall number of possible outcomes (128) and obtain the final answer of .1640. Thus, there is a 16.40% chance of five male children being born out of seven consecutive births.

$$nCm = \frac{7!}{5!(7-5)!} = \frac{7 \times 6 \times 5 \times 4 \times 3 \times 2 \times 1}{5 \times 4 \times 3 \times 2 \times 1(2 \times 1)} = \frac{7 \times 6}{2 \times 1} = \frac{42}{2} = \boxed{21}$$

<u>Desired outcome of five male children</u>

➤
➤ $\frac{21}{128} = \boxed{.1640 \text{ or a } 16.40\% \text{ chance}}$

<u>Number of possible outcomes for seven consecutive births</u>

For the next example, we not only use a different event (flips of a coin), we also state the question in a different format: "What is the probability of flipping *three or fewer heads* out of eight consecutive flips of a coin?" This question is phrased in a manner nearly identical to that used for calculating probabilities using a *Z*-score distribution in Chapter 6 (i.e., an IQ of 80 or less). Because flips of a coin are discrete outcomes, however—heads or tails versus an endless array of possible values associated with Z distributions (this distinction will be discussed in greater detail shortly)—we determine the probability of this event using the combination formula. Further, this formula must be used more than once to be able to answer the entire question.

Mathematically, the question is actually fourfold. We are questioning the probability of flipping 3, 2, 1, and zero heads out of 8 consecutive flips of a coin. Thus, we must make four separate combination calculations: (1) for the probability of getting three heads, (2) for the probability of getting two heads, (3) for the probability of getting one head, and (4) for the probability of getting zero heads (students often forget to calculate the probability of zero heads). Then, because we are interested in the possibility of all of these outcomes happening, designated by the *or* statements, we add up each probability to get the final answer.

Before undertaking the formula calculations, we again first must determine the overall number of ways that 8 consecutive flips of a coin can occur. There are two possible outcomes for each independent event (a flip of a coin—heads or tails) and we are interested in eight consecutive events (flips), so we take 2 to the eighth power. The resultant answer tells us there are 256 different ways (combinations) for 8 consecutive flips to occur.

$$\text{Overall number of possible combinations is } 2^8 = \boxed{256}$$

Next we independently calculate the combination values, each of which is then divided by the value of 256. These calculations are completed as follows:

$$nCm = \frac{8!}{3!(8-3)!} = \frac{8 \times 7 \times 6 \times 5 \times 4 \times 3 \times 2 \times 1}{3 \times 2 \times 1(5 \times 4 \times 3 \times 2 \times 1)} = \frac{8 \times 7 \times 6}{3 \times 2 \times 1} = \frac{336}{6} = \boxed{56}$$

$$\text{and thus } \frac{56}{256} = \boxed{.2187 \text{ or a } 21.87\% \text{ chance}}$$

and

$$nCm = \frac{8!}{2!(8-2)!} = \frac{8 \times 7 \times 6 \times 5 \times 4 \times 3 \times 2 \times 1}{2 \times 1(6 \times 5 \times 4 \times 3 \times 2 \times 1)} = \frac{8 \times 7}{2 \times 1} = \frac{56}{2} = \boxed{28}$$

$$\text{and thus } \frac{28}{256} = \boxed{.1093 \text{ or a } 10.93\% \text{ chance}}$$

and

$$nCm = \frac{8!}{1!(8-1)!} = \frac{8 \times 7 \times 6 \times 5 \times 4 \times 3 \times 2 \times 1}{1 \times (7 \times 6 \times 5 \times 4 \times 3 \times 2 \times 1)} = \frac{8}{1} = \boxed{8}$$

$$\text{and thus } \frac{8}{256} = \boxed{.0312 \text{ or a } 3.12\% \text{ chance*}}$$

(continues on following page)

(continued from previous page)

and

$$nCm = \frac{8!}{{}^{**}0!(8-0)!} = \frac{8 \times 7 \times 6 \times 5 \times 4 \times 3 \times 2 \times 1}{1 \times (8 \times 7 \times 6 \times 5 \times 4 \times 3 \times 2 \times 1)} = \frac{1}{1} = \boxed{1}$$

and thus $\dfrac{1^{***}}{256} = \boxed{.0039 \text{ or a } .39\% \text{ chance}}$

*If one thinks about it, it makes sense that there are eight ways in which a head can occur; one head for each of the eight consecutive flips of the coin with the other seven flips all being tails.
**As noted earlier, a zero (0) factorial is always equal to 1.
***With eight flips of a coin, there is literally only one way that zero heads can occur: all tails.

Because there is an "or" statement in the original question, the final operation requires us to add together each of the probabilities to obtain an overall probability, the final answer.

$$.2187 + .1093 + .0312 + .0039 = \boxed{.3631 \text{ or a } 36.31\% \text{ chance}}$$

In other words, there is a 36.31% chance of flipping three heads or fewer out of 8 consecutive flips of a coin.

Obviously, using combinations in this manner could answer an endless array of questions with reference to this or any other set of similar events. So let's propose another question using heads and flips of a coin: "What is the probability of flipping 4 to 6 heads out of 8 consecutive flips of a coin?" In other words, what is the probability of getting 4 *or* 5 *or* 6 heads out of 8 consecutive flips of a coin?

In the preceding example we determined that the overall number of possible outcomes for 8 consecutive flips is 256 and the same is true for this example. Next, we calculate separately each independent event of interest; thus, we calculate the probability of getting 4 heads, 5 heads and 6 (4 to 6 heads) out of 8 consecutive flips. These calculations are shown below, and on the top of the following page:

$$nCm = \frac{8!}{4!(8-4)!} = \frac{8 \times 7 \times 6 \times 5 \times 4 \times 3 \times 2 \times 1}{4 \times 3 \times 2 \times 1(4 \times 3 \times 2 \times 1)} = \frac{8 \times 7 \times 6 \times 5}{4 \times 3 \times 2 \times 1} = \frac{1680}{24} = \boxed{70}$$

and thus $\dfrac{70}{256} = \boxed{.2734 \text{ or a } 27.34\% \text{ chance}}$

and

$$nCm = \frac{8!}{5!(8-5)!} = \frac{8 \times 7 \times 6 \times 5 \times 4 \times 3 \times 2 \times 1}{5 \times 4 \times 3 \times 2 \times 1(3 \times 2 \times 1)} = \frac{8 \times 7 \times 6}{3 \times 2 \times 1} = \frac{336}{6} = \boxed{56}$$

and thus $\dfrac{56}{256} = \boxed{.2187 \text{ or a } 21.87\% \text{ chance}}$

and

$$nCm = \frac{8!}{6!(8-6)!} = \frac{8 \times 7 \times 6 \times 5 \times 4 \times 3 \times 2 \times 1}{6 \times 5 \times 4 \times 3 \times 2 \times 1(2 \times 1)} = \frac{8 \times 7}{2 \times 1} = \frac{56}{2} = \boxed{28}$$

and thus $\dfrac{28}{256} = \boxed{.1093 \text{ or a } 10.93\% \text{ chance}}$

To obtain the final answer, sum the three separate answers together to find that there is a 60.14% chance of flipping 4 to 6 heads out of 8 consecutive flips of a coin.

$$.2734 + .2187 + .1093 = \boxed{.6014 \text{ or a } 60.14\% \text{ chance}}$$

Probability Distributions for Combinations

You may have noted a pattern emerging in the last two problems. That is, the calculation for five and six heads resulted in the same answers obtained for three and two heads. The reason that these answers are identical is that we are merely observing part of a probability distribution for a set of discrete events.

Flips of a coin or gender of a child are considered discrete events because they can only occur in fixed categories: heads or tails, male or female. Discrete events such as this are also reflective of a nominal level of measurement; per se, no numerical value can be directly applied to them. Z distributions, on the other hand, reflect continuous variables: weights, heights, income levels, etc. These types of variables represent a literally infinite number of possible outcomes and, as such, they are considered an interval/ratio level of measurement. Nevertheless, we can apply the notion of a probability distribution to both types of variable. Z-score distributions and continuous variables already have been discussed, so we now turn our attention to discrete probability distributions.

Reusing the example concerning 8 flips of a coin to construct a probability distribution, most of the information needed has already been completed in previous examples. A probability distribution for 8 flips of a coin must consider all possible outcomes; for this example that is 26 possible combinations. One easy way to do this task is to calculate the probability for each outcome (zero to 8 heads), which can alternatively be viewed as zero to 8 tails. We have already calculated the probabilities for zero to 6 heads, so we can simply re-list these values. To construct a complete distribution of combinations, however, we must also calculate the probabilities associated with 7 and 8 heads (as will be shown, in a sense we have already done this by calculating the probabilities associated with 1 head and zero heads). Both of these calculations are completed on the top of the following page.

$$nCm = \frac{8!}{7!(8-7)!} = \frac{8 \times 7 \times 6 \times 5 \times 4 \times 3 \times 2 \times 1}{(7 \times 6 \times 5 \times 4 \times 3 \times 2 \times 1)1} = \frac{8}{1} = \boxed{8}$$

and thus $\dfrac{8}{256} = \boxed{.0312 \text{ or a } 3.12\% \text{ chance}}$

and

$$nCm = \frac{8!}{8!(8-8)!} = \frac{8 \times 7 \times 6 \times 5 \times 4 \times 3 \times 2 \times 1}{(8 \times 7 \times 6 \times 5 \times 4 \times 3 \times 2 \times 1)1} = \frac{1}{1} = \boxed{1}$$

and thus $\dfrac{1}{256} = \boxed{.0039 \text{ or a } .39\% \text{ chance}}$

We can now combine all eight of the calculations concerning 8 consecutive flips (6 from previous examples and 2 from the above example) to construct the probability distribution found in Table 7.2.

Several noteworthy observations can be made about this distribution. First, when all the combinations are added together they do equal the number of all possible combinations: 256. Second, when all the probabilities of occurrence are added together they equal 1.00 or 100%. This should not be surprising because they don't, in fact, represent *all* (100%) of the ways that 8 flips of a coin can occur. Third, exactly like a *Z*-score distribution, the above distribution is symmetrical in shape. That is, other than its midpoint of 4 heads (like the mean in a *Z* distribution), all other values have an exact corresponding value on the other side of the distribution. Moreover, just like the tail regions of the *Z*-score distribution, the further one gets away from the midpoint value of four heads the more the probability of the given occurrence decreases. Finally, by graphing this information we can create an illustration (a histogram) that clearly represents the

Table 7.2   Discrete Probability Distribution for Eight Flips of a Coin

Number of Heads Out of Eight Flips	Number of Combinations Out of Total Possible	Probability of Occurrence
0	1/256	.0039
1	8/256	.0312
2	28/256	.1093
3	56/256	.2187
4	70/256	.2734
5	56/256	.2187
6	28/256	.1093
7	8/256	.0312
8	1/256	.0039
Sum of Combinations = 256		Probabilities = 1.00

shape of a *Z* distribution: a bell-shaped curve. This is done in Figure 7.1, and has the bell shape of a *Z* distribution superimposed on it.

Chapter Summary and Conclusions

This chapter explored several ways to determine the probability of certain events. It discussed basic probabilities in terms of how they can solve problems involving independent events, "or" statements and "and" statements. Examples used in these problems involved several different types of events from which probabilities can be determined (e.g., drawing a card, predicting sex of a child at birth, flipping a coin). Next an overview of factorials was given and then applied to permutations and combinations. Combinations were demonstrated to have additional statistical meaning in that a probability distribution was constructed using them. Probabilities, although applied in a slightly different manner than in this chapter, have increasing importance throughout the remainder of this text.

Figure 7.1   Discrete Probability Distribution

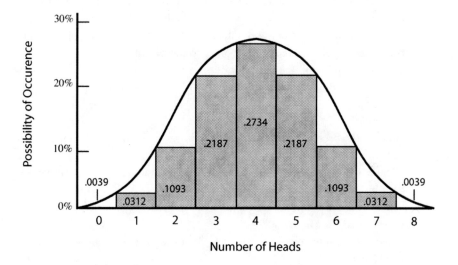

Number of Heads

Key Terms to Remember

- Basic Probabilities
- Independent Events
- "Or" Statements
- "And" Statements
- Gambler's Fallacy
- Factorials
- Permutations
- Combinations

Practice Exercises

1. Referring back to Cartoon 7.1, and all things considered equal:
   a. What was the probability of Opus's mother having a girl instead of Opus?
   b. If Opus's mother wanted three more children, what is the probability of her having a girl, and then a boy, and then another girl?
   c. If Opus was playing cards, what is the probability of his randomly drawing (in a single draw) an ace or the queen of hearts out of a full deck of shuffled cards?
   d. How about a black 4 or any face card (a king, a queen, or a jack)?
   e. If Opus was flipping a balanced coin, what is the probability of his getting five heads in row?
   f. If he was tossing a balanced die and flipping a balanced coin, what is the probability of his getting a 6 on the die and then a head on the coin?

2. Using factorials with permutations:
   a. What is the probability of selecting a club and then a heart out of 4 cards representing each suit (clubs, hearts, spades, and diamonds)?
   b. What is the probability of (randomly) selecting the top 3 finishers of a bike race comprised of 7 bikers in the exact order of their finishing?
   c. What is the probability of (randomly) selecting the top 2 finishers of a horse race comprised of 11 horses in the exact order of their finishing?

3. Using factorials with combinations:
   a. What is the probability of getting 2 heads out of 7 flips of a balanced coin? (Obviously, order is no longer relevant.)
   b. What is the probability of having 1 female penguin out of 9 consecutive penguin births?
   c. What is the probability of having 3 or fewer male penguins out of 12 consecutive births?
   d. What is the probability of having 5 to 8 female penguins out of 12 consecutive births?
   e. What is the probability of Opus's getting a date with one of these flightless female fowl? (Obviously given Opus's dating history and his rather sexist attitudes, the probability of his even making a successful first impression, let alone getting a date, is rather small. Nevertheless, per se, there is no definitive way to answer this question.)

8

Constructing Confidence Intervals

The last two chapters demonstrated techniques that determined probabilities for continuous and discrete outcomes; for example, there is a 50% chance the next person you will meet will have an IQ of 100 or less, or there is a 12.5% chance of your flipping a coin and getting three consecutive heads. In this chapter, some of these basic ideas about probability theory are used to construct *confidence intervals*. Moreover, the previous two chapters explored descriptive mathematical techniques, and this chapter introduces the notion of *inferential statistics*. As such, this is the first chapter to delve exclusively into *sample statistics*.

During political campaigns the news media often makes statements such as, "If the election were held today, candidate A would have 52% of the votes while candidate B would have 47% of the votes." In this hypothetical case they might add: "However, due to sampling error of five percentage points" (this is also referred to as a confidence limit) "the election appears to be a dead heat and too close to predict a winner." Similar statements are made during actual elections, and newscasters might report, "With 10% of the precincts reporting, we are predicting candidate C to be the winner over candidate D by a margin of 60% to 39%." What do these figures represent? How do the pollsters arrive at these figures? With 52% clearly being more than 47%, and a large enough margin to win most elections, why is the election still reported as a dead heat?

Answering each of these questions in turn, the figures of 52% and 47% represent proportions of a sample of registered voters, expressed in terms of which candidate those in the sample say that they plan to vote for in the upcoming election. In other words (and referring all the way back to Chapter 1), these proportions are inferential statistics calculated from a sample that was drawn from a larger population.

(As an aside, if these figures [52% and 47%] were for an upcoming presidential election and we wanted to predict the winner, the population our sample would be drawn from comprises all registered voters in the United States. Conversely, if the figures were for the elected position of mayor of the town or city you reside in, the population would be all registered voters in your town or city.)

How such figures are actually calculated and why they point to a dead heat is what the rest of this chapter is devoted to explaining. At this point, however, there are some simple observations we can make. Using the values of 52% and 47% and with corresponding margins of sampling error equal to 5%, we are actually being told that the true percentage of people who support candidate A is somewhere between 47% and 57% (52% ± 5%) of the voters while the proportion that supports candidate B is somewhere between 42% and 52% (47% ± 5%). Because there is considerable overlap between the actual proportions of people that may support candidate A versus candidate B, it cannot be stated conclusively that either candidate appears to have a clear-cut lead.

To answer the above questions more completely, this chapter discusses how to calculate the statistical concepts of the standard error of the mean, confidence limits and levels (using the previously discussed *Z* distribution and a newly introduced *t* distribution), and alpha levels; taken all together, these terms equal a confidence interval. This chapter also explores a statistical technique that tells the sample size required for a stated margin of error. While all these new terms may seem somewhat overwhelming, in application they really are quite easy to both calculate and understand. Quite simply, what confidence intervals do is estimate population parameters. While an array of different confidence intervals exists to estimate nearly every conceivable population parameter, to keep things simple only estimates of population means are discussed in this chapter.

Samples

Before undertaking any actual calculations for confidence intervals, we should review briefly what samples and statistics enable us to do. To assist in this discussion, below is the figure that initially appeared in Chapter 1 (Figure 8.1). This figure is important to this chapter's material because it points out the two things that samples and corresponding statistics do with regard to population parameters: (1) estimate, and (2) hypothesis test. The first, estimates of population parameters, is what this chapter is all about, while hypothesis testing is largely addressed by chapters 9 through 13.

To this point, the discussion primarily has been concerned with two different types of sample statistics: means and standard deviations. Until now, however, we have had no way to assess how accurate these and other statistics are in terms of the population parameters

Figure 8.1   Population Parameters/Sample Statistics

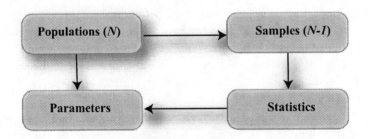

1. Estimate Population Parameters
2. Hypothesis Testing

they estimate. That is, while sample means, standard deviations, and other descriptive statistics are the best estimates we have for each corresponding parameter, these figures by themselves tell us nothing about how accurate they are. Accuracy, in this context, means how much the sample statistic potentially deviates from the parameter it is estimating.

This is exactly what confidence intervals do; they enable us to determine the accuracy of our initial estimates. To accomplish this, information from the population and the sample (or, more typically, just from the sample) is used to calculate the given estimate's accuracy. Moreover, and building upon the material discussed in the previous two chapters, confidence intervals also make estimates of accuracy in terms of probability values. In sum, confidence intervals are probability estimates of the true parameter value in terms of its occurrence between constructed boundaries.

Confidence Intervals Using a Population Standard Deviation

Below is the formula used to calculate a confidence interval when the population standard deviation is known. Given this information, what the formula estimates is an unknown population mean.

<u>Confidence Interval When σ is Known</u>

$$CI = \bar{x} \pm (Z_{\alpha/2})\left(\frac{\sigma}{\sqrt{n}}\right)$$

Before we explore the formula in its complete form, it is much easier to introduce and explain each of its four sub-parts individually. These parts are: the *standard error of the mean*, the *confidence level*, the *alpha level*, and the *confidence limits*. Once each of these components is explained, there is only one more step required to construct a confidence interval.

Cartoon 8.1 serves as a backdrop for the discussion that follows in this section. This cartoon is representative of a measure that the authors have administered in many of our courses (including statistics) called the BEM Sex Role Inventory (BSRI). The BSRI measures something called psychological androgyny. To this end, the scale is comprised of 60 questions that assess each respondent's stereotypical attributes of instrumentalness (construed as traditional masculine characteristics—Ward Cleaver) and expressiveness (construed as traditional feminine characteristics—June Cleaver). Of the 60 questions, 20 measure instrumentalness, 20 measure expressiveness, and 20 are filter items that don't measure anything per se. Further, the 60 questions ask the respondent to answer how applicable each one-word item is to them on a seven-point scale. After the scale is completed, the 20 masculine scores and the 20 feminine scores are separately added together, and then each divided by 20—this gives two average scores: one for masculinity and one for femininity.

Cartoon 8.1   BLOOM COUNTY

(As an aside, respondents whose average masculine and feminine scores are within one whole point of each other are considered psychologically androgynous. This means that, psychologically, they have nearly equal amounts of traditional male and female personality characteristics. Many contemporary social commentators view psychological androgyny as a positive trait.)

Also, while the BSRI is an ordinal-level measurement, the confidence interval statistical technique was initially created with the assumption that only interval/ratio-level data should be used. The reason for this assumption is beyond the scope of this text. Needless to say, as with our example, this assumption is regularly violated; that is, it is rather commonplace for social scientists to construct confidence intervals using ordinal-level data. Violating this assumption potentially draws into question any findings, however, so always make note of circumstances where lower levels of measurement have been used.

Before proceeding, let's quickly review what is found in the confidence-interval formula. As noted regarding the original formula, we assume that the population standard deviation value is already known. Although it is actually fairly uncommon to know the population standard deviation when calculating a confidence interval, there are instances, such as in industry, where this value may be known. Further, as demonstrated in the next section, using a population standard deviation versus a sample standard deviation entails the use of different set of standardized scores (a corresponding Z distribution versus a t distribution, which is introduced later) to calculate a confidence interval.

With the above provisions in mind, we are finally ready to apply an actual data set to the abstract discussion we have thus far undertaken. The first author administered the BSRI in a course he taught and found the 36 students that attended class that day had an average expressive score of 4.2 and an average instrumental score of 4.8 (once again, on a scale of 1 to 7). We'll also say that the standard deviation values for *all* the students at the university he teaches are 1.5 for the expressive scores and 1.8 for the instrumental scores. Thus, in this case, we are treating our 36 students as a nonrandom sample and *all* students at the university as the population. (Ideally, we would have generated a random sample from all of the university students. Only then can we assume that our sample is truly representative.)

Utilizing the information from this data set, we first construct a confidence interval for the expressive scores to estimate what the actual expressive average (population mean) is for all students at the university. To this end, we must calculate the *standard error of the mean*. To determine this value, we take the population standard deviation and divide it by the square root of the sample size. This sub-part of the overall confidence interval formula is mathematically represented below.

Formula for the Standard Error of the Mean

$$\sigma / \sqrt{n}$$

Without becoming mired in too technical a discussion, following are some important observations that we can make about what the standard error of the mean represents. Recall that a standard deviation represents the amount of standardized variance found in a given set of scores. Because we divide the standard deviation by the square root of the sample size (n), the size of the final answer for this operation is directly determined by both the amount of standardized variance and the sample size. In slightly different terms, this means that the larger the standard deviation and/or the smaller the sample, the larger the standard error of the mean will be. Conversely, the smaller the standard deviation and/or the larger the sample, the smaller the standard error of the mean will be. As we will see, because the size of a confidence interval is a measure of the accuracy of the estimate of the population mean, a smaller standard error of the mean value is always desired. In other words, using a smaller standard error value results in a more accurate estimate.

Below we have placed the appropriate BEM expressive values into the standard error of the mean formula (n = 36; σ = 1.5) to obtain the answer of .25.

$$\frac{\sigma}{\sqrt{n}} = \frac{1.5}{\sqrt{36}} = \frac{1.5}{6} = \boxed{.25 *}$$

*Standard Error of the Mean for the BEM Expressive Scores

The next sub-part that we must calculate and define is the *confidence level*. This is represented by the portion of the confidence interval formula that has the notation of a Z with a new subscript ($\alpha / 2$). What it represents is an actual Z value. To keep things simple, for our purposes this is always one of two Z-score values: 1.96 and 2.58. That is, in subsequent calculations for confidence intervals where the population standard deviation is known, one of these two values is always used.

Although the values of 1.96 and 2.58 are now treated as givens, it is still helpful to discuss briefly how they are derived. These values reflect two different confidence levels. Taking the Z value of 1.96 first and tracing its calculations, we must define what it represents: a confidence level, which in this case is 95%. A confidence level of 95% indicates that our final answer, the confidence level itself, will contain the true population mean that it is estimating 95 times out of 100. This is more clearly demonstrated shortly.

A 95% confidence level also tells us that we have an error level of 5%; that is, 5% of the time our estimate is wrong—in error. The error level is more correctly referred to as an *alpha level* and is represented by the symbol α, the subscript found next to the Z. To determine an alpha level, take the value of one and subtract the given confidence level from it. In the present example, this is $1 - .95 = .05$ or a 5% alpha level. Next, as the subscript instructs, we divide the alpha level by 2; for this example, $.05 / 2 = .025$. Referring to Appendix 1 and its corresponding Z scores, we look in the Small-Part column for the probability value of .025 and find that the attendant Z value is 1.96.

Reapplying these steps to the Z value of 2.58, we first must note that this value represents a confidence level of 99%. This says that the corresponding alpha level is 1%, derived by taking $1-.99 = .01$. Next, we take the alpha level of .01, and divide it by 2, to give us the value of .005. Once again, we look this value up in the Small-Part column found in Appendix 1, and find that it falls between two Z scores: 2.57 and 2.58. Many statisticians often use the larger value of 2.58 to simplify subsequent calculations, so we also use this value.

Now that we have determined how the values of 1.96 and 2.58 are derived, a few more important observations are warranted before continuing. The values of 95% and 99%, as previously noted, are the confidence levels most commonly used in the social sciences. For this reason, and to simplify our discussion, only these confidence levels are used for Z scores. In other words, we no longer have to refer to Appendix 1 or do any additional calculations for this component of the formula. It is important, however, to note that numerous other confidence levels, such as 98% or 99.9%, can also be used (the next type of confidence interval discussed in this chapter considers these levels). Finally, the confidence levels of 95% and 99% and their corresponding alpha levels of .05 and .01, in reference to Z scores, represent the same thing and sometimes are used interchangeably in subsequent discussions.

We are now ready to calculate the confidence limits: the final sub-part of the confidence interval formula. Confidence limits also sometimes are called the "margin of error," and in the next section they are referred to as such. To calculate the confidence limits, the appropriate Z value (1.96 or 2.58) is multiplied by the standard error of the mean. Because the confidence level is usually arbitrarily set (usually determined by how accurate an estimate of the population mean the given researcher wants), the calculations for both the 95% level and the 99% level are completed below.

$$\underline{\text{Confidence Limit}}$$

$$95\% \text{ level} = (1.96)(.25) = \boxed{.490}$$

$$\left(Z_{\alpha / 2}\right)\left(\frac{\sigma}{\sqrt{n}}\right) \quad \text{for}$$

$$99\% \text{ level} = (2.58)(.25) = \boxed{.645}$$

All that's left to do to get the final answer, the confidence interval, is to add and subtract ($\pm$) the confidence limits from the sample mean; for this case, recall that our sample of 36 students had an expressive average of 4.2. Found below is the original confidence interval formula, all of the original values for each confidence interval, the calculations for both confidence levels (.05 and .01), and the two resultant confidence intervals.

For Expressive Average

Confidence Intervals for the Alpha Levels of .05 and .01

$$CI = \bar{x} \pm (Z_{\alpha/2})(\sigma / \sqrt{n})$$

For Alpha Level .05

$$4.2 \pm (1.96)(1.5 / \sqrt{36}) = 4.2 \pm .49 = \boxed{(3.71 < \mu < 4.69), .05}$$

For Alpha Level .01

$$4.2 \pm (2.58)(1.5 / \sqrt{36}) = 4.2 \pm .645 = \boxed{(3.555 < \mu < 4.845), .01}$$

The presentation format of these confidence intervals, and why there is a difference between the two, warrants some further discussion. Because the given confidence interval is an estimate of the true population mean, the population mean is placed in the middle of the constructed interval. Directly to the left and right of the population mean (μ; "mu") are two symbols that signify that the true mean is greater than the lowest part of the interval estimate (referred to as a *lower limit*) and less than the highest part (referred to as an *upper limit*). (As a somewhat ridiculous aside, some of our students have inferred the signs of greater and less than to be the equivalent to the fast forward and reverse buttons on their VCRs.) Directly to the right of the given interval is the alpha level used in its calculation.

To put all of this into English, the first confidence interval informs us that the population mean for the expressive scores (June Cleaverness) at the university is somewhere between the values of 3.71 and 4.69. Further, with the alpha level set at .05 (confidence level 95%) we assume that this estimate is correct 95 times out of 100; 95% of the time the true population mean will fall between 3.71 and 4.69. Conversely, we also assume that the estimate is in error 5% of the time; we expect the true population mean to fall outside the above confidence interval 5 times out of 100. In total, we can state that we are 95% confident that the population mean for expressiveness at the university falls between the values of 3.71 and 4.69. Alternatively, for the second confidence interval we are 99% confident that the population mean for expressiveness falls between the values of 3.555 and 4.845.

Most of you have probably noticed that as our confidence level goes up (in this example, from 95% to 99%), the corresponding width of the confidence interval also increases. The reason for this (beyond the obvious larger Z value used in the calculation of the confidence interval) is that as we become more confident that the true population mean is found within our estimate, the size of the interval must increase. A helpful way to

Figure 8.2   *Z*-Score Distribution

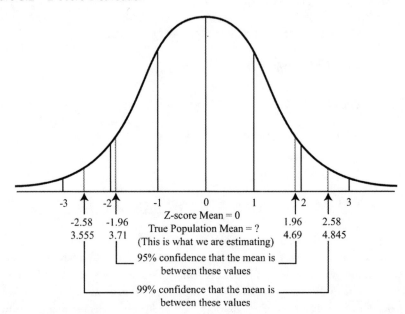

demonstrate this relationship is to superimpose both of the confidence intervals we have constructed onto the normal (*Z* score) distribution. This is done in Figure 8.2.

In a simplistic sense, by applying the constructed intervals onto the normal distribution we theoretically demonstrate that our constructed interval represents 95% or 99% of all estimated scores. Thus, correspondingly, this is how confident we are that the population mean we are estimating falls between the given interval's upper and lower limits. After all, any given mean is calculated from a distribution of actual scores.

For review purposes, let's construct the two confidence intervals for the instrumental scores (Ward Cleaverness). The mean instrumental score for the 36 students, once again, was 4.8 with an already-known population standard deviation of 1.8. Instead of going through each of the sub-parts to calculate this confidence interval, the reproduced formula and the calculations for each alpha level (.05 and .01) are presented at the top of the opposite page. If any of the values or calculations are problematic, please refer to the step-by-step discussion above for the expressive scores.

We should note two of the most obvious differences between the confidence intervals on the opposite page and those previously constructed. First, because the instrumental mean is .6 greater than the expressive mean, the constructed intervals cover a different part of the 1–7 score range of the BSRI. Second, because the standard deviation for the instrumental scores (1.8) is larger than that for the expressive scores (1.5), the widths of the resultant confidence intervals are larger: .98 at .05 and 1.29 at .01 for the expressive scores versus 1.168 at .05 and 1.548 at .01 for the instrumental scores. This demonstrates the importance of the size of the standard deviation; as it increases the width of the confidence interval also increases. Of course, again, one way a researcher can compensate for

For Instrumentality Average

Confidence Intervals for the Alpha Levels of .05 and .01

$$CI = \bar{x} \pm (Z_{\alpha/2})(\sigma / \sqrt{n})$$

For Alpha Level .05

$$4.8 \pm (1.96)(1.8 / \sqrt{36}) = 4.8 \pm .588 = \boxed{(4.212 < \mu < 5.388), .05}$$
$$(.3)$$

For Alpha Level .01

$$4.8 \pm (2.58)(1.8 / \sqrt{36}) = 4.8 \pm .774 = \boxed{(4.026 < \mu < 5.574), .01}$$
$$(.3)$$

this is to increase the sample size, which always decreases the width of the confidence interval. This relationship is more clearly demonstrated below.

Summarizing the above confidence intervals, at the .05 alpha level, we can estimate that 95 times out of 100 the population mean of instrumental scores for all university students will fall between 4.212 and 5.388; 5 times out of 100 it will fall outside. At the .01 alpha level we can estimate that 99 times out of 100 the population mean will fall between 4.026 and 5.574; 1 time out of 100 it will fall outside.

Sample Size Required for a Given Margin of Error

When the population standard deviation is known, as with the above confidence intervals, this information can help researchers and pollsters estimate what size sample is required for a predetermined margin of error. As already noted, the margin of error is the same thing as a confidence limit. Mathematically, when the population standard deviation and confidence level are both known, we can predetermine the sample size required for a given confidence interval. The formula to do this is derived from the original confidence-interval formula using the same simple algebraic logic that tells us that $Z = 1 / X$ thus $X = 1 / 2$ or $4 = 1 / X$ thus $X = 1 / 4$. By algebraically transforming the original confidence interval formula (e = the margin of error) we find:

$$\text{If } \quad e = (Z_{\alpha/2})\left(\frac{\sigma}{\sqrt{n}}\right), \text{ then } n = \left(\frac{(Z_{\alpha/2})(\sigma)}{e}\right)^2$$

One very practical application of this formula that corporations often use is to test products' quality control. For instance, light-bulb companies often make the claim that a given bulb lasts 400 hours or that batteries for mechanical rabbits will last 40 hours. Taking the latter example of batteries and mechanical rabbits, say we want to know what size sample of batteries is required (number of batteries to be tested) to have a 2-hour margin of error. From previous tests we know the population standard deviation is 4 hours. All we have to do to complete the formula is set the alpha level; for the first calculation it is set at .05. The original formula, all relevant values ($Z = 1.96$, $\sigma = 4$, and $e = 2$), and all calculations are found below:

$$n = \left(\frac{(Z_{\alpha/2})(\sigma)}{e}\right)^2 = \left(\frac{(1.96)(4)}{2}\right)^2 = \left(\frac{7.84}{2}\right)^{2*} = (3.92)^2 = \boxed{16**}$$

* We must also note that students using this formula often forget to square the final answer; make sure you don't!

** One immediate point of clarification: while 3.92 squared equals 15.3664, since we are dealing with whole sampling units required for a given margin of error, always round up to the next whole unit. After all, it would be impossible to have a sample of 15.3664 batteries.

The final answer tells us that we need a sample of 16 batteries to have a confidence limit of 2 hours. Further, we are 95% confident in this estimate of the sample size required. To validate this conclusion, we can take the predicted sample size required (15.3664 for the actual calculation) along with the other given values and plug them into the original confidence interval formula to find that:

$$e = (Z_{\alpha/2})(\sigma / \sqrt{n}) = (1.96)(4 / \sqrt{15.3664}) = \boxed{2}$$

Alternatively, let's say that we want the margin of error for our batteries to be within one-half hour (.5). Using the same alpha level of .05 and population standard deviation as in the previous example (4), but different margin of error ($e = .5$) in this case, we have completed the appropriate calculations below:

$$n = \left(\frac{(Z_{\alpha/2})(\sigma)}{e}\right)^2 = \left(\frac{(1.96)(4)}{.5}\right)^2 = \left(\frac{7.84}{.5}\right)^2 = (15.68)^2 = \boxed{246}$$

Thus, to decrease the margin of error by 1.5 hours (from 2 hours to .5 hours), we must drastically increase the sample size from 16 to 246 batteries. Referring back to the original confidence-interval formula, this relationship clearly demonstrates the importance of sample size in determining the width of a confidence interval.

As noted, the alpha level has the same effect on the sample size. For instance, in our first example above, with the alpha level at .01, we need a sample of 27 instead of 16, while the sample size required for the second example would increase from 246 to 427. All of this has significant implications for pollsters and industry when determining how large a sample to draw for research. It costs money to increase a given sample size, and to be only slightly more accurate or confident in one's estimate is often not worth it.

Confidence Intervals Using a Sample Standard Deviation

Thus far, the discussion of confidence intervals has assumed that we already know the population standard deviation value; however, as noted, we seldom know this value. Like a sample mean, the best estimate of a population standard deviation is the sample standard deviation. Below is the formula used to calculate a confidence interval using a sample standard deviation.

Confidence Interval Using *s*

$$CI = \bar{x} \pm (t_{\alpha/2})(s / \sqrt{n})$$

Although this formula appears very similar to the previous one used, there are some important differences. To begin with the obvious, instead of using a population standard deviation, we now use a sample standard deviation value. Moreover, while the use of a sample standard deviation value does not change the format of the actual calculations, it does require that we now use a *t* value instead of a *Z* value. As such, before we can actually construct a confidence interval with this new formula, we must explain its accompanying distribution and how to use it.

The *t distribution* is found in Appendix 2 (please refer to it for the following discussion). The two pages of this appendix have a format different from that used for the *Z* distribution. Instead of column headings for what part of the distribution we are concerned with, the column for the *t* distribution has alpha levels. One set of column headings is for *one-tailed values* whereas the second set of column headings is for *two-tailed values*. The easiest way to construct this type of confidence interval is with two-tailed values, so only the two-tailed column headings and their corresponding values are used in this chapter.

On the left side of the table are found what are called degrees of freedom, signified by "df." Degrees of freedom are determined by subtracting the value of one from the sample size: $n - 1$. The reason that degrees of freedom are determined using $n - 1$ is that we are estimating a population parameter; this is the same reason the denominator in the standard deviation formula is $n - 1$. In other words, because we are estimating a population mean, the absolute minimum number of values (observations) that would potentially have to change for our estimate to equal the mean is one. Thus, fixing one degree of freedom leaves us with an estimate that takes into account potential sampling error.

By combining these two pieces of information, alpha level and df, we can determine any *t*-critical value. Before undertaking the complete confidence-interval formula, let's first practice determining some *t*-critical values. Given a sample of 16 and an alpha level of .05, what is the corresponding *t*-critical value? First we determine the degrees of freedom by simply subtracting one from the sample size; $16-1 = 15$ df. Next we look down the row headings to 15 df, and then proceed to the column heading of alpha .05, to ascertain that the *t*-critical value for this example is 2.131.

Box 8.1   William Gosset, Guinness, and the *t* Distribution

The *t* distribution is actually based on the student's *t* distribution. The creator of this distribution, William Gosset, was an employee of Guinness Brewery in Dublin, Ireland. He developed this distribution as a technique to deal with small samples of barley and hops and other conditions of production to ensure the quality of his brewery's product. The reason that this distribution does not bear his name is that one of the conditions of his employment was that he could not personally take credit for any of his publications; he simply signed all his works "Student." This is why this distribution is called Student's *t*.

For the next example, what is the corresponding t-critical value for a sample of 10 with an alpha level of .001? (As an aside, a .001 alpha level is the same thing as a confidence level of 99.9%; that is, the resultant confidence interval, if it were completed for this example, would contain the true mean value an estimated 999 times out of 1000.) To answer the question, we first determine the degrees of freedom (10 – 1 = 9 df), find this row heading combined with the column heading of .001, and find the *t*-critical value of 4.781.

Finally, let's say we have a sample of 37 and want to know what corresponding *t*-critical value is at the .02 alpha level. The .02 column heading is easy to locate, but what do we do with 36 df (37 – 1 = 36 df) when this row heading is not listed? In situations such as this where the df value falls between two listed values, you should always take the next lowest value on the table, in this case 30 df. This gives a more conservative estimate and prevents the need for an additional step called extrapolation. Thus, with 36 df (30 df) at the .02 alpha level the corresponding *t* value is 2.457.

We are now ready to construct a confidence interval using this new distribution. To assist in this discussion, we offer Cartoon 8.2. More specifically, our current research interests are the number of "thinking responses" or inquiries students make per semester (or quarter) in a statistics class taught with the text that you are presently using. We randomly sample 16 students currently enrolled in statistics classes at a large university that are using this text to determine the average number of "thinking responses" they make in these types of classes. They are then watched for a semester's period. We find that the average (x bar) of "thinking responses" is 30 with a sample standard deviation (*s*) of 5 such responses for our sampled 16 students.

With the alpha level set at .05 and .001, we use this information to construct two confidence intervals to estimate what the population mean is. The population, in this case, is all students attending statistics classes at the given university that are using this text.

We use the following four basic steps to construct this type of confidence interval:

1. Derive the standard error of the mean
2. Determine the *t*-critical value
3. Multiply these two values together, to give us our confidence limits
4. Add and subtract the confidence limits from the sample mean to give us the confidence interval.

The formula to do this and all these steps for both confidence intervals (.05 and .001) are completed below; however, as this is our first example of this type of confidence interval, we will briefly outline each step for the .05 interval.

Once again, to determine the standard error of the mean, take the sample standard deviation (5) and divide it by the square root of n (the square root of $16 = 4$); 5 divided by 4 equals 1.25. Next, refer to Appendix 2 to find that the t critical value is 2.131; column heading of .05 with 15 degrees of freedom ($n - 1$; $16 - 1 = 15$ df). We multiply these two values together (the t critical by the standard error of the mean) to derive the confidence limit of 2.6637. Finally, add and subtract this value from our sample mean (30 thinking responses) to obtain the confidence interval of $(27.3363 < \mu < 32.6637)$, .05.

Confidence Intervals for Alpha Levels Set at .05 and .001

$$CI = \bar{x} \pm (t_{\alpha/2})(s / \sqrt{n}) \quad \text{Confidence Interval Using } s$$

For Alpha Level .05

$$30 \pm (2.131)(5 / \sqrt{16}) = 30 \pm 2.6637 = \boxed{(27.3363 < \mu < 32.6637), .05}$$
$$(1.25)$$

For Alpha Level .001

$$30 \pm (4.073)(5 / \sqrt{16}) = 30 \pm 5.0912 = \boxed{(24.9088 < \mu < 35.0912), .001}$$
$$(1.25)$$

Summarizing these confidence intervals, for the first one with the alpha level set at .05, we are 95% confident that the true sample mean occurs between the values of 27.3363 and 32.6637. In other words, we are estimating that the average number of "thinking

Cartoon 8.2   DOONESBURY

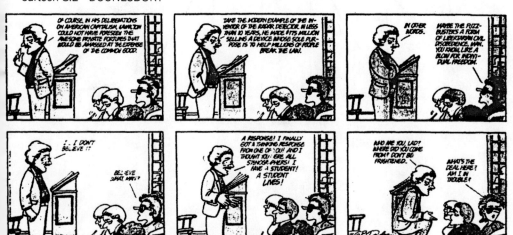

Box 8.2   Differences Between *t* and *Z* Distributions

Although the *t* distribution is very similar to the *Z* distribution (since it was created specifically to deal with smaller sets of numbers, samples, especially those less than 30), there are also some significant differences. To begin with, as illustrated in Figure 8.3, the *t* distribution is much flatter, with thicker tail regions than the *Z*. The reason for this is that as a sample size decreases the corresponding potential for sampling error increases. In slightly different terms, this means that as the sample size decreases, the scores tend to become more evenly dispersed throughout the distribution. This is in direct contrast to the *Z* distribution, where most of the scores tend to occur right around the mean.

To further demonstrate this difference between distributions, with the *Z* distribution at plus or minus two standard deviations (1.96 to be exact), we expect to find 95% of all the scores in this region. However, with a sample of 6 (5 df) it takes more than two-and-one-half standard deviations (2.571) to make this same conclusion. Both of these examples are also illustrated in Figure 8.3.

On the other hand, as the sample size increases, the shape of the *t* distribution becomes more and more like that of the *Z* distribution. Referring to Appendix 2, if one looks at the row heading of 120 df under the .05 column heading, the critical value is 1.98, almost the same as that of *Z* distribution at this level. Moreover, just below this value is the row heading of infinite (4) and the expected 1.96.

Figure 8.3   *Z* and *t* Distributions

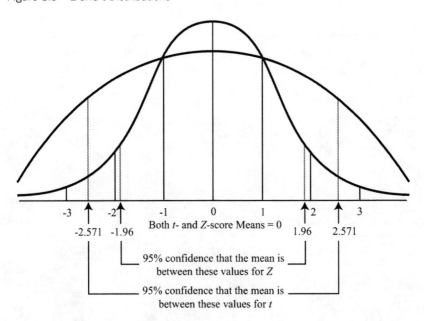

responses" made by statistics students using this text at our hypothetical university (the population) is found between these values 95 times out of 100; 5 times out of 100 the population mean falls outside of this interval.

The second confidence interval, alpha level of .001, is much larger. The reason for this, once again, is that we are much more confident that the true population mean is found within our constructed interval. Stated in the context of the resultant answer, 999 times out of 1000 the true population mean is expected to occur between the values of 24.9088 and 35.0912 and only 1 time out of 1,000 is it expected to fall outside of this interval. Thus, we can be quite confident that most students using this text at this university will make somewhere between 25 and 35 "thinking responses" per semester.

Chapter Summary and Conclusions

This chapter began with a discussion of inferential statistics and what they enable us to do: estimate population parameters and hypothesis test. Dealing exclusively with the former, two techniques to estimate population means were outlined. The first technique was a confidence interval when the population standard deviation is known. It was noted that because the population standard deviation is typically not known, this type of confidence interval is not widely used. Next was an outline of an algebraic variant of this first confidence-interval formula that enabled us to determine the sample size required for a given margin of error.

The second, more widely used technique that was explored next utilized a sample standard deviation and a newly introduced t distribution to construct confidence intervals. Also noted was that there are other techniques of estimation for proportions and other population parameters.

The next chapter builds upon the confidence intervals presented in this chapter and uses them to investigate the second thing sample statistics enable us to do: hypothesis test.

Key Terms to Remember

- Samples
- Standard Error of the Mean
- Inferential Statistics
- Margin of Error
- Populations
- Confidence Level
- Parameters
- Confidence Limits
- Alpha Levels
- Z Distribution
- Confidence Intervals
- t Distribution

Practice Exercises

1. Using Cartoon 8.2 again as a backdrop, let's say that we are interested in the number of "thinking responses" made in a statistics class that does not use this text. We find the following:

Mean (μ) = 22 Thinking Responses
Population Standard Deviation (σ) = 4.5 Thinking Responses
$n = 25$
    a. Calculate the standard error of the mean.
    b. With the confidence level set at 95%, what are the confidence limits for this mean?
    c. Construct a confidence interval using the confidence limits.

2. Say that we have the following information on the average life of a 100-watt light bulb:
Mean (μ) = 400 hours
Population Standard Deviation (σ) = 36 hours
$n = 144$
    a. Calculate the standard error of the mean.
    b. With the confidence level set at 99%, what are the confidence limits for this mean?
    c. Construct a confidence interval using the confidence limits.

3. We are given the following information on the average amount of time spent daily in lines (such as at the grocery store, the bank, or any of the numerous mazes found in your college's or university's administration buildings—all great places to spend time waiting to give other people your money):
Mean ($\overline{X}$) = 43 minutes
Standard Deviation (s) = 12 minutes
$n = 36$
    a. Calculate the standard error of the mean.
    b. With a confidence level set at 95% and 99%, what are the two different confidence limits for this mean?
    c. Construct two confidence intervals using the two different confidence limits.
    d. Explain why there is a difference between the two confidence intervals' widths.

4. Using the information in exercise 3:
    a. Repeat the questions a, b, and c (using just the 95% confidence level) with an n of 120.
    b. Why does increasing the sample size have such a drastic impact on the width of the resultant interval?

5. For females aged 40 to 49 in the United States, the average weight is 142 pounds, with a standard deviation of 27 pounds.
    a. How large a sample would we need to estimate the mean with a margin of error of 2 pounds? (alpha level .05 and .01)
    b. One-half pound? (alpha level .05 and .01)
    c. Which sample size is more economically feasible?

9

Hypothesis Testing Between Two Sets of Observations

Having explored in the last chapter how confidence intervals are constructed and what they represent, we can take these ideas one step further and show how they are also used to test hypotheses. (Recall from Chapter 1 that estimating population parameters and hypothesis testing are the two things that inferential statistics enable us to do.) While the construction of confidence intervals is important to social scientists who undertake quantitative research, perhaps an even more important function is that they enable us to test hypotheses. Quite simply, *hypothesis testing* is what almost all quantitative studies and journals ultimately report; these are the all-important findings. It is through the process of hypothesis testing that the phrase "statistically significant" is derived.

Specifically, this chapter first explores the underlying assumptions of hypothesis testing and statistical significance. These ideas are then applied to four types of statistical tests (ways to hypothesis testing); a *Z test, a dependent-sample t-test,* an *independent-sample t-test,* and a *matched t-test.* Because the remainder of this text is largely devoted to hypothesis testing, these four initial tests are viewed as starting points for understanding statistical testing.

Hypothesis Testing

All scientists are ultimately interested in explaining how and why certain things occur the way they do. For social scientists, this interest is obviously in terms explaining social phenomena. Social phenomena are a nearly inexhaustible array of every imaginable attitude, behavior, and social characteristic. What social scientists attempt to do is establish relationships of association (two variables tend to occur together) and causality (one variable is seen as bringing about a change in another variable) between different social phenomena.

Another way of viewing social phenomena is in terms of a measurable variable. For example, a measurable attitude is whether one supports the legalization of marijuana, a measurable behavior is if one smokes marijuana, and a measurable social characteristic is one's age. One possible relationship among these three variables might be that those who support marijuana legalization are more likely to smoke it than those who don't support

---

**Box 9.1   Differences Between Physical Scientists and
Social/Behavioral Scientists**

Physical scientists' research interests, in many ways, are far different from those of social/behavioral scientists. Physical scientists are interested in explaining things such as why chemical and biological reactions occur the way they do. Social/behavior scientists, on the other hand, are interested in explaining social/behavioral phenomena.

This differing emphasis has strong implications in terms of how research is undertaken. For physical scientists, most of the research they undertake is in the artificial setting of the laboratory. Such a setting enables the scientist to control for factors (variables) that may influence research outcomes (e.g., how much of a given element or chemical is used).

Although a substantial amount of social/behavioral research is done in laboratory settings, such as research undertaken by psychologists, most of it is done outside of this setting in the real world. As such, whereas physical scientists can often explain the exact effect one single variable has upon another single variable, this is simply not possible with social research. Social scientists deal with human behavior, so they are faced with research situations where numerous variables can be used to explain one variable. Moreover, some of the variables are extraneous and just associated with, but not an actual cause of, a given variable. Further, even the most carefully designed social research project seldom, if ever, takes into account all of the variables that are actually the cause of another variable. Even in laboratories, where human subjects are involved, these same problems are prevalent.

As a result, there are many more complexities that a social/behavioral scientist must deal with when she or he undertakes research. This also poses problems with statistical testing. Quite simply, while this chapter deals exclusively with *bivariate* relationships (two variables, where one is seen as potentially affecting the other), almost all social relationships are *multivariate*. That is, no one variable is the exclusive cause of change in another. More typically, there are always numerous variables that explain a given outcome, with many of them often not even being measured.

---

legalization. Moreover, we might expect that younger people are more likely to support marijuana legalization and to smoke it than older people. If this in fact was found to be true, we would conclude that age and marijuana use are both determinants—seen as causes—of attitudes about legalization.

A more formal way of viewing variable relationships of association and causality is in terms of a stated hypothesis. A stated hypothesis actually comes in two basic forms: the *null hypothesis* and the *research hypothesis* (also called the alternative hypothesis). The null hypothesis simply means *no difference*, one variable is not associated with another. Conversely, the research/alternative hypothesis simply means there is a relationship of association. For the purpose of this chapter, one way to determine if one variable is associated with or brings about a change in another variable is by comparing group means (averages) associated with a given bivariate relationship. This is actually what all the aforementioned statistical tests in this chapter do. What these tests allow us to do is to determine, statistically speaking, if there is a difference between two group means. One generic way this is presented is found below; the actual means tested for a difference varies from test to test.

As the above symbolically demonstrates, the null hypothesis tells us that there is *no* difference between the means; they are statistically equal. On the other hand, the research

Null Hypothesis	$H_0 : \bar{x} = \bar{x}$
Alternative or Research Hypothesis	$H_A : \bar{x} \neq \bar{x}$

hypothesis implies that there is a difference between two means. This is mathematically represented by the symbol of "not equal" between the two means.

Before beginning any calculations, let's apply what we have discussed thus far to Cartoon 9.1 (we use this same information when we undertake an actual test). Our current research interests are how intelligent—or dim-witted—different breeds of cows are. Reflecting on the cartoon, we decide to measure intelligence in terms of the number of times per day a cow touches an electric fence. That is, the fewer the number of times a cow runs into the electric fence, the more intelligent it is perceived as being. Let's say we know the daily average that all cows (all breeds) in the United States touch an electric fence is 10, with standard deviation of 1.5 times. We want to know if the Holsteins are more or less intelligent than all breeds of cows combined. We sample 25 Holstein cows and find that on the average they touch an electric fence 7 times a day.

Cartoon 9.1   THE FAR SIDE®

Stating this in terms of hypothesis testing, the null hypothesis holds that, statistically speaking, there is no difference between the average number of times Holsteins run into an electric fence and the national average for all cows. We must note that just because a numerical difference may exist between two means does not necessarily mean that there is a statistical difference. As we will see, nonsignificant differences are due to potential sampling error. The research hypothesis, on the other hand, holds that there is a statistical difference between the means. This is symbolically represented below (μ represents the national average (population) while the $\overline{X}$ represents the Holstein average (sample)).

Null Hypothesis $\qquad\qquad H_0 : \mu = \bar{x}$

Alternative or Research $\qquad H_A : \mu \neq \bar{x}$
Hypothesis

There are obviously two possible outcomes in reference to these two statements: There *is* or *is not* a statistical difference between the two group means. These two outcomes can be stated in more scientific terms. In the first case, if there is a statistical difference between the two means, we *reject* the null hypothesis and *fail to reject* the alternative (research) hypothesis. Conversely, if there is not a statistical difference between the two means, we *fail to reject* the null hypothesis and *reject* the alternative hypothesis. Though we may be tempted to say that we *accept* a hypothesis, it is standard practice to use the double negative *fail to reject*. This reflects the spirit of scientific skepticism; from this view we can never know whether a hypothesis is true; we can only find support for our hypothesis.

Similar to confidence intervals, we decide to reject or fail to reject the null or research hypothesis by using an alpha level. That is, dependent upon the given alpha level, we can state how confident we are that the null hypothesis has been correctly rejected. The alpha level also tells us the probability that we have rejected the null hypothesis when in fact it is true. If this is done (i.e., the null hypothesis is rejected when it is in fact true), we have committed what is referred to as a *Type I Error* (this term is discussed in detail in a moment).

Putting this into English, say the above bovine (cow) example has a present alpha level of .05 and we find that the difference between the number of times per day a Holstein touches an electric fence (7) and the national average (10) is statistically significant. As such, Holsteins are far less likely, on average, to touch the "damn" electric fence, and thus (because of this difference) we infer that they are more intelligent. Moreover, we are 95% confident that we have correctly rejected the null hypothesis. On the other hand, we also recognize that there is a 5% chance that we have rejected the null hypothesis when in fact it is true: a Type I Error. When the first actual hypothesis test is undertaken, in a moment, this becomes clearer.

Although beyond the scope of this text in terms of how it is numerically calculated, it is nevertheless important to discuss a second type of statistical error that can occur when hypothesis testing: a *Type II Error*. This type of error occurs when we do not reject the

Table 9.1   2 x 2 (Two-by-Two) Contingency Table of Type I and Type II Errors

	H_0 True	H_0 False
Reject H_0	Type I Error	Correct Rejection
Do not reject H_0	Correct Nonrejection	Type II Error

null hypothesis when in fact we should have. In other words, we fail to recognize a statistically significant difference between two means when in fact there is one. A great deal of research undertaken hopes to find a difference (some researchers' funding may even be contingent upon finding a difference), so this can be very problematic. Both the Type II Error and the previously discussed Type I Error outcomes along with the relationships of the correct rejection and acceptance of the null and research hypothesis are summarized in the 2 x 2 contingency table.

Z Test

Having discussed the abstract theoretical aspect of hypothesis testing, we now can turn to an actual application. To this end we use the bovine data (summarized below) from the discussion that has preceded, and offer the accompanying statistical formula, called a *Z test*. As denoted by the formula, the only way we can use a *Z* test is when the population mean, the population standard deviation, the sample mean, and the sample size values are all known.

What the *Z* test enables us to determine is if the difference between the two means (μ: mu and $\bar{X}$: *x* bar) is statistically significant. As the formula states, we first subtract the population mean from the sample mean. The population standard deviation is then divided by the square root of the sample size, once again referred to as the standard error of the mean. Recall from the previous chapter that, simply stated, the standard error of the mean is a standardized measure of the amount of variability and potential sampling error found around the mean of a given data set. In terms of how it is calculated, the format of the standard error of the mean differs and is dependent upon the type of test being performed. Nevertheless, all of the statistical tests in this chapter use a form of the standard error of the mean in the denominator portion of the given formula. Finally, we simply divide the resultant numerator value by the resultant denominator value to get that is called a *Z obtained*.

The *Z*-obtained value is compared against a second value called the *Z critical*. In many ways, *Z*-obtained values are similar to *Z* scores discussed in Chapter 6. That is, a *Z*-obtained value represents how much of a standardized difference there is between the two means compared. We define *Z*-critical values in a moment. However, let's first do an actual *Z*-test calculation; as shown below.

Because only two-tailed tests are presently considered, the Z-obtained value is put into brackets, which indicates that we are treating it as an absolute value with no regard to sign. Thus the final answer is $|-10|$ or 10. Near the end of this chapter (in a separate section) we discuss the difference between two-tailed and one-tailed statistical tests.

Z Test	Holstein Data
	$\mu = 10$
$\dfrac{\bar{x} - \mu}{\sigma / \sqrt{n}} = Z \text{ Obtained}$	$\bar{x} = 7$
	$\sigma = 1.5$
	$n = 25$

Recall that $\mu = 10$ represents the national average for all cows in terms of the number of times they touch the electric fence; the s represents the standard deviation for this population. The $\bar{X} = 7$ represents the Holstein average and was determined from a sample of 25. Thus,

$$\frac{7 - 10}{1.5 / \sqrt{25}} = \frac{-3}{1.5 / 5} = \frac{-3}{.3} = \boxed{|-10|} = Z \text{ Obtained}$$

Having calculated the Z obtained, we can now turn to defining what a Z-critical value is and how it is determined. Exactly like the Z-critical values used to construct confidence intervals, we use one of two values: 1.96 (alpha = .05) and 2.58 (alpha = .01). Further, while the manner in which they are derived is exactly the same (refer to Chapter 8 for a more complete discussion), the current application is slightly different. Figure 9.1 represents a Z-score distribution with the corresponding Z values of 1.96 and 2.58 located on it. In reference to Z tests, what this distribution informs us is that an obtained value must fall outside of the area represented by the critical values for there to be a significant difference. That is, the closer an obtained value is to the mean (0), the more likely that the difference is a result of sampling error. Conversely, the farther the obtained value is from the mean, especially scores beyond plus or minus 1.96, the more likely there is an actual difference.

In slightly different terms, this means that the obtained value (treated as an absolute) must be larger than the critical value for us to conclude that there is a statistically significant difference. For instance, if the obtained value is greater than 1.96, then it is significant at the .05 level. Further, this tells us that we are 95% confident that there is an actual difference between the two means; alternatively, there is a 5% chance we have committed a Type I Error and rejected the null hypothesis when it is in fact true. Moreover, the exact same thing is said when the Z-obtained value is greater than 2.58, except that now we are 99% confident that there is a difference with a corresponding 1% chance that we have committed a Type I Error.

Returning to our bovine example with the Z obtained of 10 (alpha level=.01), we obviously reject the null hypothesis and fail to reject the research hypothesis, and conclude that there is a significant difference. After all, the obtained value of 10 is much larger than 2.58. Further, an obtained value of 10 is also significant at the .05 alpha level; however,

Figure 9.1   *Z*-Score Distribution

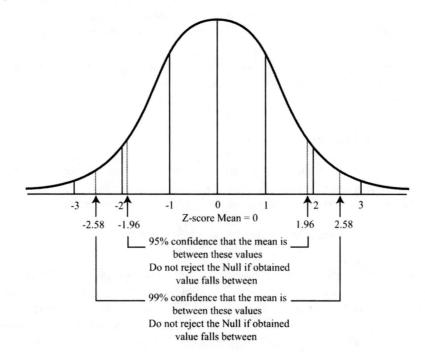

as we are even more confident at the .01 level that there is a statistically significant difference, it is obviously more desirable to reject the null at the second level (.01).

In other words, Holsteins are far less likely to touch an electric fence than all other breeds of cows combined. Moreover, while there is a 1% chance that this conclusion is in error, more importantly, we are 99% confident that it is in fact true. Thus, with an electric fence as proof, we conclude that Holsteins (as a group) are apparently more intelligent than most cows.

Using a variant of the bovine cartoon to give another example of a *Z* test, let's say that instead of Holsteins we sample 9 Jersey cows and find that their daily average for touching the electric fence is $\overline{X} = 10.5$. This information along with the appropriate calculations are found below. Also found below is a present alpha level of .05 with the noted corresponding *Z*-critical value of 1.96. Although obtained values are typically reported as either significant at the level found or not significant, to simplify our discussion we present the alpha level in this and subsequent tests.

Jersey Data

$\mu = 10$

$\overline{x} = 10.5$

$\sigma = 1.5$

$n = 9$

$$\frac{10.5 - 10}{1.5 / \sqrt{9}} = \frac{.5}{1.5 / 3} = \frac{.5}{.5} = \boxed{1}$$

$\alpha = .05,\ Z\ \text{critical} = 1.96$

With the Z obtained value of 1 in this case being smaller than the Z-critical value of 1.96, we fail to reject the null hypothesis (reject the research hypothesis) and conclude that, statistically speaking, there is not a significant difference between the two groups. In other words, although Jerseys may appear to touch the electric fence more often than the average for all breeds of cows, this difference is not statistically significant. In sum, in terms of touching the electric fence, Jerseys are apparently no more or less intelligent than the average for all cows.

Dependent-Sample *t*-Test

Sometimes when a researcher is hypothesis testing, she or he may have access to a population mean but not know the accompanying standard deviation value. In cases such as this, a different type of test is used: a *dependent-sample t-test*. Following is the actual formula.

$$\text{Dependent-Sample } t \text{ Test } = \frac{\bar{x} - \mu}{s / \sqrt{n}} = t \text{ Obtained}$$

Not only does this new test use a *sample standard deviation* in place of the population standard deviation found in the previous Z test, but (as you may have guessed by the test's name) it also requires the use of a t distribution. More specifically, the t distribution is used to determine critical values of t which are compared to obtained values of t to judge if there is a significant difference. The procedures to determine which t-critical value is used are the same ones employed to determine the t-critical values used to construct confidence intervals. Once again, the t-critical value is determined by two pieces of information: the alpha level and the degrees of freedom $(n - 1)$.

To apply what has been discussed thus far, we offer Cartoon 9.2. It is not the intent of the authors to offend any Greeks who are using this text, but rather just to have a little fun using statistics. After all, both authors are former fraternity members.

Let's say our current research interest is the amount of money spent per month on clothes by different types of male students at "All-American U." This represents a population. From a previous questionnaire administered during registration to all students at All-American U we found that male students spend an average of $50.00 per month for clothes; however, this study neglected to calculate the corresponding standard deviation. We want to know if there is a difference between the amount of money spent per month for clothing by the general male population versus by fraternity members (Bob and all those Polo shirts, but then again, he can spell his name backwards and get the same result). Thus, the null hypothesis states that there is no difference between the amount of money spent by all male students versus fraternity members at All-American U, whereas the research hypothesis states that there is a difference.

To test this, we draw a random sample of 25 fraternity members and find that they spend an average of $60.00 per month on clothing, with a sample standard deviation of $20.00. This information along with the actual *t*-test is summarized below.

Cartoon 9.2   BLOOM COUNTY

© Berkeley Breathed. Used by permission.

Though the .05 alpha level is the minimal acceptable level of significance, in this example we have chosen a more conservative level of significance. In this case, we want to be more confident that we have not committed a Type I Error. Specifically, we want to be 98% confident that we have correctly rejected the null hypothesis, and are setting our alpha level at .02. For our preset alpha level of .02, the corresponding *t*-critical value is 2.492. This value is found in Appendix 2 using 24 degrees of freedom ($n - 1$; $25 - 1 = 24$ *df*) and the present alpha level of .02.

Clothing Expenditures for Fraternity Members Versus the General Male Population at All-American U

$\mu = \$50.00$

$\bar{x} = \$60.00$

$s = \$20.00$

$n = 25$

$$\frac{\bar{x} - \mu}{s / \sqrt{n}} = \frac{60 - 50}{20 / \sqrt{25}} = \frac{10}{20/5} = \frac{10}{4} = \boxed{2.5}$$

$$\alpha = .02, \ t \text{ critical} = 2.492; \ t \text{ obtained} = 2.5$$

With the *t* obtained of 2.5 being larger than the *t*-critical value of 2.492, we obviously conclude that there is a statistically significant difference between the two groups. Thus we reject the null hypothesis and fail to reject the research hypothesis. Further we are 98% confident that we have correctly rejected the null hypothesis with a converse 2% chance that we have incorrectly rejected it when in fact it is true—a Type I Error. In total, we conclude that on the average fraternity members at All-American U spend more money on clothes than the general male population attending the university.

For our next example of a dependent-sample *t*-test, we use the same population information previously gathered at All-American U concerning expenditures on clothing ($\mu = \$50.00$). Instead of fraternity members, however, we are now interested in the average amount of money spent on clothes by male athletes—typical attire being T-shirts and sweatshirts turned inside out to get a second day's wear—versus the overall average for all male students. We sample 16 male athletes and find that they spend an average of $45.00 a month on clothing, with a sample standard deviation of $10.00. With a preset alpha level of .05 and 15 degrees of freedom, the t-critical value for this example is 2.131 (Appendix 2). All of this information and the appropriate calculations are presented below.

Clothing Expenditures for Male Athletes Versus the General
Male Population at All-American U

$\mu = \$50.00$

$\bar{x} = \$45.00$

$s = \$10.00$

$n = 16$

$$\frac{\bar{x} - \mu}{s / \sqrt{n}} = \frac{45 - 50}{10 / \sqrt{16}} = \frac{-5}{10 / 4} = \frac{-5}{2.5} = \boxed{|\text{-}2|}$$

$\alpha = .05$, t critical $= 2.131$; t obtained $= |\text{-}2|$ or 2

With a t-obtained value of 2 being less than the t-critical value of 2.131, we fail to reject the null hypothesis and reject the research hypothesis. Therefore, we conclude that there is not a statistically significant difference between the amount of money spent on clothing by male athletes versus the general male population at All-American U. Then again, if one is looking to save a little money, there might be something to be said for turning soiled sweatshirts inside out.

Independent-Samples *t*-Test

Similar to the construction of confidence intervals, typically no information about the population is available to the researcher when he or she sets out to test hypothesis and, as you have probably already guessed, such situations call for yet another type of t-test. One that is often used is called the *independent-samples t-test*. The actual formula is found below. Please note that part of the formula, s^2 pooled, is presented separately to simplify the actual calculations.

Although you should be familiar with all the symbols found within the formula, before proceeding it is still a good idea to clarify what they represent and briefly review them. While the standard error of the mean no longer appears in the same form as it has thus far, the denominator portion of the formula still represents it. That is, mathematically, the denominator portion of the formula is the standard deviation divided by the square root of n. The reason that the formula appears in this form, however, is that seldom, if ever, are two samples drawn that have the exact same sample size and/or standard deviation. As such, the denominator is mathematically a weighted standard error of the mean. In other words, similar to weighted mean, an independent-samples t-test takes into account different standard deviation values and sample sizes.

The whole formula, including the s^2 pooled portion, has only three basic symbols: (1) $\bar{X}$ for sample means, (2) s for sample standard deviations, and (3) n for sample size. The formula tests to see if there is a difference between two independent sample means, so for each symbol there is a subscript for which group the information belongs to: the subscript

Independent-Samples *t* Test	s^2 Pooled Portion of Formula
$$\dfrac{\bar{x}_1 - \bar{x}_2}{\sqrt{s^2\,pooled\left(1/n_1 + 1/n_2\right)}}$$	$$\dfrac{\left(n_1 - 1\right)s_1^2 + \left(n_2 - 1\right)s_2^2}{n_1 + n_2 - 2}$$

1 refers to sample one—group one; conversely the subscript 2 refers to sample two—group two.

We now can turn to the formula's actual calculation. To this end, we refer back to Cartoon 9.2 as a backdrop for our first example. Our current research interests are the number of organized social events per month that fraternity members attend versus non-fraternity men at All-American U. We get two lists from the registrar's office, one for fraternity members and one for non-fraternity member (all other) men at the campus. From this, we draw a sample from each of the groups, two independent samples, and find the following. Also listed is a present alpha level of .01. The actual calculations using the above formula are found below the data sets:

Fraternity Members Group 1	Non-Fraternity Men Group 2	
$\bar{x}_1 = 15$	$\bar{x}_2 = 11$	**Average Number of Social Events Per Month**
$s_1 = 3*$	$s_2 = 4$	**Standard Deviation of Events**
$n_1 = 33$	$n_2 = 29$	**Sample Size of Each Group**

(alpha=.01)

*Why do you think the standard deviation for fraternities (s=3) is smaller than that for non-fraternity members (s=4)? Since fraternity members are a more homogenous (similar) group than simply everyone else (a more heterogenous group), one expects a smaller amount of variation in this group.

$$\frac{15-11}{\sqrt{\dfrac{(33-1)(3)^2 + (29-1)(4)^2}{33+29-2}\left(\dfrac{1}{33} + \dfrac{1}{29}\right)}}$$

$$= \frac{4}{\sqrt{\dfrac{(32)(9) + (28)(16)}{60}(.0303+.0344)}}$$

$$= \frac{4}{\sqrt{\dfrac{288+448}{60}(.0647)}} = \frac{4}{\sqrt{(12.2666)(.0647)}} = \frac{4}{.8908} = \boxed{4.4903}$$

While the above calculations give us a t-obtained of 4.4903, this answer alone does not tell whether the two sample means are significantly different. To make this determination, we must decide what the t-critical value is. For this type of t-test, however, we use slightly different degrees of freedom than the previous, $n - 1$. We are dealing with *two* independent samples and this must be taken in account when determining the t-critical degrees of freedom. In other words, since two samples are used, correspondingly, two degrees of freedom must be controlled.

To do this, we take the sum of both samples and subtract the value of 2 from it; $n_1 + n_2 - 2 = t$-critical df or (for this example) $29 + 33 - 2 = 60$. (Please note that in the denominator of the s-pooled portion of the formula one finds exactly the same calculations. Some of you may prefer to simply use this portion of the formula to calculate the degrees of freedom for this type of t-test.)

Although the .05 alpha level is the minimal acceptable level of significance, in this example we will use the .01 alpha level. With 60 degrees of freedom and the alpha level preset at .01, we look in Appendix 2 and find that the t-critical value for this example is 2.66.

Now we can finally determine if there is a significant difference. With a 4.4903 t-obtained being larger than the 2.66 t-critical, we conclude that there is a significant difference between the two groups; thus, we reject the null hypothesis and fail to reject the research hypothesis. With the alpha level at .01, we also conclude that there is a 1% chance that we have committed a Type I Error; alternatively, we are 99% confident that we have correctly rejected the null hypothesis. In other words, fraternity members apparently attend significantly more organized social events per month than non-fraternity members. Given the number of private mixers and other types of parties that fraternities sponsor, this finding is really not that surprising.

For our next example of an independent-samples t-test, let's say we now want to know if there are differences in the dating behaviors of fraternity versus non-fraternity men. That is, during a school year does one group go out on more dates with different women than the other? Once again, we draw two independent samples. The data and accompanying calculations are presented on the opposite page.

With a t-obtained of 1.3114, we must compare it to a t-critical value that has 38 degrees of freedom with an alpha level of .05. Referring once again to Appendix 2 we find that, although there are t-critical values for 30 df and 40 df, a t-critical for 38 df is not listed. To simplify matters in cases such as this, you should always take a larger, more conservative critical value associated with the next numerically lower degrees of freedom. For this example, use 30 df. With the alpha set at .05, the corresponding t-critical value is 2.042. (To give a few more examples, if we have 100 df then we would use the lesser value of 60 df; if we have 55 df, then we would use 40 df.)

Because the t-obtained (1.3114) is smaller than the t-critical value (2.042) for $df = 30$, we conclude that there is not a statistically significant difference between the two groups. Thus, we fail to reject the null hypothesis and reject the research hypothesis. In other words, there is no difference in the dating behaviors of fraternity men versus non-fraternity men.

Fraternity Members	Non-Fraternity Members	
Group 1	Group 2	
$\bar{x}_1 = 8$	$\bar{x}_2 = 7$	Average Number of Dates per School Year
$s_1 = 1.5$	$s_2 = 3$	Standard Deviation of Dates
$n_1 = 19$	$n_2 = 21$	Sample Size of Each Group

$$(alpha=.05)$$

$$\frac{8-7}{\sqrt{\dfrac{(19-1)(1.5)^2 + (21-1)(3)^2}{19+21-2}\left(\dfrac{1}{19}+\dfrac{1}{21}\right)}}$$

$$= \frac{1}{\sqrt{\dfrac{(18)(2.25)+(20)(9)}{38}(.0526+.0476)}}$$

$$= \frac{1}{\sqrt{\dfrac{40.5+180}{38}(.1002)}} = \frac{1}{\sqrt{(5.8026)(.1002)}} = \frac{1}{.7625} = \boxed{1.3114}$$

Difference (Matched or Paired) *t*-Test

The *difference t-test*, also referred to as a matched or paired *t*-test, is somewhat different from the *Z* test and *t*-tests explored thus far. What distinguishes a difference *t*-test is that whereas the previous tests used two separate group means, this test uses two different means obtained from the same group. That is, a difference *t*-test typically uses a single group of people, derives two means from them, and then tests to see if there is a difference between them. Obviously, however, the two means compared are measurements of the same variable. The manner in which this is typically applied (there are other applications, e.g., twins research) is to give a pre-test, then some sort of treatment, followed by a post-test to determine if the treatment brought about a measurable change.

As usual, the easiest way to clarify what has been abstractly stated thus far is with another cartoon problem. Cartoon 9.3 on p. 163 serves as a backdrop to the last few problems discussed in this chapter. To begin with and reflecting on the cartoon, let's say we want to know if listening to heavy-metal music increases or decreases the number of pages a given student reads nightly.

We randomly select seven (*n* = 7) individuals attending All-American U and measure the number of pages they read per school night listening to no music (the pre-test). Next, we have these same individuals listen to heavy-metal music (the treatment) while they are reading. As they listen to the music, we also measure the number of pages they read per school night (the post-test). Our findings are reported in Table 9.2. Found below is the formula (and its sub-parts) used for calculating a difference *t*-test.

Table 9.2   Heavy Metal/Reading Data

	Number of Pages Read	
Individual	No Music	Listening to Heavy Metal
1	34	37
2	31	43
3	18	27
4	36	33
5	31	39
6	30	30
7	38	41

<u>Difference t-Test Formula</u>

$$\frac{\bar{d}}{s_d / \sqrt{n}}$$

where:

$$\bar{d} = \frac{\Sigma d}{n} \quad \text{and} \quad s_d = \sqrt{\frac{\Sigma d^2 - (\Sigma d)^2 / n}{n - 1}}$$

There are new symbols found in this formula, so before doing any calculations we first must explain what the formula actually asks us to do. To begin with, because this is a difference t-test, it asks us to determine the difference between two sets of scores. In mathematical terms, a "difference" ultimately refers to subtraction.

Referring to the actual formula, in the numerator portion is a d with a bar above it ($\bar{d}$). Symbolically similar to a sample mean, this formula sub-part indicates that we are to calculate the mean difference of the scores. To accomplish this, take each individual's first score and subtract their corresponding second score from it (e.g., individual 1: 34 – 37 = –3). Next, as the formula notes, all the resultant scores are added together and then divided by the sample size.

The symbol of s with d subscript (s_d) represents the standard deviation of difference. Beginning with the left symbol in the numerator, this tells us to take the sum of the differences squared. That is, each individual difference score is squared and then summed. The right-hand portion of the denominator, alternatively, tells us to take the sum of the differences (the same value used in the mean calculation), square the resultant value, and then divide it by the sample size ($n = 7$). In the denominator is the same operation that is associated with a regular sample standard deviation: $n - 1$, or the sample size minus one.

Now apply these instructions to the above data set. Although all the calculations are completed below, because this is the first use of this formula we walk you through each of the operations.

First, in addition to the original data set, we have added a column for the individual differences and a column for each of these values squared. Below each new column is found its sum; each of these values is required in subsequent calculations. Please note that when the differences are summed, we must be especially careful when adding negative values or the resultant answer will be wrong (e.g., $-3 + -12 = -15$, or $-6 + 3 = -3$). This is why each difference score has clearly been designated as having a negative or positive value.

Next we calculate the mean difference. Recall that this is obtained by taking the sum of the differences and dividing it by the sample size: $-32 / 7 = -4.5714$. After this, calculate the standard deviation of differences: 5.3183. Having derived these two initial values,

Cartoon 9.3   BLOOM COUNTY

combined with the sample size value, simply place all of these values into their appropriate locations in the actual formula and get a t obtained of -2.1665. (In other words, both the mean difference and the standard deviation of differences first must be separately calculated before the t obtained can be derived.)

As with the previous t-test, to determine the t-critical we preset an alpha level (.05 for this example) and determine the degrees of freedom. There are seven individuals in this example, so simply take $n - 1 = df$ or $7 - 1 = 6$ df. (Note that even though we have two measurements of seven, 14 total, just one variable is measured [pages read], so our n is the actual number of subjects involved in the experiment.) This gives us a t-critical value of 2.447. Again, all of the above discussion is summarized in Table 9.3 (the intermediate calculations) and below with the final calculations:

Mean Difference

$$\bar{d} = \frac{-32}{7} = \boxed{-4.5714}$$

Standard Deviation of Differences

$$s_d = \sqrt{\frac{\Sigma d^2 - (\Sigma d)^2 / n}{n - 1}} = \sqrt{\frac{316 - (-32)^2 / 7}{7 - 1}} = \sqrt{\frac{316 - 1024 / 7}{6}}$$

$$= \sqrt{\frac{316 - 146.2857}{6}} = \sqrt{\frac{169.7143}{6}} = \sqrt{28.2847} = \boxed{5.3183}$$

Difference t test

$$\frac{\bar{d}}{s_d / \sqrt{n}} = \frac{-4.5714}{5.3183 / \sqrt{7}} = \frac{-4.5714}{5.3183 / 2.6457} = \frac{-4.5714}{2.0101} = \boxed{|-2.2742|}$$

alpha=.05, df=6 (7-1=6); thus t critical 2.447

The above calculations complete, we now can determine whether there is a statistically significant difference. Because the t-obtained value of $|-2.2742|$ is smaller than the t-critical value of 2.447, we conclude that there is not a significant difference; we fail to reject the null hypothesis, and reject the alternative hypothesis. Thus, we conclude that listening to heavy-metal music versus no music has no appreciable effect on the number of pages read nightly by these 7 research subjects.

If we were actually researching this topic, we would probably still report that listening to heavy-metal music does appear to increase the number of pages read; however, the increase is not statistically significant. One way that we could probably demonstrate this relationship to be statistically significant is to increase our sample size. Whenever sample sizes are increased, mathematically it makes the denominator value smaller (the square root of n), and thus the t-obtained often becomes larger. Further, when the sample size increases the corresponding *t*-critical value becomes smaller, which makes it easier to find significance. Both of these factors make it easier to reject the null hypothesis. Of course, this also assumes that if more subjects were tested, the relationship would continue in this manner. A second, easier way that this relationship can be demonstrated as significant is discussed in Box 9.2 on p. 166 using a one-tailed *t*-critical value.

Table 9.3   Intermediate Steps for Heavy Metal Difference Test

Individual	No Music	Listening to Heavy Metal	d (Difference)	d² (Difference Squared)
1	34	37 (34-37)	-3	9
2	31	43 (31-43)	-12	144
3	18	27 (18-27)	-9	81
4	36	33 (36-33)	+3	9
5	31	39 (31-39)	-8	64
6	30	30 (30-30)	0	0
7	38	41 (38-41)	-3	9
			-32	316

To ensure a clear understanding of how to calculate a difference *t*-test, following is one last example based upon Cartoon 9.3. We replicate the previous experiment with 10 individuals; however, instead of having them listen to heavy metal music, we have them listen to Barry Manilow recordings. Again we measure the number of pages read per night not listening to any music (pre-test), and then the number of pages read listening to Barry Manilow music. Table 9.4 (on the following page) represents our findings and the intermediate calculations. Found below are the appropriate formulas and corresponding calculations. The alpha level again is preset at .05.

Mean Difference

$$\bar{d} = 57/10 = \boxed{5.7}$$

Standard Deviation of Differences

$$s_d = \sqrt{\frac{\Sigma d^2 - (\Sigma d)^2 / n}{n-1}} = \sqrt{\frac{635 - (57)^2 / 10}{10-1}} = \sqrt{\frac{635 - 3249/10}{9}}$$

$$= \sqrt{\frac{635 - 324.9}{9}} = \sqrt{\frac{310.1}{9}} = \sqrt{34.4555} = \boxed{5.8698}$$

Difference *t* test

$$\frac{\bar{d}}{s_d / \sqrt{n}} = \frac{5.7}{5.8698 / \sqrt{10}} = \frac{5.7}{5.8698 / 3.1622} = \frac{5.7}{1.8562} = \boxed{3.0707}$$

alpha = .05, df = 9 (10 - 1 = 9); thus *t* critical = 2.262

Table 9.4   Intermediate Steps for Barry Manilow Difference Test

Individual	No Music	Listening to Barry Manilow	d (Difference)	d^2 (Difference Squared)
1	33	23	+10	100
2	29	31	-2	4
3	19	12	+7	49
4	38	29	+9	81
5	33	20	+13	169
6	32	30	+2	4
7	39	42	-3	9
8	25	18	+7	49
9	22	21	+1	1
10	37	24	+13	169
			57	635

Box 9.2   One-Tailed Versus Two-Tailed Critical Values

In an attempt to simplify the material presented in this chapter, all alpha levels are preset and we only use two-tailed critical values to determine significance. When social scientists are undertaking actual research projects, however, they seldom preset levels of significance and often use *one-tailed critical values.* In both cases, there are researcher advantages for not using the simplified format that we have followed.

Actual researchers almost always report the level to which the *t* (or *Z*) obtained is significant. In the Barry Manilow example, for instance, we obtained a *t* value of 2.9634 and noted that because it is larger than the *t*-critical value of 2.262 (alpha = .05, 9 df), it is significant at this level. While this test is significant at the .05 level, moreover, it is also significant at the .02 level, but it is not significant at the .01 level.

Refer to Appendix 2 and follow along the row heading of 9 degrees of freedom: the df for this problem. Note that the *t* obtained value of 2.9634 is larger than the *t*-critical values at both .05 and .02 alpha levels but it is not larger than the *t*-critical value at the .01 alpha level: 3.250. Thus, this problem is more appropriately reported as statistically significant at the .02 alpha level. With this example, obviously it is to a researcher's advantage to report this finding significant at the .02 level rather than the .05 level. After all, we are more confident at this level because there is a diminished possibility of a Type I Error.

Further, in many research reports and journals this finding would be reported with the following symbol: $p < .02$. Not only does this inform us that significance is obtained at the .02 level, but—further—the probability that a Type I Error has been committed is less than 2%. Thus p (probability) < (less than) .02. What if in another example we were presented with $p < .01$? This informs us that the probability that a Type I Error has been committed is less than 1%. Sometimes you may see the symbols of $p > .05$. This simply states that the probability of a Type I Error is greater than .05, and thus it is not significant at this level. For almost all social scientists, the alpha level of .05 is the minimum to report a given relationship as statistically significant.

As noted, often a researcher's whole project is contingent upon his or her demonstrating statistical significance. If researchers can hypothesize the direction of the relationship prior to testing it, they can use a one-tailed t-critical value. This is symbolically represented in the research hypothesis as $\overline{X}_1 > \overline{X}_2$ or $\overline{X}_1 < \overline{X}_2$ instead of the previously utilized $\overline{X}_1 \neq \overline{X}_2$. When the use of a one-tailed value is possible, the corresponding t-critical values are always smaller than their two-tailed counterparts; thus, it is often much easier to find statistical significance using one-tailed values.

In the previous example (number of pages read by subjects listening to no music versus heavy metal music), we were unable to find statistical significance. If, however, we had some previous reason to believe that listening to heavy metal music might increase the number of pages read (such as previous research that had demonstrated this or a similar relationship), we could have treated this as a one-tailed t-test. That is, instead of using the critical t value of 2.447 (which resulted in the conclusion that there was not a significant difference), we could use the t-critical value of 1.943 (look to one-tailed column heading with 6 df, alpha level = .05). Had we hypothesized the direction of this relationship, we would have used the t-critical value of 1.943. And with a t-obtained value of | −2.1665 |, we would have concluded this relationship to be statistically significant at the .05 alpha level. Then again, those of you who listen to this type of music probably already knew this.

With a t obtained of 3.0707 and the t-critical value of 2.262, we conclude that listening to Barry Manilow music has a statistically significant effect on the number of pages read. Specifically, and reflecting the raw numbers in the data set, listening to Barry Manilow music significantly reduces the number of pages read per night. This is in direct contrast to the previous example, where listening to heavy metal music led to more pages being read. Recall, however, that this relationship was not found to be statistically significant. Regardless, because this is significant, we reject the null hypothesis and fail to reject the research hypothesis. As such, we are 95% confident that we have correctly rejected the null hypothesis; however, there is still a 5% chance of a Type I Error. In sum, don't listen to Barry Manilow music if you have a lot of pages to read in a short period of time.

Chapter Summary and Conclusions

This chapter has explored techniques of hypothesis testing. To this end, specifically the techniques of the Z test, dependent-sample t-test, independent-samples t-test, and difference t-tests were presented. All four of these tests made comparisons of some form of group means to determine whether there were statistical differences between them. Determining which of these tests is used is dependent upon the information available to the researcher and/or the manner in which the data was collected. In variant forms, the underlying assumptions of these tests and the actual tests themselves are reapplied in the statistical tests found in the remaining chapters.

Key Terms to Remember

- Bivariate Relationships
- Multivariate Relationships
- Null Hypothesis
- Research Hypothesis
- Type I Errors
- Type II Errors
- Z Tests
- Dependent-Sample t-Test
- Independent-Samples t-Test
- Paired t-Test
- One-Tailed t-Critical Values
- Two-Tailed t-Critical Values

Practice Exercises

1. Referring again to the bovine data and the electric fence, we want to know how intelligent the breed of Brown Swiss are—the cows used to make Miss Swiss Hot Chocolate. We sample 9 Brown Swiss cows and find they touch the electric fence an average of 13 times per day. The combined information gives us the following:

$$\mu = 10; \bar{X} = 13; \sigma = 1.5; n = 9$$

   a. Using the appropriate test (alpha = .05), is the Brown Swiss mean statistically different than that of the national average?
   b. What does this tell us in the context of the null and research hypothesis?

2. We now want to know if the breed of Guernsey cows is more or less intelligent than the national average. We sample 25 Guernsey cows and find that they touch the electric fence an average of 10.5 times per day. The combined information gives us the following:

$$\mu = 10; \bar{X} = 10.5; \sigma = 1.5; n = 25$$

   a. Using the appropriate test (alpha = .05), is the Guernsey mean statistically different than that of the national average?
   b. What does this tell us in the context of the null and research hypotheses?

3. Using Cartoon 9.2, instead of fraternity members we are now interested in sorority members and the amount they spend monthly on clothes. Once again, from a questionnaire administered at All-American U we know the average amount of money spent by all women is $60.00. We randomly sample 36 sorority members and find that they spend an average of $75.00 per month on clothes, with a corresponding standard deviation of $24.00. The combined information gives us the following:

$$\mu = \$60.00; \; \overline{X} = \$75.00; \; \sigma = 24.00; \; n = 36$$

a. Using the appropriate test (alpha = .05, two-tailed), are the averages statistically different?

b. What is the highest level of Significance (smallest alpha level) achieved?

c. What does this tell us in the context of the null and research hypotheses?

d. Test the hypothesis that sorority members spend more money than the population of women at All-American U (a one-tailed hypothesis) at the .05 alpha level. What is the highest one-tailed level of significance achieved?

4. We now are interested in the number of alcoholic beverages consumed per week by students at different universities. We draw two independent samples of students, one from All-American U (1), and one from All-American State University (2). We find the following.

$$\overline{x}_1 = 18 \qquad\qquad \overline{x}_2 = 14$$
$$s_1 = 2.5 \qquad\qquad s_2 = 1.5$$
$$n_1 = 15 \qquad\qquad n_2 = 12$$

a. Using the appropriate test (alpha = .001), is there a statistically significant difference between the two groups in terms of weekly consumption of alcoholic beverages?

b. What is the highest level of significance (smallest alpha level) achieved?

c. What does this tell us in the context of the null and research hypotheses?

d. Test the hypothesis that students at All-American U consume more alcoholic beverages than students at All-American State University (a one-tailed hypothesis) at the .05 alpha level. What is the highest one-tailed level of significance achieved?

5. Similarly, we are interested in the number of parties attended per semester by students at the above universities; once again, one sample is drawn from All-American U (1), and one from All-American State University (2). We find the following:

$$\overline{x}_1 = 25 \qquad\qquad \overline{x}_2 = 21$$
$$s_1 = 4 \qquad\qquad s_2 = 3$$
$$n_1 = 15 \qquad\qquad n_2 = 12$$

a. Using the appropriate test (alpha = .02), is there a statistically significant difference between the two groups in terms of the number of parties each attends per semester?

b. What is the highest level of significance (smallest alpha level) achieved?

c. What does this tell us in the context of the null and research hypotheses?

d. Test the hypothesis that students at All-American U attend fewer parties per semester than students at All-American State University (a one-tailed hypothesis) at the .05 alpha level. What is the highest one-tailed level of significance achieved?

Table 9.5   Country Music/Reading

Individual	Number of Pages Read	
	No Music	Listening to Country Music
1	33	21
2	31	32
3	18	16
4	36	33
5	31	24
6	30	22
7	38	41
8	24	15
9	23	12

6. Now we want to know if listening to country music increases or decreases the number of pages read per night. We sample 9 research subjects and find the data listed in Table 9.5.

a. Using the appropriate test (alpha = .05), does listening to country music have a statistically significant effect on the number of pages read per night? What sort of effect does it have?

b. What is the highest level of significance (smallest alpha level) achieved?

c. What does this tell us in the context of the null and research hypotheses?

d. Test the hypothesis that listening to country music decreases the number of pages a person reads, compared to the number of pages read with no music, (a one-tailed hypothesis) at the .05 alpha level. What is the highest one-tailed level of significance achieved?

7. Finally, we want to know if listening to the blues increases or decreases the number of pages read per night. We sample 12 research subjects and find the data listed in Table 9.6.

a. Using the appropriate test (alpha = .05), does listening to the blues have a statistically significant effect on the number of pages read per night? What sort of effect does it have?

b. What is the highest level of significance (smallest alpha level) achieved?

c. What does this tell us in the context of the null and research hypotheses?

d. Test the hypothesis that listening to blues music decreases the number of pages a person reads, compared to the number of pages read with no music (a one-tailed hypothesis), at the .05 alpha level. What is the highest one-tailed level of significance achieved?

Table 9.6   Blues/Reading Data

	Number of Pages Read	
Individual	*No Music*	*Listening to The Blues*
1	23	31
2	21	42
3	28	26
4	31	43
5	18	34
6	20	32
7	32	51
8	34	25
9	33	22
10	29	31
11	23	22
12	33	36

10

Simple Regression and Correlation

This text has largely explored univariate (single-variable) statistical techniques. In the last chapter we began to consider bivariate (two-variable) statistical techniques. This was presented in the context of comparing two groups' means to determine if a statistically significant difference existed (e.g., breed of cow and number of times it touches the electric fence). Although the techniques discussed to this point are all important and meaningful ways of analyzing variables, they tell us very little about the form or potential strength of a relationship that exists between two variables.

Further, the last few chapters have been primarily concerned with relationships between nominal and interval-ratio or ordinal variables. The statistical techniques in this chapter deal with bivariate relationships between two interval-ratio variables in terms of whether, and how strongly, they are associated together. Specifically, this chapter first explores a simple graphing technique called a scattergram that is used to illustrate relationships between two variables. Next we delve into the important statistical technique of simple linear regression, Pearson's r, and the newly introduced t-test of significance. Similar techniques for ordinal and nominal variables are also considered. Before proceeding, however, a brief review of independent and dependent variables and a discussion of causality is warranted.

Independent/Dependent Variables and Causality

Almost all research is based on the notion of causality. In the last chapter we implicitly introduced the idea of causality in terms of whether a given variable was seen as bringing about a measurable change in another group's mean. Quite simply, causality is the notion that one event or series of events causes another event or series of events to occur. In more scientific terms, one variable is seen as bringing about—causing—a change in another variable.

The specific terms used to describe the relationship between two variables are *independent* (X) and *dependent* (Y) *variables*. As previously discussed, the independent variable is seen as bringing about a change in a dependent variable—the dependent variable is seen as a function of the independent variable. Conversely, the independent variable is seen as a determinant of the dependent variable.

A simple example of this type of relationship is a person's income (the dependent variable) seen as a function of years of education (the independent variable). Alternatively, the grade you receive in this class (the dependent variable) is seen as a function of the number of hours spent studying (the independent variable). In other words, years of education and hours spent studying are seen as determinants of, respectively, one's income and course grades.

While both of these examples make sense intuitively, unfortunately, due to extraneous (unaccounted for) factors that are often not measured, we are never able absolutely to conclude causality. That is, while the relationship of hours spent studying as a determinant of the grade you receive in this class makes sense, potential other factors (such as previous math classes taken, type of school one attends, whether one is employed, or has children or other special obligations while attending school) can all potentially affect one's course grade. In other words, while two variables may be associated together—they tend to occur together—it does not follow automatically that one causes the other to change.

Moreover, as just demonstrated, most if not all variable relationships in the social sciences involve several, often numerous, independent variables. Typically these "other" variables are not accounted for in a given research design. For instance, the potential determinants of one's grade listed above is far from complete—type of textbook and the instructor you have while taking this course could be added to the list. As such, it is impossible to conclude absolutely that one variable is the cause of another. In the social sciences, at best, we make educated and logical inferences about independent and dependent variable relationships.

A somewhat humorous example that summarizes the above discussion is the often-noted relationship between fire trucks and fire damage. In numerical terms, as more fire trucks and firefighters respond to a fire there is a strong tendency for more damage to occur. One could conclude that fire trucks (or firefighters) are the independent variable and fire damage is the dependent variable; that is, an increase in the number of fire trucks leads to increased damage. Of course, this is ridiculous. Nevertheless, one could conclude wrongly that the fire trucks are the cause of the damage. In reality, however, the larger the fire, the more fire trucks that are required to put it out; and the larger the fire the more damage it causes.

Scattergrams

One easy way to represent a relationship of association between two variables is graphically with a *scattergram*. Similar to histograms and frequency polygons, scattergrams entail the graphic charting of two variables. This is accomplished by the use of intersecting axes; the horizontal axis represents the independent variable, while the vertical axis represents the dependent variable. A dot is used to represent each measurement of the independent variable in comparison to the dependent variable.

An easier way to discuss scattergrams is with an actual example. Taking a short break from cartoon examples but still using one that is absurd but somewhat humorous is the

Table 10.1   Soda and Urination Data

Individual's Name	Number of 12-ounce Sodas Consumed (X)	Number of Times Research Subject Urinated in the Following 3-hour Period (Y)
Rick	1	2
Janice	2	1
Paul	3	3
Susan	3	4
Cindy	4	6
John	5	5
Donald	6	5

data set found in Table 10.1 for 7 research subjects. The independent variable, under the heading X, is the number of 12-ounce sodas consumed by these 7 research subjects. The dependent variable, under the heading Y, is the corresponding number of times each subject urinated in a three-hour period immediately following the consumption of the sodas. To keep this presentation simple, we have rank ordered the observations of the independent variable.

Two preliminary observations are warranted. First (as you have probably noticed from the data set), as the amount of soda consumed increases, correspondingly, and not surprisingly, there is an increase in the number of times the research subject visits the bathroom. Second, while this example may appear completely absurd, as an undergraduate in college Steve Schacht worked in a federally sponsored nutrition research center where similar experiments were undertaken.

For this data set, the scattergram's horizontal axis represents the X variable and the vertical axis represents the Y variable. A dot is placed where the observations of the X and Y variables for each individual meet. As shown in Figure 10.1, the first dot for individual 1 is found at the intersection of 1 for X and 2 for Y. The rest of the dots representing each individual are also plotted and the resultant picture is called a scattergram. Due to such a small sample size, the scattergram represented in Figure 10.1 is fairly neat in presentation. Many scattergrams, however, plot hundreds (sometimes thousands) of cases, which often results in a jumble of dots.

A picture emerges from the scattergram that enables the inference that there is a positive linear relationship between the independent and dependent variables. Linear simply means that the relationship between those two variables resembles a straight line. Specifically, one of the best ways to represent the relationship between these two variables is to fit a straight line through the pattern of the scattergram. In a sense, this fitted line is an average of where the actual dots occur. The next section addresses this mathematically. For now, however, we simply estimate where this line goes and get the illustration of a regression line placed over the previously constructed scattergram (Figure 10.2).

Figure 10.1   Scattergram for Soda and Urination Data

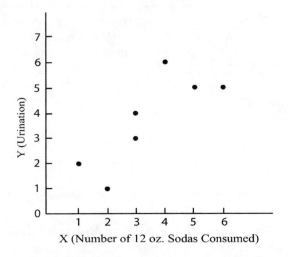

Figure 10.2   Scattergram With Estimated Regression Line

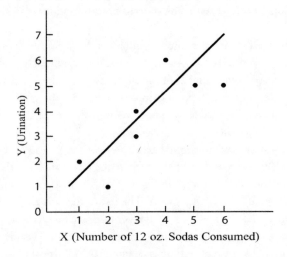

This new depiction clearly shows that as the line goes from left to right it correspondingly rises in reference to the Y axis. With each increase of the X variable comes a corresponding increase in the observed Y variable. This type of relationship is referred to as a positive linear relationship. Conversely, in cases where each increase of X results in a corresponding decrease in the observed Y variable, the relationship is referred to as an inverse (negative) relationship. Although beyond the scope of this text, there exist other types of linear relationships that do not follow a straight line. An example of one of these, graphically presented in Figure 10.3, is called a curvilinear relationship.

Figure 10.3   Curvilinear Relationship

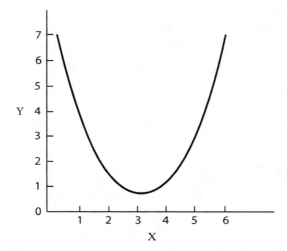

Finally, we are sometimes presented with situations where no discernible pattern emerges. That is, the dots in the scattergram are so dispersed that no lines can be fitted in any meaningful manner. In these cases, the variables are probably not associated together. The scattergram found in Figure 10.4 represents an unrelated X and Y variable relationship.

Figure 10.4   Scattergram of an Unrelated *X* and *Y* Variable Relationship

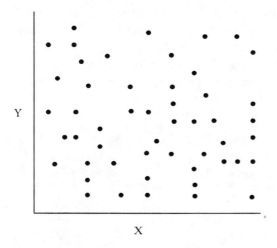

Simple Linear Regression

While a scattergram provides a picture of a relationship between two variables, it does not indicate exactly where the fitted line actually belongs. For the above example we simply guessed. A precise statistical technique that mathematically indicates the line's position is called a least-squares regression line, also referred to as a simple linear regression. In a limited sense, this line is a mathematical average between the observed X and Y values. The actual equation to do this, found below, should look familiar: it is the mathematical equation for plotting a straight line. Found below the equation are the definitions for each of its parts.

Equation for a Straight Line
(Least-Squares Regression)

$$Y = a + bX$$

Where:

Y = Dependent Variable: seen as a function of (or predicated by) the independent variable (X);

X = Independent Variable: the dimension or characteristic that is seen as the determinant or cause of the dependent variable (Y);

b = Slope of the Line: rise (or drop) divided by run;

a = Y-intercept: where the value of X = 0 and the line intercepts the Y axis.

Before introducing an example that requires actual mathematical operations to determine the slope (b) and the Y-intercept (a), we present an exact linear relationship from the physical sciences. This is not only a simple way to illustrate what the slope and intercept are, but it also gives readers some practice plotting the least-squares regression line.

A simple example of an exact linear relationship is converting Celsius to Fahrenheit: two different measure of temperature. In converting these different measures of temperature it is commonly known that the slope (b) is 9/5 (1.8) and the Y-intercept (a) is 32. Stating this in slightly different terms, for each degree of Celsius added, a corresponding 1.8 increase is found on the Fahrenheit scale. Further, the value of (0) on the X axis (representing Celsius) is equal to 32 on the Y axis (representing Fahrenheit). Not only is this where the Y-intercept occurs, moreover, this also represents the temperature where water freezes on both scales. In increments of 10 for X, each score was calculated and then its corresponding dot was placed on Figure 10.5. When the dots are then connected, we have a straight line that represents an exact linear relationship.

Table 10.2   Replicated Soda and Urination Data

Individual's Name	Number of 12-ounce Sodas Consumed (X)	Number of Times Research Subject Urinated in the Following 3-hour Period (Y)
Rick	1	2
Janice	2	1
Paul	3	3
Susan	3	4
Cindy	4	6
John	5	5
Donald	6	5

Figure 10.5   An Exact Linear Relationship

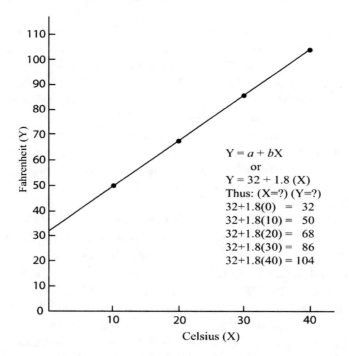

$Y = a + bX$
or
$Y = 32 + 1.8 (X)$
Thus: (X=?) (Y=?)
32+1.8(0)   =   32
32+1.8(10) =   50
32+1.8(20) =   68
32+1.8(30) =   86
32+1.8(40) = 104

As noted earlier, due to unknown extraneous factors, there are probably no exact linear relationships in the social sciences—and there really are very few in the physical sciences. As a result, we are forced to fit (calculate) a line. To assist in this discussion the data set on soda and urination (Table 10.2) is used. Also, the relationship between soda and urination is not an exact linear relationship, so the formulas used to calculate the slope (b) and Y-intercept (a) are introduced below.

Formula for Calculating a and b

$$b = \frac{\Sigma XY - \dfrac{(\Sigma X)(\Sigma Y)}{n}}{\Sigma X^2 - \dfrac{(\Sigma X)^2}{n}} \qquad a = \bar{y} - b\bar{x}$$

Although there are no new symbols introduced (and all of them should be quite familiar by now), for these first calculations go through the mathematical operations required for each formula. Beginning with the slope (b), the numerator portion of this formula requires first individually multiplying each X value by each Y value and then summing these values ($\Sigma XY = 104$). Next, take the sum of the X observations ($\Sigma X = 24$) and multiply it by the sum of the Y observations ($\Sigma Y = 26$) to find that $(24)(26) = 624$. This value, 624, is then divided by n = 7 (the sample size), which gives the value of $624/7 = 89.1428$. Then, as the formula requires, the value of 89.1428 is subtracted from the value of 104 (104 − 89.1428 = 14.8572). The resultant answer of 14.8572 is the solution to the numerator portion of the slope formula.

The denominator requires that each X value first be squared, and then these values are summed; the sum of the X values squared is 100. Next, the sum of all the X values (ΣX = 24) is squared; 24 squared = 576. This value, 576, is divided by n (n = 7); 576/7 = 82.2857, and then subtracted from the value of 100. Thus, 100 − 82.2857 = 17.7143, the denominator solution to the formula. Finally, the numerator value is divided by the denominator value, with the resultant answer being the slope; 14.8572/17.7143 = .8387 = b.

An observation is warranted before turning to the intercept formula. Because the answer calculated above for the slope is a positive value (.8387), this immediately shows that there is a positive relationship between X and Y variables. If, conversely, a negative value had resulted from the calculations, then the relationship between the X and Y variables would have been negative and inverse.

As most of you probably have noted, to calculate the value of the Y-intercept (a) one must first calculate the slope. The Y-intercept formula also requires the calculation of the means for the X and Y variables. This is accomplished by simply taking the sum of the Xs (ΣX = 24) and the sum of the Ys (ΣY = 26) and separately dividing each of these values by the sample size (n = 7); 24/7 = 3.4285 = the mean of X, while 26/7 = 3.7142 = the mean of Y. These values are plugged into the formula to give 3.7142 − (.8387) (3.4285) = 3.7142 − 2.8754 = .8388 = a.

A summary of all these calculations is provided below (intermediate calculations are presented in Table 10.3). Also found is the previous scattergram with the least-squares regression line plotted from the final derivation of Y = a + bX or Y = .8388 + (.8387)X (Figure 10.6). (Please note that seldom, if ever, are the slope and intercept values this close.)

$$b = \frac{104 - (24)(26)/7}{100 - (24)^2/7}$$

$$= \frac{104 - 89.1428}{100 - 82.2857}$$

$$= \frac{14.8572}{17.7143} = \boxed{.8387}$$

$$a = 3.7142 - (.8387)(3.4285)$$

$$= 3.7142 - 2.8755 = \boxed{.8387}$$

Least-Squares Line $(Y = a + bX)$
or
$Y = .8387 + (.8387)X$

$.8387 + (.8387)(0) = .8387$
$.8387 + (.8387)(1) = 1.6774$
$.8387 + (.8387)(2) = 2.5161$
$.8387 + (.8387)(3) = 3.3548$
$.8387 + (.8387)(4) = 4.1935$
$.8387 + (.8387)(5) = 5.0322$
$.8387 + (.8387)(6) = 5.8709$

Apparently the consumption of soda does have an effect on the number of times our subjects visit the bathroom. More specifically, with a positive slope we conclude that increased soda consumption apparently leads to increased urination. Moreover, soda and

Table 10.3   Intermediate Calculations for Soda/Urination Data

	X	Y	X^2	XY
1	1	2	1	2
2	2	1	4	2
3	3	3	9	9
4	3	4	9	12
5	4	6	16	24
6	5	5	25	25
7	6	5	36	30
	24	26	100	104

Figure 10.6   Scattergram and Plotted Least-Squares Regression Line

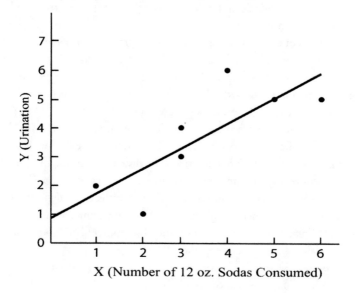

urination are apparently related. The strength of this relationship, however, cannot be assessed using a least-squares regression line, an additional measure called a correlation coefficient is needed to make that determination.

Pearson's *r* Correlation Coefficient

For continuity purposes, instead of giving the customary second example at this point, we now turn to the calculation of what is called a Pearson's-*r* correlation coefficient. (A second example for calculating the least-squares regression line and what follows is given as a summary problem at the end of this chapter.) Whereas the calculation and plotting of the least-squares regression line gives a clear picture of what sort of relationship exists between two variables (positive or negative), it tells nothing about the strength of the relationship. This is determined by using the correlation coefficient.

Before giving the actual Pearson's-r formula, it is helpful to first understand what it represents. On Figure 10.7 (and exactly as it was previously presented) is the plotted least-squares regression line and the scattergram for the soda/urination data set. Also imposed onto this figure is a horizontal line representing the mean of the Y variable (3.7142). The amount that each observation deviates from the mean of Y, called the sum of squares, is determined by two factors: regression and error. If the observations are very close to the fitted line, we can infer that most of the deviation is due to regression. Deviation due to regression means the amount of variance in the dependent variable (Y) that is explained—inferred, as caused—by variation in the independent variable (X). Conversely, if the observed values are found predominantly away from the fitted line in no discernible pattern, we then can infer that most of the deviation is attributable to error (also called residual variance).

Both of these types of deviation are also graphically presented in Figure 10.7. So, with individual 2, who consumed two 12-ounce sodas and urinated once, we see that the amount of variation to the least-squares line is illustrated as due to regression while the amount it goes beyond the observed value is illustrated as a result of error. To reiterate, individuals who are given two 12-ounce sodas are expected to urinate 2.5162 times, but our research subject who drank two 2-ounce sodas only urinated once. As such, and in simplistic terms, the difference between the expected and observed value, 2.5162 − 1 = 1.5162, is the amount of variance due to error. The distance from the mean of Y to the expected value is, conversely, the amount of variance due to regression: 3.7142 − 2.5162 = 1.198. In other words, this is the amount of variation in the dependent variable that is seen as being caused by the independent variable. Remember, however, that although we are inferring causality, all that can be demonstrated absolutely is the amount that two variables are correlated—associated—together.

A more precise way of measuring this is using the Pearson's-r correlation coefficient formula. The resultant answer (squared, as will be shown) from this formula tells exactly how much variation is attributed to regression versus error. The answer this formula gives is on a scale of 0 to 1 (actually −1 to +1; in cases where a negative coefficient is given, this shows a negative inverse relationship). The closer the final answer is to the value of 1, the more the two variables are associated together and the greater the amount of variability in the dependent variable is attributed to regression. Conversely, the closer the final answer is to 0, the less the variables are associated together; as such, more of the variability is inferred as due to error. What the actual formula does is to determine the amount of deviation due to regression and then divide this value by the total amount of deviation in X and Y.

The actual Pearson's-r formula is given below and looks very similar to the previously discussed slope (b) formula, except that now we must take the square root of the previous denominator of X and multiply it by the square root of the Y calculation. What this

Figure 10.7   Estimated Amount of Deviation Due to Error and Regression

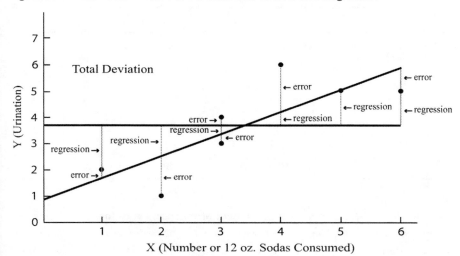

does is mathematically determine the amount of variance shared between the two variables, called covariance (the numerator portion of the formula), and divide this value by the total amount of variance for each variable (the denominator portion of the formula). These calculations were completed earlier, so here we have simply presented the actual calculations for this problem below the formula, and Table 10.4 is offered to assist in this presentation. (Note: As is done below, the resultant square-root values in the denominator are multiplied together.)

Pearson's-*r* Formula

$$\frac{\Sigma XY - ((\Sigma X)(\Sigma Y)/n)}{\sqrt{\Sigma X^2 - ((\Sigma X)^2/n)}\sqrt{\Sigma Y^2 - ((\Sigma Y)^2/n)}}$$

Calculations

$$r = \frac{104 - (24)(26)/7}{\sqrt{100 - (24)^2/7}\sqrt{116 - (26)^2/7}} = \frac{14.8572}{\sqrt{17.7143}\sqrt{19.4286}}$$

$$= \frac{14.8572}{(4.2088)(4.4077)} = \frac{14.8572}{18.5511} = \boxed{.8008}$$

With a Pearson's-*r* (correlation coefficient) of .8008, the variables of soda and urination are strongly related (associated). Further (as we discovered when calculating the slope), because the answer is positive, the relationship between the two variables is a strong, positive one. While the answer (.8008) shows that the two variables are strongly

Table 10.4   Intermediate Steps for Soda/Urination Data (Pearson's-r Formula)

	X	Y	X^2	Y^2	XY
1	1	2	1	4	2
2	2	1	4	1	2
3	3	3	9	9	9
4	3	4	9	16	12
5	4	6	16	36	24
6	5	5	25	25	25
7	6	5	36	25	30
	24	26	100	116	104

associated together, it does not tell the amount of variance that is due to regression versus error. To answer this question we use what is called the *coefficient of determination*: the total variation of the Y variable that is a function of variation in the X variable. This is derived by squaring the value of the obtained correlation coefficient (shown below).

$$r = .8008 \qquad r^2 = \boxed{.6412} = \text{Coefficient of Determination}$$

From this final answer, we can now infer that 64.12% of the variance in the dependent variable is due to regression. Conversely, we can also infer that 35.88% (1 − .6412 = .3588) of the variance in the dependent variable is due to error: unexplained variance. Thus, we conclude (although not absolutely) that 64.12% of the number of times our 7 respondents urinated is attributable to the number of sodas consumed, while 35.88% of the number of times each urinated is error or unexplained variance. The obvious conclusion is that drinking soda causes one to urinate, and the more soda someone drinks the greater number of times he or she will urinate.

Testing for Significance

We now have a clear picture of what the relationship between soda and urination looks like and how strong it is, but we do not know if the relationship is statistically significant. A variant for of the *t*-test found below is used to determine this.

$$t \text{ test for Pearson's } r = r\sqrt{\frac{n-2}{1-r^2}}$$

The formula requires first taking the sample size and subtracting 2 from it; 7 − 2 = 5. Then we take the value of 1 and subtract r squared from it; 1 − .6412 = .3588. Next, the value of 5 is divided by .3588 (5/.3588 = 13.9353); we then take the square root of this value to get 3.733. This value of 3.733 is multiplied by r (.8008), which gives us the final answer—a *t* obtained of 2.9893.

As with previous *t*-tests, the obtained value is now compared to a critical value. While the *t*-critical value is discerned using the familiar alpha level, the determination of degrees of freedom (df), however, is slightly different with this type of *t*-test. We are dealing with two variables, so we use $n - 2 = df$ instead of the previous $n - 1$. Thus for the present example we take $7 - 2$, giving 5 df. Setting the alpha level at .05, the corresponding *t*-critical value is 2.571. A *t*-obtained of 2.9893 is larger than the critical value of 2.571, so we conclude that the more sodas one drinks the more likely one is to urinate, and that this relationship is statistically significant. All of the steps for calculating this type of *t*-test applied to the soda/urination example are mathematically summarized below.

<u>*t* test for Soda/Urination Data</u>

$$r\sqrt{\frac{n-2}{1-r^2}} = .8008\sqrt{\frac{7-2}{1-.6412}} = .8008\sqrt{\frac{5}{.3588}}$$

$$= .8008\sqrt{13.9353} = (.8008)(3.733) = \boxed{2.9893} = t \text{ obtained}$$

(alpha = .05, 5 df = *t* critical = 2.571)

Summary Example

To give a second set of examples for all of the formulas that have been discussed in the chapter, we offer the following summary example based upon Cartoon 10.1. This cartoon is also used for the Practice Exercises.

The following data set (see Table 10.5) represents a 12-month period of January 1 through December 24. The independent variable (X) is the number of complaints per month about Santa's herd of reindeer. The dependent variable (Y) is the current size of Santa's reindeer herd at the end of each month.

Table 10.5   Complaints and Herd Size Data

Month	Number of Complaints Received Per Month (X)	Current Size of Herd (Y)
January	2	25
February	1	24
March	3	24
April	4	23
May	3	22
June	5	20
July	4	20
August	7	18
September	8	17
October	10	14
November	11	12
December	14	9

The data also reflect a negative relationship culminating in the month of December with the traditional nine reindeer left to pull Santa's sled. In other words, each month leading up to Christmas sees more complaints with fewer reindeer left in Santa's herd. (This relationship can also be conceptualized as a positive one; that is, more complaints lead to more reindeer being turned into venison. This example, however, is presented as a negative, inverse relationship to give you an idea of some of the minor differences in plotting and calculation.) Using the previously explored formulas, we now demonstrate mathematically what type of relationship exists, and what its strength is and whether it is statistically significant.

As before, we first plot the data in the form of a scattergram (Figure 10.8). Once again, the independent variable (number of complaints) is the horizontal axis, and the dependent variable (size of herd) is the vertical axis.

Having constructed the scattergram, we next calculate the least-squares regression line—the slope (b) and the intercept (a). The data and the intermediate operations that are used in the formulas are found on Table 10.6 on p. 189. To aid in this presentation, below are the slope and intercept formulas and the final calculations.

Formulas for Slope (b) and Intercept (a)

$$b = \frac{\Sigma XY - (\Sigma X)(\Sigma Y) / n}{\Sigma X^2 - (\Sigma X)^2 / n} \qquad\qquad a = \bar{y} - b\bar{x}$$

$$= \frac{1144 - (72)(228) / 12}{610 - (72)^2 / 12} \qquad\qquad = 19 - (-1.2584)(6)$$

$$= \frac{1144 - 1368}{610 - 432} \qquad\qquad = 19 - (-7.5504)$$

$$= \frac{-224}{178} = \boxed{-1.2584} \qquad\qquad = \boxed{26.5504}$$

Finding a slope of -1.2584 confirms that this is a negative relationship. Further, when a negative slope value is used to calculate the least-squares line (below), we actually make this value minus after it has been multiplied by each value of X. To calculate the intercept for this example, when a negative value is subtracted we actually add it—minus a minus means we add the value; $19 - (-7.5504) = 26.5504$. Given the values of the slope (b) and the intercept (a), the resulting least-squares line formula is used to find the expected values of Y for each possible value of X. These computations are presented in Table 10.7. Using the expected Y values we have plotted the least-squares regression line over the previously constructed scattergram (see Figure 10.9, p. 188).

With the observed values falling very close to the plotted regression line, as the above graphically represents, there obviously is a very strong linear relationship that is inverse.

Cartoon 10.1   THE FAR SIDE®

© Chronicle Features, 1980   12-22

And I've only one thing to say about all these complaints I've been hearing about . . . venison!

To mathematically demonstrate the strength of the relationship, again we use the Pearson's-*r* formula. Both the formula and the actual calculations for this data set are presented below. The coefficient of determination value, *r* squared, is also found below:

<u>Pearson's-r Formula</u>

$$\frac{\Sigma XY - (\Sigma X)(\Sigma Y)/n}{\sqrt{\Sigma X^2 - (\Sigma X)^2/n}\sqrt{\Sigma Y^2 - (\Sigma Y)^2/n}}$$

Calculations

$$r = \frac{1144 - (72)(228)/12}{\sqrt{610 - (72)^2/12}\sqrt{4624 - (228)^2/12}} = \frac{-224}{\sqrt{178}\sqrt{292}}$$

$$= \frac{-224}{(13.3416)(17.088)} = \frac{-224}{227.9812} = \boxed{-.9825}$$

$$r = -.9825; \qquad r^2 = \boxed{.9653} = \text{Coefficient of Determination}$$

Figure 10.8   Scattergram for Venison Data

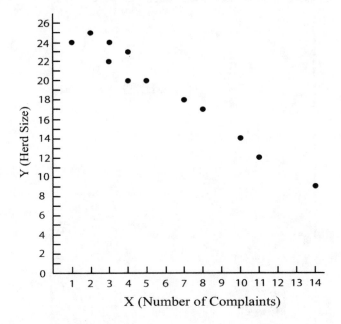

Figure 10.9   Plotted Least-Squares Regression Line for Venison Data

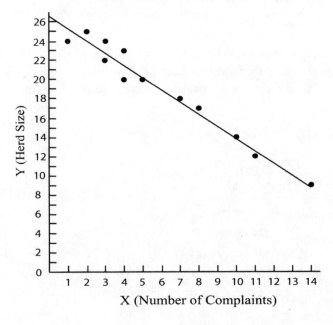

Table 10.6   Intermediate Calculations for Complaints and Herd Size Data

Month	Number of Complaints Received Per Month (X)	Current Size of Herd (Y)	XY	X^2	Y^2
January	2	25	50	4	625
February	1	24	24	1	576
March	3	24	72	9	576
April	4	23	92	16	529
May	3	22	66	9	484
June	5	20	100	25	400
July	4	20	80	16	400
August	7	18	126	49	324
September	8	17	136	64	289
October	10	14	140	100	196
November	11	12	132	121	144
December	14	9	126	196	81
Sums	72	228	1144	610	4624

Table 10.7   Values of Y Predicted for Complaints and Herd Size Data

Least-Squares Line = $Y = a + bX$	
$Y = 26.8388 + (-1.2584)X$	(continued)
$26.5504 + (-1.2584)(0) = 26.5504$	$26.5504 + (-1.2584)(7) = 17.7416$
$26.5504 + (-1.2584)(1) = 25.292$	$26.5504 + (-1.2584)(8) = 16.4832$
$26.5504 + (-1.2584)(2) = 24.0336$	$26.5504 + (-1.2584)(9) = 15.2248$
$26.5504 + (-1.2584)(3) = 22.7752$	$26.5504 + (-1.2584)(10) = 13.9664$
$26.5504 + (-1.2584)(4) = 21.5168$	$26.5504 + (-1.2584)(11) = 12.708$
$26.5504 + (-1.2584)(5) = 20.2584$	$26.5504 + (-1.2584)(12) = 11.4496$
$26.5504 + (-1.2584)(6) = 19.00$	$26.5504 + (-1.2584)(13) = 10.1912$
	$26.5504 + (-1.2584)(14) = 8.9328$

The obtained r value is negative, which again indicates that this is a negative, inverse relationship. Once the r value of $-.9825$ is squared, the resultant coefficient-of-determination value of $.9653$ is quite high on a scale of 0 to absolute 1. Moreover, this value allows us to infer that 96.53% of Santa's herd size is explained by the number of complaints received in a given month; only 3.47% is due to unexplained variance—error. In other words, complaints have a deadly effect on Santa's reindeer herd. While this is obviously significant, as presented at the top of the following page, the t-test for this data set must be completed.

$$t \text{ Test for Pearson's r} = r\sqrt{\frac{n-2}{1-r^2}}$$

t Test For Complaints/Herd Size Data

$$= -.9825\sqrt{\frac{12-2}{1-.9653}} = -.9825\sqrt{\frac{10}{.0347}}$$

$$= -.9825\sqrt{288.1844} = (-.9825)(16.9759) = \boxed{-16.6788} = t \text{ obtained}$$

(alpha = .001, 10 df = *t* critical = 4.587)

In sum, we conclude that an increase of complaints leads to a statistically significant reduction in Santa's herd size. This may explain how Santa gets his reindeer to fly. That is, if you are a reindeer and lucky enough to have made it to Christmas, given the alternative you would probably fly, too.

Box 10.1

While all the examples used in this chapter have used interval-ratio variable relationships, situations often dictate that ordinal and nominal variables must be used. These circumstances require the use of different measures of association. Although Pearson's *r* has the explicit assumption that interval-ratio data are used in its calculation, this assumption is often violated. Researchers and statisticians have offered various explanations for violating this assumption of using interval-ratio data (and it has become fairly commonplace to do so), but the authors still think it important that readers understand that other statistical techniques have been developed to deal with this problem. It is beyond the scope of an introductory statistics textbook to explore these alternative measures of association, so we have simply outlined them in Table 10.8.

Table 10.8   Types of Correlation Coefficient for Relationships Among Ordinal and Interval-Ratio Variables

		Independent Variables		
		Interval/Ratio	*Ordinal*	*Nominal*
Dependent Variable	Interval-Ratio	Pearson *r*	Biserial *r*	Point Biserial *r*
	Ordinal	Biserial *r*	Spearman's Rho	Phi
	Nominal	Point Biserial *r*	Phi	Phi

Chapter Summary and Conclusions

This chapter introduced a new way of conceptualizing bivariate relationships. It first examined such relationships in terms of a graphic illustration, a scattergram, and then built upon the scattergram to demonstrate that, using a least-squares regression formula, a straight line can be determined and plotted to represent the entire data set. While this information gave a general idea of whether the relationship was positive or negative and what it looked like, additional formulas are needed to determine the strength of the relationship and whether it is statistically significant. To this end, we used the Pearson's-r formula, a coefficient of determination (r squared), and a newly introduced t-test. This chapter ended by noting that, dependent upon what type of variable is being used, there are several other measures of association that can be utilized.

Key Terms to Remember

- Independent Variables
- Scattergram
- Dependent Variables
- Least-Squares Regression Line
- Notion of Causality

- Pearson's-r Correlation Coefficient
- Slope
- Coefficient of Determination
- Y-Intercept
- Pearson's-r/t-test

Practice Exercises

1. The data set in Table 10.9 refers to Cartoon 10.1. As labeled, the independent variable represents the (previously given) number of complaints per month for Santa's reindeer. The dependent variable represents the number of reindeer turned into venison.
   a. Construct a scattergram with this data set. What type of relationship appears to exist between number of complaints and reindeer becoming venison?
   b. Calculate the slope (a) and intercept (b) for this data.
   c. Plug the calculated slope and intercept values into the least-squares regression line (Y = a + bX), and then plot it over the previously constructed scattergram.
   d. Calculate the Pearson's-r correlation coefficient for this data set.
   e. Using the appropriate t-test, determine whether the relationship between number of complaints and number of reindeer becoming venison is statistically significant.
   f. Having made all of these calculations, what would you conclude about the relationship between the number of complaints and the number of reindeer becoming venison?

Table 10.9   Complaints and Venison Data

Month	Number of Complaints Received Per Month (X)	Number Turned Into Venison (Y)
January	2	1
February	1	2
March	3	3
April	4	2
May	3	5
June	5	8
July	4	7
August	7	10
September	8	9
October	10	13
November	11	16
December	14	13

2. Again, the data set in Table 10.10 refers to Cartoon 10.1. The independent variable is the age of the reindeer and the dependent variable represents the number of complaints received in a year's time. The data set obviously assumes that these 10 reindeer did not become venison in the (year-long period) of measurement.

    a. Construct a scattergram with this data set. What type of relationship appears to exist between reindeer age and number of complaints received in a year?

    b. Calculate the slope (a) and intercept (b) for this data set.

    c. Plug the calculated slope and intercept values into the least-squares regression line $(Y = a + bX)$, and then plot it over the previously constructed scattergram.

    d. Calculate the Pearson's-r correlation coefficient for this data set.

    e. Using the appropriate t-test, determine whether the relationship between complaints and number of reindeer becoming venison is statistically significant.

    f. Having made all of these calculations, what can you conclude about the relationship between age and the number of complaints received?

3. The data set in Table 10.11 again refers to Cartoon 10.1. In this study, we are interested in whether Santa displaces any of his anger at the reindeer's complaints toward elves. Here, the independent variable is the number of complaints from the reindeer, while the dependent variable represents the number of elves that Santa kicks in a given month.

    a. Construct a scattergram with this data set. What type of relationship appears to exist between the number of reindeer complaints received in a month and the number of elves kicked?

Table 10.10   Age and Complaints Data

Reindeer's Name	Age of Reindeer (X)	Number of Complaints Received for the Year (Y)
Rudolph	1	20
Donner Jr.	1	15
Dasher II	3	17
Blitzen	3	14
Dancer	4	15
Prancer	5	11
Comet	5	8
Cupid	5	10
Donner Sr.	7	9
Dasher III	10	8

Table 10.11   Complaints and Elves Kicked Data

Month	Number of Complaints Received Per Month (X)	Number of Elves Kicked (Y)
January	2	6
February	1	2
March	3	5
April	4	1
May	3	7
June	5	4
July	4	3
August	7	8
September	8	3
October	10	12
November	11	3
December	14	5

b. Calculate the slope (a) and intercept (b) for this data set.

c. Plug the calculated slope and intercept values into the least-squares regression line (Y = a + bX), and then plot it over the previously constructed scattergram.

d. Calculate the Pearson's-*r* correlation coefficient for this data set.

e. Using the appropriate *t*-test, determine if the relationship between complaints and the number of elves getting kicked is statistically significant.

f. Having made all of these calculations, what can you conclude about the relationship between the number of complaints received from reindeer and the number of elves Santa kicked?

4. For this example, assume that we want to assess the relationship between the average number of toys that children request each month and the number of elves that Santa kicks. The data is presented in Table 10.12. Here, the independent variable is the average number of toys requested by children each month, while the dependent variable represents the number of elves that Santa kicks in a given month.

   a. Construct a scattergram with this data set. What type of relationship appears to exist between number of toys requested and the number of elves that Santa kicks in a month?
   b. Calculate the slope (a) and intercept (b) for this data set.
   c. Plug the calculated slope and intercept values into the least-squares regression line (Y = a + bX), and then plot it over the previously constructed scattergram.
   d. Calculate the Pearson's-r correlation coefficient for this data set.
   e. Using the appropriate t-test, determine if the relationship between the average number of toys children ask for each month and the number of elves getting kicked is statistically significant.
   f. Having made all of these calculations, what can you conclude about the relationship between the number of toys children request each month and the number of elves Santa kicked?

5. For any of the above exercises where the correlation was not significant, how many observations/cases (what size n) must be added for the correlation to be significant? This, of course, assumes that adding new observations does not change the strength or direction of the original relationship identified. Report both the number of new observations/cases needed and the resulting total sample size. Remember that the degrees of freedom for correlations is $n - 2$.

Table 10.12   Toys Asked for and Elves Kicked Data

Month	Average Number of Toys Asked for Each Month (X)	Number of Elves Kicked (Y)
January	0	12
February	1	9
March	1	8
April	3	7
May	4	4
June	5	2
July	5	1
August	6	4
September	8	6
October	9	8
November	10	10
December	12	12

11

One-Way Analysis of Variance (ANOVA)

Chapter 9 explored various techniques of hypothesis testing where two group means were compared to determine whether there was a significant difference between them. This chapter explores situations where three or more group means are compared. The specific statistical technique to accomplish this is called *Analysis of Variance,* hereafter referred to as ANOVA (the actual ANOVA procedure is also referred to as an *F* test).

More specifically, this chapter first outlines some of the advantages and theoretical assumptions that explain why ANOVA is often utilized as a statistical technique. It then presents an eighteen-step procedure for completing an ANOVA. When statistical significance is determined using ANOVA, subsequent statistical tests are often undertaken. One of these tests, called an *LSD t-test,* is also explored in terms of its calculations and what it represents. The chapter ends with some simple examples of *ANOVA summary tables* and how to interpret them.

Advantages and Theoretical Assumptions of ANOVA

Like many statistical tests, ANOVA originated from studies in agriculture. Researchers in the agricultural sciences often study things such as the effects of different levels of irrigation on land plots with varied levels and types of fertilizers. In investigations such as this, the researcher is often faced with situations where dozens of group means must be compared. This translates into literally hundreds of potential *t*-tests; anything more than eleven groups correspondingly results in a minimum of 100 possible *t*-tests.

To determine the number of possible *t*-tests that can be performed for 7 group means, simply plug 7 into a formula to find that there are 21 possible *t*-tests. These calculations are found below with the actual formula (*J* represents the number of groups).

$$\frac{J(J-1)}{2} \quad \text{or} \quad \frac{7(7-1)}{2} = \frac{42}{2} = \boxed{21}$$

The calculation of 21 *t*-tests is no more difficult than the amount of time it takes to complete them; however, undertaking a large number of *t*-tests, such as 21, does present a theoretical dilemma. That is, if we had 20 possible *t*-tests (referred to as 20 to simplify the discussion) and the alpha level was set at .05, how many t values would we expect to find significant when, in fact, they are not significant?

The question actually is what's the probability of committing a *Type I Error* and reject-ing the null hypothesis when in fact it is true? (To refresh your memory, you may want to refer to Chapter 9 for a more comprehensive discussion of Type I Errors.) With 20 t-tests, alpha level set at .05, due to potential sampling error we expect one of these t-tests to be found significant when in fact it is not: once again, a Type I Error.

It is because of this potential predicament that when a researcher is undertaking an analysis involving the calculation of numerous potential t-tests, an additional test is need-ed to guard against the committing of Type I Errors. This is why the statistical procedure of ANOVA was created. Additionally, while this technique was created to deal with situ-ations of three or more group means, it can also be used with just two group means. ANOVA enables researchers to determine statistically if additional tests (including t-tests and an array of other tests) are warranted. Quite simply, if one obtains a significant F value using ANOVA, then subsequent statistical tests are typically undertaken. Conversely, if an F value that is not significant is obtained, the subsequent tests should not be undertaken. This is made clearer through the actual calculations.

The actual ANOVA statistical test tells whether there is more variance *between* the groups than that which is found *within* all of the groups. More specifically, given any set of numbers we almost always find variability. One way the variability within a group is measured and represented is with a variance value (the actual calculations for this formu-la are found in Chapter 5). The variability between groups is measured in a similar man-ner. What the ANOVA formula represents, as a final answer, is the amount of variability between the groups divided by the amount of variability within the groups. In other words, the *obtained F value* is a *ratio value*.

As demonstrated below, if there is measurably more variability between the groups than within them, the obtained-ratio value (F) will be found to be statistically significant. Conversely, if the amount of variability between the groups is close to or less than the amount of variability found within the groups, the obtained F value will be close to or less than one; such an answer would be statistically insignificant.

Applying the *null* and *research hypothesis* to ANOVA, we find that, instead of state-ments of one mean being or not being statistically equal, these potential relationships are stated in slightly different terms. When three or more group means are compared, the null hypothesis states that none of the means is significantly different—all of them are equal. Conversely, the research hypothesis holds that two or more of the means are statis-tically different, not equal. If statistical significance is found using ANOVA, it says that two or more of the means are not equal, but it does not specify which of the means are not equal. Subsequent statistical tests, such as the LSD t-test, are used to determine which of the groups means are actually statistically different. Both the null and research hypoth-esis for an ANOVA are mathematically represented below.

<u>Null Hypothesis</u>   <u>Research Hypothesis</u>

$H_0: \mu_1 = \mu_2 = \mu_3$ H_A : One or more group means are not equal.

One final preliminary observation is warranted. As with previous tests, once an obtained value is derived, this value has to be compared to a critical table value to determine if there is statistical significance. Because this is an *F* test, not surprisingly, a new set of *F*-critical values, found in Appendix 3, is used to make this determination. For simplicity, the table values found in Appendix 3 list *F-critical values* at two alpha levels: .05 and .01. Here, as for previous critical values, we are making a statement of probability of the likelihood of a Type I Error having been committed. In other words, even when using ANOVA, due to sampling error the potential still exists that a Type I Error was committed, even though this technique does greatly diminish the probability that a Type I Error is committed with subsequent tests. Remember that these tests cannot be performed unless a significant *F* value is obtained.

One-Way Analysis of Variance (ANOVA)

We now turn to the actual calculations used to complete an ANOVA. To assist in this discussion we use Cartoon 11.1 (found on the following page). Our current research interests are the effects of different types of liquids poured "off" a duck's back.

We randomly select three groups of 10 ducks (30 ducks total) for this experiment. For this technique to be used in a theoretically appropriate manner, the selection of the research subjects—ducks—and their placement into each of the groups should be done randomly. Group 1 receives the treatment of one ounce of acid poured "off" each duck's back. Group 2 receives the treatment of one ounce of vinegar poured "off" each duck's back. Group 3 is our control group and no treatment is given; nothing is poured "off" any of their backs. (Although a control group is often utilized when undertaking an ANOVA, it need not be.) Each group of ducks is then observed for twenty-four hours to determine the number of feathers each of them loses or gains during this period. The findings for this experiment are reported in Table 11.1.

Some of the symbols found in this table are being presented for the first time, so let's review all of them. To begin with, the table reports the finding for our three groups of ducks in terms of the number of feathers lost or gained at the end of the twenty-four-hour period. This is indicated by the very top column headings. Under these column headings are the sub-headings of *s#*; X.1, X.2, or X.3; and X.1, X.2, or X.3 squared. The symbol *s#* simply represents research subjects (ducks) for a given group (e.g., X31 or X93). The column headings X.1, X.2, and X.3 indicate which group the observation is taken from. Thus, for instance, research subject X42 lost one feather as a result of participating in this experiment while subject X31 lost 10 feathers.

The column heading X.1, X.2, and X.3 squared are used for calculation purposes and are any observed value squared. Finally, at the *bottom* of each group's X and X squared columns are spaces reserved for their totals: (1) the upper row represents the sum of all the observed values for the given group and (2) the lower row of the matrix represents the sum of all the observed values squared for the given group.

Cartoon 11.1   THE FAR SIDE

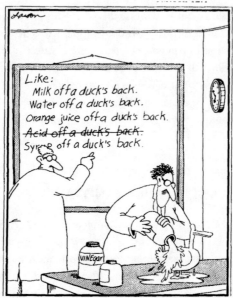

Table 11.1   Liquids off a Duck's Back Data

One-way Analysis of Variance for Feathers Lost (or Gained)

	Group 1			Group 2			Group 3	
s #	X.1	X.1²	s #	X.2	X.2²	s #	X.3	X.3²
X11	-8		X12	+2		X13	-3	
X21	-9		X22	-6		X23	+2	
X31	-10		X32	-4		X33	-3	
X41	-8		X42	-1		X43	+2	
X51	-11		X52	-1		X53	+4	
X61	-15		X62	+4		X63	-1	
X71	-16		X72	-3		X73	-3	
X81	-7		X82	-2		X83	-2	
X91	-12		X92	-4		X93	+2	
X101	-14		X102	-5		X103	-3	
ΣX.1			ΣX.2			ΣX.3		
ΣX.1²			ΣX.2²			ΣX.3²		
(n_1=10)			(n_2=10)			(n_3=10)		

Group 1 = One ounce of acid poured "off" a duck's back
Group 2 = One ounce of vinegar poured "off" a duck's back
Group 3 = Control group; no treatment given

The first step asks us to find the sum of all the X values. This is accomplished by summing the observed values separately for each of the groups, and then adding together the groups' summed values. The i and j subscripts found in the formula simply denote, from beginning to end, the sum of all observed values. With the present or similar examples (where both negative and positive values are summed), be very careful to differentiate between these two types of values; otherwise any subsequent answers are incorrect. These operations are completed in a revised table of raw scores (Table 11.2) and are mathematically represented and completed as follows.

Step 1:   The sum of $\Sigma X_{ij} = \Sigma X1 + \Sigma X2 + \cdots + \Sigma X_j$

For this example: $\Sigma X1 + \Sigma X2 + \Sigma X3 = -110 + -20 + -5 = \boxed{-135}$

Step two also requires calculations to be made in the table of raw values. To this end, first square each observation of X (answers are found in column two for each group), then separately sum these values for each group, and finally add together the three group sums to get one final answer. The completed operations for this step are found below and in the revised table (Table 11.2) of raw values.

Step 2:   The sum of $\Sigma X_{ij}^2 = \Sigma X_1^2 + \Sigma X_2^2 + \Sigma X_3^2 + \cdots + \Sigma X_j^2$

For this example: $\Sigma X1_1^2 + \Sigma X2_2^2 + \Sigma X3_3^2 = 1300 + 128 + 69 = \boxed{1497}$

Table 11.2   Intermediate Steps for Liquids off a Duck's Back Data

One-way Analysis of Variance for Feathers Lost (or Gained)

Revised Table With Squared and Summed Table Values Included.

Group 1			Group 2			Group 3		
s #	X.1	X.1²	s #	X.2	X.2²	s #	X.3	X.3²
X11	-8	64	X12	+2	4	X13	-3	9
X21	-9	81	X22	-6	36	X23	+2	4
X31	-10	100	X32	-4	16	X33	-3	9
X41	-8	64	X42	-1	1	X43	+2	4
X51	-11	121	X52	-1	1	X53	+4	16
X61	-15	225	X62	+4	16	X63	-1	1
X71	-16	256	X72	-3	9	X73	-3	9
X81	-7	49	X82	-2	4	X83	-2	4
X91	-12	144	X92	-4	16	X93	+2	4
X101	-14	196	X102	-5	25	X103	-3	9
ΣX.1	-110		ΣX.2	-20		ΣX.3	-5	
ΣX.1²		1300	ΣX.2²		128	ΣX.3²		69
(n_1=10)			(n_2=10)			(n_3=10)		

Group 1 = One ounce of acid poured "off" a duck's back

Group 2 = One ounce of vinegar poured "off" a duck's back

Group 3 = Control group; no treatment given

The next operation is not required in terms of obtaining the final answer; nevertheless, Step 3 does give us an interesting, alternative look at our data set. This step asks us to sum all the X values, as we did in Step 1, and then divide this value by the total number of observations for all groups. We represent the latter symbol as N, which in this case is 30. Even though we are actually dealing with a sample, we use an uppercase N instead of a lowercase n to aid in subsequent calculations. A subsequent ANOVA step, as will be shown, uses lower-case n's to represent individual group sizes (e.g., the n for group 1 is 10).)

What the final answer for Step 3 actually shows is that the grand (total) mean for all observations is –4.5. In our example, this shows that our 30 ducks lost an average of 4.5 feathers.

$$\text{Step 3:} \quad \frac{\Sigma X_{ij}}{N} = \frac{(Step1)}{N} = \frac{-135}{30} = \boxed{-4.500}$$

A further observation is warranted: Steps 1 and 3 are the only ones where negative answers can be obtained, otherwise, every other ANOVA step involves the squaring of values; therefore, all other resultant answers, including the final answer, are always positive values.

We now can make calculations that represent the total amount of variance found in each of the groups. This is also referred to as the total square sum of scores (divided by n). First the sum of X for each group is separately squared and then the resultant answer is divided by the group size. These calculations need not be done separately when each of the group sizes is the same; this is true for the case at hand ($n_1 = 10$, $n_2 = 10$, and $n_3 = 10$). Because most data sets do not entail equal group sizes, however, each of the three calculations is done separately (listed as Steps 4, 5, and 6) below:

Obtain the $\Sigma\left(\Sigma X_{ij}\right)^2 / n_{ij}$ for each available group.

$$\text{Step 4:} \quad \frac{\Sigma(X.1)^2}{n_1} = \frac{(-110)^2}{10} = \frac{12100}{10} = \boxed{1210}$$

$$\text{Step 5:} \quad \frac{(\Sigma X.2)^2}{n_2} = \frac{(-20)^2}{10} = \frac{400}{10} = \boxed{40}$$

$$\text{Step 6:} \quad \frac{(\Sigma X.3)^2}{n_3} = \frac{(-5)^2}{10} = \frac{25}{10} = \boxed{2.5}$$

The next step is really what the formula prior to Steps 4 through 6 asked for: the total square sum of scores divided by n. In simpler terms, to complete Step 7, add together the results of Steps 4, 5, and 6.

$$\text{Step 7:} \quad \Sigma\left(\frac{\left(\Sigma X_{ij}\right)^2}{n_{ij}}\right) = \text{Step 4} + \text{Step 5} + \text{Step 6} =$$

$$1210 + 40 + 2.5 = \boxed{1252.5}$$

Step 8 is an intermediate operation and requires that we sum all the observed X's, square this value, and then divide it by the total number of subjects (N). In other words, take the value of Step 1, square it, and then divide this answer by N. This step is mathematically presented as follows.

$$\textbf{Step 8:}\quad \frac{\left(\Sigma X_{ij}\right)^2}{N_{ij}} = \frac{\left(Step1\right)^2}{N_{ij}} = \frac{(-135)^2}{30} = \boxed{607.5}$$

At this point, all of the answers for subsequent operations are further summarized on what is called an *ANOVA* (Table 11.3). This table, along with the summarized eighteen steps (Table 11.4), is found at the end of all of the calculations. In turn, each of the new symbols in Table 11.3 is explained as its corresponding calculations are made. Not only is this table an efficient way to summarize meaningful information about our data set and the mathematical computations we have made, but some of the values (other than the final answer) are used in subsequent statistical tests.

Step 9, the result of which is the first to be placed in the ANOVA summary table, tells how much variability between the groups is present; this is referred to as the sum of squares (SS) between groups. To obtain this value, subtract Step 8 from Step 7, to obtain the value 645. This value—645—is placed in the table under the column heading SS and the row heading Between.

Step 9: The sum of squares between groups = Step 7 - Step 8
$$= 1252.5 - 607.5 = \boxed{645}$$

Similarly, Step 10 provides the answer that is placed in the table for the SS within groups. This value is obtained by taking the sum of all individually squared values (Step 2) and subtracting the total square sum of scores value (Step 7). The obtained value of 244.5, reported below, is placed in the table under the column heading SS and the row heading Within.

Step 10: The sum of squares within groups = Step 2 - Step 7
$$= 1497 - 1252.5 = \boxed{244.5}$$

Although the next step is not required for subsequent calculations, we have included Step 11 as a way to check whether previous answers are correct. This step, which gives the value for the *total* sum of squares, is frequently reported in articles and papers that have used an ANOVA statistical technique. Further, for calculation purposes this value is needed for some of the subsequent ways ANOVA Summary Tables are explored. As reported below, the answer is obtained by taking the sum of all squared values (Step 2) and subtracting the result of Step 8 from it. This gives us the answer of 889.5, which is placed in the table under the column heading SS and the row heading of TOTAL.

To check previous calculations, Step 9's answer is compared to the separately derived answer of the SS within added to the SS between (645 + 245.5). In the case at hand, both

values equal 889.5. If, however, these values are not equal, a mistake has been made somewhere in the previous calculations and one must go back and correct the error. Although
the potential still exists for these two answers to be equal even when errors have been
made in previous calculations, this comparison nevertheless is a fairly easy way to check
for possible mistakes.

Step 11: The TOTAL sum of squares = Step 2 - Step 8
$$= 1497 - 607.5 = \boxed{889.5}$$

As you become more proficient at completing ANOVA summary tables, the remaining steps should come more automatically. For the first few times through these steps,
however, each of the required steps is listed explicitly.

Step 12 represents the number of groups in the analysis and, because this is a sample,
one of these groups (conceptualized as a degree of freedom) is fixed. To mathematically
find the degree of freedom between groups take the total number of groups (represented
by the symbol J) and subtract the value of 1 from it. In this case, the answer is 2; $J - 1$ or
$3 - 1 = 2$. Thus, as reported below and on the ANOVA summary table, there are 2 df
between groups for this example.

Step 12: The between degrees of freedom = $J - 1 = 3 - 1 = \boxed{2\ df}$

Next we determine the within groups degrees of freedom. Using an ANOVA procedure, each group, in a sense, is treated as a sub-sample—a discrete, separate set of individuals. As such, one degree of freedom from each individual group is fixed.
Mathematically, as found below and reported in the ANOVA table, this is obtained by
taking the value of N and subtracting the number of groups (J) from it.

Step 13: The within degrees of freedom = $N - J = 30 - 3 = \boxed{27\ df}$

Although the next step is another operation not required for any subsequent calculations, it is still a quick way to check whether the calculations for Step 12 and Step 13 are
correct. Step 14 represents the *total* degrees of freedom, and is obtained by subtracting
the value of 1 from N (as shown below).

Step 14: The TOTAL degrees of freedom = $N - 1 = 30 - 1 = \boxed{29\ df}$

We now can determine the between and within mean-square (MS) values. The *mean-
square (MS) values*, in a limited sense, represent the average amount of variability between
and within the groups. The *mean-square-between (MSB)* value is determined by taking the
sum-of-squares between value and dividing it by the degrees of freedom between. In other
words, we take the value from Step 9 (645) and divide it by that of Step 12 (2) to get the
MSB (reported below and in the table) of 322.5.

Step 15: The mean square (MS) between $\dfrac{SSbetween}{dfbetween} = \dfrac{Step\,9}{Step\,12} = \dfrac{645}{2} = \boxed{322.5}$

Similarly, to obtain the *mean square within* (*MSW*-Step 16), divide the sum-of-squares within value by the within degrees of freedom. That is, divide the result of Step 10 (244.5) by that of Step 13 (27 df), which equals 9.0555.

$$\textbf{Step 16: The mean square } (MS) \textbf{ within} = \frac{SSwithin}{dfwithin} = \frac{Step10}{Step13} = \frac{244.5}{27} = \boxed{9.0555}$$

Step 17 gives the *F-obtained* value. As noted, *F*-obtained values are simply ratio values that compare the amount of variability found between versus within groups. As such, this calculation requires dividing the mean square between (*MSB*) by the mean square within (*MSW*) to get the *F*-obtained ratio value. For the present calculation, we take the value from Step 15 (322.5) and divide it by that from Step 16 (9.0555) to get an *F*-obtained of 35.6137.

$$\textbf{Step 17: } F \textbf{ obtained } = \frac{MSbetween}{MSwithin} = \frac{Step15}{Step16} = \frac{322.5}{9.0555} = \boxed{35.6137}$$

As with previous obtained values from various other statistical tests explored in this text, we are now required to compare the *F*-obtained with the *F*-critical value to determine if there is statistical significance. Critical values of *F*, once again, are found in Appendix 3.

Listed at the top of each of the tables in Appendix 3 is an explanation that first-row values are for the .05 alpha level whereas second-row values are for the .01 alpha level. Within the actual tables are column headings for the numerator degrees of freedom and row headings for the denominator degrees of freedom. These represent values that have already been calculated and are found in our ANOVA summary table. Numerator degrees of freedom are between df while denominator degrees of freedom are within df.

In the present analysis, the ANOVA summary table (Table 11.3), shows that there are 2 between *df* (numerator degrees of freedom) and 27 within df (denominator degrees of freedom). Using these values we simply look to the appendix and find that the *F*-critical value at alpha level .05 is 3.35 and at .01 it is 5.49.

The final determination to make is whether there is a statistically significant difference. As with *Z* tests and *t*-tests, if the obtained value is larger than the critical value, we conclude that there is statistical significance. In the present case, because the *F*-obtained value of 35.6137 is larger than 3.35 or 5.49, it is considered significant at both of these levels. Significance at an alpha of .01, however, is more desired than significance at the .05 level, so report the *F*-obtained significance at this more desirable level.

Differing somewhat from how significance was previously denoted, on an ANOVA summary table we report it significant using a "$p < .05$" or "$p < .01$" representation. Because the obtained value of 35.6139 is significant at the .01 alpha level, it is reported as such with a $p < .01$. What $p < .01$ tells us is that not only is our obtained value significant at the .01 level, but that the probability that a Type I Error has been committed is less than 1% (.01 chance). This step, Step 18, and the format in which it is reported in the ANOVA summary table are found below.

Table 11.3   ANOVA Summary Table for Duck Data

Source	SS	df	MS	F	p
Between	645	2	322.5	35.6137	p<.01
Within	244.5	27	9.0555		
TOTAL	889.5	29			

Step 18:   Determining F-critical value $= F$ crit.

(determined by alpha level and numerator and denominator = degrees of freedom)

F crit. $\frac{2(numerator\ df)}{27(denominator\ df)}$ $=$ alpha $.05 = F$ crit. $\frac{2}{27} = \boxed{3.35}$ and

alpha $.01 = F$ crit. $\frac{2}{27} = \boxed{5.49}$ with $35.6139 > 5.49$;
thus, it is reported in the table as $\boxed{p< .01}$ and statistically significant.

As a hypothetical aside, if the F-obtained value was 4 in the present example, how would we report this? Because this value is larger than 3.35 but less that 5.49, we would report this F-obtained to be significant at the .05 level; $p < .05$. Alternatively, if we had obtained an F-obtained value of 3, we would leave the table blank or simply write "not significant."

While an F-obtained of 35.6137 clearly shows that one or more of the means are significantly different, as noted at the beginning of this chapter, it doesn't tell which of the groups actually is different. In the terms of the data set, while we are sure that one or more of the treatments of acid and vinegar is causing the ducks to lose a significant number of feathers, we are not sure if this is in comparison to the control group, to each other, or to both.

Table 11.4   18 Steps for ANOVA Summarized

	Steps		
1.	−135	10.	244.5
2.	1497	11.	889.5
3.	−4.5	12.	2
4.	1210	13.	27
5.	40	14.	29
6.	2.5	15.	322.5
7.	1252.5	16.	9.0555
8.	607.5	17.	35.6137
9.	645	18.	p<.01

Although there is an array of appropriate statistical techniques that can be used to determine which groups are actually different, we now explore one of the simplest and widely used of these test: an LSD *t*-test.

Least-Significant-Difference (LSD) *t*-Test

To use an LSD test or an array of similar statistical tests, we must first obtain an *F* value that is significant at least at the .05 alpha level. (Although some researchers use an alpha level of .10, as previously noted, we always use the more common .05 alpha level as our minimum). In the analysis we are undertaking, not only is an *F*-obtained of 35.6137 significant at the .05 level, but it is also significant far beyond the .01 level. As such, it is obviously appropriate for us to undertake subsequent test to determine definitively which of the means is statistically different.

The actual formula used to make this determination, found below, should look quite familiar to you. In fact, the formula for the LSD *t*-test is nearly identical to a test we explored in Chapter 9: an independent-samples *t*-test. The only real difference between the two formulas is that we already know what the s^2 pooled value is using and LSD *t*-test, whereas for the independent samples *t*-test we had to calculate this value. As noted below, with an LSD *t*-test simply use the mean square within (*MSW*) value found in our previously constructed ANOVA summary tables as the s^2 pooled value.

Using the *MSW* value in calculations has one important advantage beyond the obvious (that we do not need to calculate this value separately). Since the *MSW* value is derived from the within df, the df used to determine the *t*-critical value (Appendix 3) is the same as the ANOVA within df. (Recall that the more df we have, the easier it is to find statistical significance.) For the present example, even though in any given LSD *t*-test a group of 10 is compared to another group of 10 (20 total), because the *MSW* value was determined using 27 within *df*, we use the more advantageous value of 27 *df*. Thus, offering a preset alpha level of .01 with 27 *df*, the corresponding *t*-critical value for the following *t*-tests is 2.771.

$$\text{LSD } t \text{ test} = \frac{\bar{x}_i - \bar{x}_j}{\sqrt{MSW\left(1/n_i + 1/n_j\right)}}$$

The reason an *i* and *j* subscript are listed on the means and the "*n*'s" of this formula is that when dealing with more than two means, there are obviously more than two groups to compare. Thus, we are instructed to undertake all possible tests, that is, *i* to *j* or from beginning to end. In the present example of three group means, there are three corresponding *t*-tests we can undertake: group 1 versus group 2, group 1 versus group 3, and group 2 versus group 3. To this end, the appropriate calculations for these three LSD *t*-tests are completed below. Please note the following four provisions as you review the calculations for an LSD *t*-test.

1. As the formula requires, we must calculate a separate mean value for each of the groups.

2. The *MSW* value is taken from the previously constructed ANOVA summary table, and in this case it is 9.0555.

3. In the actual calculations, algebraically when you minus a minus—subtract a negative value from another negative value—this is the same as adding it. Thus $(-11) - (-2) = -9$; if this is still confusing, think of it in terms of integers.

4. In cases such as the present one, where each of the group sizes is equal (10), once the denominator portion of the first calculation (1.3458) has been completed, we do not need to recalculate it for subsequent tests.

$$\bar{x} = (\Sigma X)/n \quad \text{or} \quad \begin{aligned} \bar{x}_1 &= -110/10 = \boxed{-11} \\ \bar{x}_2 &= -20/10 = \boxed{-2} \\ \bar{x}_3 &= 5/10 = \boxed{-.5} \end{aligned}$$

Step 1. The LSD t test for group 1 versus group 2 is:

$$\frac{-11-(-2)}{\sqrt{(9.0555)(.20)}} = \frac{-9}{1.3457} = \boxed{-6.6879}$$

t obtained $= |-6.6879| > 2.771 = \quad t$ critical. Thus, group 1 is statistically different from group 2 at the .01 alpha level.

Step 2. The LSD t test for group 1 versus group 3 is:

$$\frac{-11-(-.5)}{\sqrt{(9.0555)(.20)}} = \frac{-10.5}{1.3457} = \boxed{-7.8026}$$

t obtained $= |-7.8026| > 2.771 = \quad t$ critical. Thus, group 1 is statistically different from group 3 at the .01 alpha level.

Step 3. The LSD t test for group 2 versus group 3 is:

$$\frac{-2-(-.5)}{\sqrt{(9.0555)(.20)}} = \frac{-1.5}{1.3457} = \boxed{-1.1146}$$

t obtained $= |-1.1146| < 2.771 = \quad t$ critical. Thus, group 2 is NOT statistically different from group 3 at the .01 alpha level.

As indicated above, while group 2 is not statistically different from group 3, we can conclude that group 1 is significantly different from both group 2 and group 3. So, in reference to the original data set, what does this mean? Quite simply, the acid is causing the ducks in this treatment group to lose a statistically significant number of feathers in comparison to the ducks in the other treatment group and the control group. Vinegar, on the other hand, with this sample size does not appear to bring about a significant loss of feathers in comparison to the control group. Thus, if we are ducks concerned with keeping our feathers we should obviously avoid having acid poured off our backs!

Cartoon 11.2   FRANK & ERNEST

Reprinted by permission of Newspaper Enterprise Association, Inc.

Analyses Using ANOVA Summary Table

As noted, an alternative approach to undertaking ANOVA is to practice doing this type of analysis using just ANOVA summary tables. Approaching ANOVA in this manner is less time consuming because it entails far fewer calculations—only eight steps—than does our previous use of actual raw data and its accompanying eighteen steps. Further (like most statistical techniques), the more you do the actual ANOVA calculations, the more likely you are to understand what the statistical technique actually measures. We think that the last eight steps and what they measure, however, are the most critical to accomplishing this learning goal. As a result, the Practice Exercises section of this chapter reviews this alternative way of approaching ANOVA in detail in addition to providing several practice examples.

We next introduce Cartoon 11.2, and use our current research interests to gauge the success of different types of sex education classes. To this end, we draw a random sample of 48 research subjects and randomly assign them to four groups of 12. Three of the groups (the treatment groups) reflect different approaches to teaching sex education, whereas the members of the control group receive no instruction. A test is administered at the end of the semester with results that yield a sum of squares within value of 220 and a total SS value of 265; the SS-between value is unknown. This limited information is found in an incomplete ANOVA summary table (Table 11.5). Our task is to fill in all of the missing values.

Although there are several pieces of information that most of you could fill in immediately, it's important to discuss the table as an incremental, step-by-step procedure. As such, the first thing to determine is the missing SS-between value. To do this, subtract the SS-within

Table 11.5   Incomplete ANOVA Summary Table for Sex Education Data
                ($J = 4$; $N = 48$)

Source	SS	df	MS	F	p
Between					
Within	220				
TOTAL	265				

Table 11.6   Completed ANOVA Summary Table for Sex
Education Data ($J = 4$; $N = 48$)

Source	SS	df	MS	F	p
Between	45	3	15	3	$p<.05$
Within	220	44	5		
TOTAL	265	47			

from the total-SS to determine the missing value; in this case, $265 - 220 = 45$ SS between. Conversely, if only the SS-between and total-SS values are given, subtract the SS-between from the total to get the missing value. Finally, if just the SS-between and SS-within are listed, add these two values together to get the total-SS (for this example, $45 + 220 = 265$).

The remaining steps are discussed in the terms of Step 12 through Step 18 presented in the original ANOVA, and they should start to be somewhat automatic with practice. All the steps are briefly outlined and summarized below in a completed ANOVA summary table (Table 11.6).

Steps 12, 13, and 14 are used to ascertain the degrees of freedom found in three different applications. Step 12 requires a determination of the $J - 1$ = between df, or (for the present analysis) $4 - 1 = 3$ between df. The next step, 13, tells how many within df are present: $N - J$ = within df, or (for the present example) $48 - 4 = 44$ within df. Finally, Step 14 asks for the total df; $N - 1$ = total df, or $48 - 1 = 47$ total df.

Steps 15 and 16 have us determine two different mean-square values. Step 15 is the SS-between value divided by the df between, or (for this example) the MS-between = $45/3$ = 15. Similarly, Step 16 finds the SS-within divided by the df within, or (for this example) the MS-within = $220/44 = 5$.

The remaining steps result in an F-obtained value (Step 17) which is then compared to an F-critical value to determine if there is statistical significance (Step 18). The F-obtained value is derived by dividing the MSB by the MSW; or $15/5$ = an F-obtained value of 3. The F-critical values are found in Appendix 3 and are determined by the numerator and denominator df taken directly from the ANOVA summary table.

In this example, we have 3 numerator df and 44 denominator df; as such, the corresponding F-critical values are 2.82 (alpha = .05) and 4.26 (alpha = .01). Thus, with an F-obtained of 3, it is significant at the .05 level ($3 > 2.82$) but it is not significant at the .01 alpha level ($3 < 4.26$); as such, $p < .05$ is reported in the table below.

Reflecting on the ANOVA summary table, we can also conclude that one or more of the treatment groups and/or control group is significantly different from one or more of the other(s). We do not know the sum of X totals (e.g., $\Sigma X.1$) which would enable determination of group means for each of the groups, so we cannot do the subsequent LSD tests.

Table 11.7   Incomplete ANOVA Summary Table for
Sex Education Data ($J = 3$; $N = 30$)

Source	SS	df	MS	F	p
Between	260				
Within					
TOTAL	313.5				

Table 11.8   Completed ANOVA Summary Table for
Sex Education Data ($J = 3$; $N = 30$)

Source	SS	df	MS	F	p
Between	260 /	2	130	65.6101	p<.01
Within	53.5 /	27	1.9814		
TOTAL	313.5	29			

For the next example, which is also based upon the sex education cartoon (Cartoon 12.2), we now have three groups of 10, (30 randomly placed research subjects). The research question, similarly, is whether different types of sex education classes are more successful than others. The population from which the sample is drawn is ninth grade students at a local junior high school.

The subjects in group 1 receive traditional sex education instruction for the period of one semester and then are tested on the material. The subjects in group 2 receive traditional sex education and stork-theory instruction for the same period of one semester, and then are tested on the material. Members of group 3 are given no formal sex education instruction; they are simply tested (the control group). The actual test is a ten-item instrument and has scores ranging from 10 (100% correct) to 0 (0% correct).

As found in Table 11.7, for this example we know what the SS-between and the total-SS values are, and we also know what the sum of X totals are for each group: $\Sigma X.1 = 85$, $\Sigma X.2 = 35$, $\Sigma X.3 = 15$. If appropriate, our F-obtained is significant and knowing these values enables the completion of subsequent LSD t-tests.

Now that these operations are familiar to you, we have dropped the step-by-step format. If any of the current material becomes confusing, then you can refer to one of the previous examples. All of the operations are also found in a completed ANOVA summary table (Table 11.8). Note that there are three division symbols in the table where these operations are appropriately undertaken.

First, the missing *SS*-within value must be determined; so subtract the given *SS*-between value from the total *SS*, or 313.5 − 260 = 53.5. Next determine the *df* between (*J* − 1, or 3 − 1 = 2 *df* between), *df* within (*N* − *J*, or 30 − 3 = 27 *df* within), and total *df* (*N* − 1, or 30 − 1 = 29 total *df*). The derived between and within *df* values are then divided into their corresponding *SS* values to give the *MSB* and *MSW* values: *MS* between = *SS* between/between *df*, or 260/2 = 130; and *MS* within = *SS* within/within *df*, or 53.5/27 = 1.9814.

To get the *F*-obtained ratio value, simply divide the *MSB* value by the *MSW* value: *F*-obtained = *MSB/MSW*, or 130/1.9814 = 65.6101. The *F*-obtained value is then compared to two *F*-critical values (which are determined by using 2 numerator and 27 denominator *df*: alpha = . 05, *F* critical = 3.35; alpha = . 01, *F* critical = 5.49). Because the *F*-obtained value is larger than both of these critical values, report the answer statistically significant at the .01 alpha level; *p* < .01.

We know that two or more of the groups, in terms of scores on the 10-point test, are significantly different, but we do not know which one(s). To make this determination again use an LSD *t*-test. Of course, this is now possible because we know what the sum of X totals are for each group: $\Sigma X.1 = 85$, $\Sigma X.2 = 35$, $\Sigma X.3 = 15$. To assist in the calculations, the LSD *t*-test formula is replicated below:

$$\text{LSD } t \text{ Test} = \frac{\bar{x}_i - \bar{x}_j}{\sqrt{MSW\left(1/n_i + 1/n_j\right)}}$$

As the formula asks, we must first calculate mean values for each of the groups. The three mean values and the rest of the *t*-test calculations are all found below. The alpha levels are preset at .05 with 27 *df*; thus, the *t* critical = 2.052.

$$\bar{x} = (\Sigma X)/n \quad \text{or} \quad \begin{aligned} \bar{x}_1 &= 85/10 = \boxed{8.5} \\ \bar{x}_2 &= 35/10 = \boxed{3.5} \\ \bar{x}_3 &= 15/10 = \boxed{1.5} \end{aligned}$$

Step 1. The LSD *t* test for group 1 versus group 2 is:

$$\frac{8.5 - 3.5}{\sqrt{(1.9814)(.20)}} = \frac{5}{.6295} = \boxed{7.9428}$$

t obtained = 7.9428 > 2.052 = *t* critical. Thus, group 1 is statistically different from group 2 at the .05 alpha level.

Step 2. The LSD *t* test for group 1 versus group 3 is:

$$\frac{8.5 - 1.5}{\sqrt{(1.9814)(.20)}} = \frac{7}{.6295} = \boxed{11.1199}$$

t obtained = 11.1199 > 2.052 = *t* critical. Thus, group 1 is statistically different from group 3 at the .05 alpha level.

Step 3. The LSD *t* test for group 2 versus group 3 is:

$$\frac{3.5 - 1.5}{\sqrt{(1.9814)(.20)}} = \frac{2}{.6295} = \boxed{3.1771}$$

t obtained = 3.1771 > 2.052 = *t* critical. Thus, group 2 is statistically different from group 3 at the .05 alpha level.

Summarizing the calculations, we find that the 10 subjects that receive just traditional sex education instruction answered an average of 8.5 (or 85%) of the questions correctly. This is very much in contrast to the 3.5 (35%) average of the other treatment group and the 1.5 (15%) average of the control group. Not surprisingly, our LSD t-tests support this apparent difference; the scores for those who receive just traditional sex education (group 1) instruction are statistically different from those in groups 2 and 3. Further, those in the second treatment group who receive instruction in both traditional sex education and stork-theory teachings are found to score significantly higher than those in the control group.

Interpreting these findings in the context of the actual data set enables us to conclude that, while a mixture of both traditional sex education and stork-theory teachings (group 2) does bring about a significant increase in the number of questions answered correctly, such an approach makes no sense in light of the 85% correct response found for group 1. In other words, while the mixed approach of group 2 is better than nothing (as seen for group 3), providing students with only a traditional sex-education emphasis (group 1) leads to the best-informed students. Perhaps the disgruntled student in the cartoon can get stork-theory teachings elsewhere (for instance, where most of us get our sex education—from parents and peers).

Chapter Summary and Conclusions

This chapter explored the statistical technique of ANOVA. This technique was created for—and is largely used—in situations where three or more group means are to be compared. ANOVA enables us to make an initial determination of whether subsequent tests are to be undertaken. That is, while ANOVA tells if one or more of the group means is significantly different from one or more of the other group means, it does not tell which of the actual means may be different. To make this determination (but only when a significant F is obtained), there exists an array of different statistical tests that determine differences between group means. For our purposes, we explored a technique called an LSD t-test. This type of test, very similar to the independent-samples t-test presented in Chapter 9, enables us to determine which of the group means are or are not different from each other, and to make specific conclusions about the data sets from which they are calculated.

Key Terms to Remember

- Sum of Squares (SS) Between
- Sum of Squares (SS) Within
- Total Sum of Squares (SS)
- Between Degrees of Freedom (df)
- Within Degrees of Freedom (df)
- Total Degrees of Freedom (df)
- Mean Square Between (MSB)
- Mean Square Within (MSW)
- F-Obtained
- F Critical
- LSD t-Test
- ANOVA Summary Table

Practice Exercises

1. Using Cartoon 9.2 as a backdrop for the data found in Table 11.9, our current research interests are whether different types of sex education have an effect on correct responses given on a sex-education test (20 questions). The population we sample is 3 groups of 8 from our 9th grade students ($N = 24$). Respondents in group 1 are given traditional sex education, and then tested on the material. Respondents in group 2 are given traditional sex education combined with stork-theory teachings, and then tested on the material. Finally, respondents in group 3 (the control group) are given no education, and simply are tested.

   a. Using the 18 steps for undertaking ANOVA, construct an ANOVA summary table for this data set.

   b. Is there a significant difference between two (or more) of the groups? Why or why not?

Table 11.9   Sex Education Data

One-way ANOVA for Numbers of Sex Ed. Test Questions Correct

s#	Group 1 X.1	X.1^2	s#	Group 2 X.2	X.2^2	s#	Group 3 X.3	X.3^2
X11	18		X12	12		X13	7	
X21	14		X22	10		X23	6	
X31	11		X32	8		X33	7	
X41	13		X42	8		X43	8	
X51	14		X52	11		X53	5	
X61	16		X62	9		X63	6	
X71	20		X72	8		X73	7	
X81	14		X82	9		X83	9	
ΣX.1			ΣX.2			ΣX.3		
ΣX.1^2			ΣX.2^2			ΣX.3^2		
(n_1=8)			(n_2=8)			(n_3=8)		

(All for randomly selected respondents given a sex education test)
Group 1 = Traditional sex education.
Group 2 = Traditional sex education and stork-theory teachings
Group 3 = Control, given no treatment (no sex education)

2. Using the information determined above, calculate the t-test values comparing each group (3 t-tests). Also, indicate whether the obtained t values are significant at the 99% confidence level (alpha = .01).

3. Table 11.10 is an ANOVA summary table for two groups with 20 respondents in each ($N = 40$). Fill in all of the missing values. (Remember that, although ANOVA was created and is most often utilized in situations where three or more group means are present, it can be used to compare just two groups.)

Table 11.10   ANOVA Summary Table for Two Groups of 20

Source	SS	df	MS	F	p
Between					
Within	380				
TOTAL	410				

4. Following is an ANOVA summary table (Table 11.11) for four groups with 10 respondents in each ($N = 40$). Fill in the missing values.

Table 11.11   ANOVA Summary Table for Four Groups of 10

Source	SS	df	MS	F	p
Between	4,800				
Within					
TOTAL	19,200				

5. Following is an ANOVA table (Table 11.12) for three groups with 11 respondents in each ($N = 33$). Fill in the missing values.

Table 11.12   ANOVA Summary Table for Three Groups of 11

Source	SS	df	MS	F	p
Between					
Within	90				
TOTAL	132				

6. For Practice Exercise 5, say we are also given the following information.

$\bar{x}_1 = 22$; $\bar{x}_2 = 16.5$; $\bar{x}_3 = 11$

Using this combined information and the appropriate test (alpha = .05), determine whether there a significant difference between the groups.

12

Factorial Analysis of Variance: ANOVA with More than One Independent Variable

Chapter 11 explored the ANOVA technique for testing hypotheses when there are more than two groups. ANOVA enables one to determine whether group means are significantly different from one another, while reducing the overall risk of committing a Type I Error (which is saying that means are different, when in fact they are not). While the ANOVA is concerned with situations where there is one independent variable, the Factorial ANOVA deals with hypotheses involving more than one independent variable. We will limit discussion of factorial ANOVA to situations where there are two independent variables (often referred to as a Two-Way ANOVA). However, the procedures presented can be adapted to test more complex hypotheses involving more than two independent variables.

This chapter first outlines the logic and advantages of using factorial ANOVA procedures and distinguishes between the influence of independent variables examined in isolation (main effects) and the influence of independent variables when they are considered together (interaction effects). Then, using a nineteen-step procedure, the calculations for completing a two-way factorial ANOVA are presented.

Advantages and Assumptions of the Factorial ANOVA

The next time you get a chance, ask any of your instructors about the relationship between any single independent variable (IV) and a related dependent variable (DV); odds are, no matter what variables you pick, the answer will be "it depends." This is true for just about all relationships between variables in the social and behavioral sciences. Whether an IV has an effect on a DV almost always depends on a variety of factors. For example, the outcome may depend on who the participants are, what characteristics the participants have, where the study is being conducted, when the study is being conducted, and often even how and why the study is being conducted. As such, when researchers find new relationships between variables, the next step is to find out whether that relationship holds all of the time or whether it depends on any other factors, such as those just mentioned.

Assume, for example, that a researcher has tested the effect of watching either 4 hours of *South Park* episodes or 4 hours of television static (IV) on the number of Cheezy Poofs participants eat during a one-half-hour post-viewing period in the lab (DV). As you may know, *South Park* is a television cartoon featuring four boys, Stan, Kyle, Eric, and Kenny; one of them (Eric) has an unnatural attraction toward snack foods, especially Cheezy Poofs.

Evaluating the data, the researcher finds that the *South Park* group does eat a small but significantly larger amount of Cheezy Poofs (3.90) than the static group (2.40). The researcher also notices, however, that almost half of the participants in the non–*South Park* group ate a rather large number of Cheezy Poofs. Upon further inquiry, it turns out that one-half of all the subjects who participated in the study were of the opinion that *South Park* was the most offensive and morally reprehensible show on TV (they hated it). The other half either had no opinion or really liked the show. By splitting the original two groups (*South Park* and non–*South Park*) into four sub-groups, based on original group membership and *South Park* liking, an interesting pattern appears in the data.

Table 12.1 shows that people who watched *South Park* ate more Cheezy Poofs than those who did not (respective means are presented in the row labeled Column Means), and that people who hated *South Park* generally ate fewer Cheezy Poofs than people who liked it (respective means are presented in the column labeled Row Means).

By examining the group means in the column labeled Watched *South Park*, we can see that the sub-group of people who watched *South Park* and like the show ate many more Cheezy Poofs than the sub-group who watched *South Park* and hate the show, with respective means of 7.40 and 0.40. Further, by examining the group means presented in the column labeled Watched TV Static, we see that the people who watched static and like *South Park* ate more Cheezy Poofs than the sub-group that watched static and hate *South Park*, with respective means of 3.80 and 2.40.

Finally, the group means within the rows indicate that, while watching *South Park* increased the number of Cheezy Poofs eaten for people who like *South Park*, for the sub-group of individuals who hate *South Park*, watching *South Park* had the opposite effect. Those who hate the show and watched it ate fewer Cheezy Poofs compared to those who hated it and did not watch it. So, what can we say about whether watching *South Park* causes people to eat more Cheezy Poofs? Well, *it depends*. Specifically, it depends on whether the respondent likes *South Park*.

It is extremely important for researchers to be able to identify the "it depends" relationships when suspecting that they might exist. The preceding example presented a simple 2 x 2 (read: two-by-two) design, and we could use a series of *t*-tests to assess the differences between all of the possible sub-group means to find out if "it depends."

This example requires a total of six tests. Two are needed to separately compare the means for each independent variable—that is, we need a test to compare the means for the *South Park* and non–*South Park* groups, and a test to compare the Like *South Park*

Table 12.1   Number of Cheezy Poofs Eaten,
Separated by Viewing Condition and Attitude Toward *South Park*

	Watched South Park	*Watched Television Static*	*Row Means*
Like South Park	10	6	
	9	5	5.60
	8	3	($n=10$)
	6	3	
	4	2	
Group Means	7.40	3.80	
	($n=5$)	($n=5$)	
Hate South Park	1	2	
	1	2	0.70
	0	1	($n=10$)
	0	0	
	0	0	
Group Means	0.40	1.00	
	($n=5$)	($n=5$)	
Column Means	3.90	2.40	
	($n=10$)	($n=10$)	

and Hate *South Park* groups. It also requires four more tests to compare each of the viewing sub-groups at each level of the *South Park* attitudes variable (i.e., Watched *South Park* and Like it, Watched *South Park* and Hate it, etc.). As mentioned in Chapter 11, running such a large number of tests is problematic in that it inflates the likelihood that a Type I Error (saying two means are significantly different, when in fact they are not) would be committed.

After running six tests, each using the $p = .05$ alpha level, our true alpha level is 6(.05) = .30. That means, due to sampling error, every time we did a study like this there is a 30% chance that we will say our results are meaningful when in fact they are not. Further, if we had more groups, say 3 different TV-viewing groups (*South Park*, *Saved by the Bell*, and a no-TV control), then we would have 6 sub-groups and the number of required analyses for this 3 x 2 design would increase to 14, as would our potential for committing a Type I Error (14(.05)=.70).

Similarly, we could have more complex studies where we have 3 independent variables. For example, with a 2 x 2 x 2 design we have 2 independent variables, each with two groups (or levels), so we would have 8 sub-groups requiring 15 total tests. Obviously, we need a way to test the "it depends" hypothesis and still control Type I Error rates.

Like ANOVA, factorial ANOVA enables the testing of the relationships among a large number of means using fewer tests than otherwise would be required. More specifically, factorial ANOVA enables researchers to test whether the effects of one IV are moderated or influenced by the effects of another IV, while keeping the potential for committing Type I Errors to a minimum. Factorial ANOVA does this by lumping all the possible tests that could be done on the independent variable groups and their sub-group combinations into larger tests that are evaluated at the .05 alpha level. Unlike ANOVA, rather than giving a single overall statistic, factorial ANOVA gives three or more statistics, depending upon the number of IVs being considered.

This chapter only covers situations where there are two IVs, so there are only three statistics to consider. Of the statistics dealt with here, two of the F statistics really are simple One-Way ANOVAs for all practical purposes. The third F is slightly more complex in what it represents, but no more complicated to calculate. As you become familiar with factorial ANOVA, you probably will find that it is simply a logical extension of the ANOVA method you already know.

Main Effects

The first two statistics obtained from the two-way factorial ANOVA are usually referred to as *main effects*. Essentially main effects describe the relationship between a single IV and the DV. With respect to the *South Park* and Cheezy Poofs example, there are two main effects to consider: The main effect of TV viewing condition (4 hrs. of *South Park* vs. 4 hrs. of static) regardless of whether they like it, and the main effect of attitude toward *South Park* (like it vs. hate it) regardless of what they watched.

The main effects of the factorial ANOVA are nearly the same as the F obtained from the ANOVA procedure presented in Chapter 11. Recall that the F ratio is obtained by dividing up the total variance in the DV into two parts: (1) variance that is shared by the independent and dependent variable ($MS_{between}$) and (2) the variance that is left over (MS_{error}). F is obtained by dividing the $MS_{between}$ by the MS_{error}. This is exactly the way to obtain F for the main effects of the factorial ANOVA. When conducting the factorial ANOVA, however, we "chop up" (partition) the total variance for both IVs at the same time. This usually means that there is less leftover variance in the DV (error); making the denominator of the F ratio smaller and the overall F statistic larger.

Figure 12.1 consists of three diagrams representing the variability in a set of independent and dependent variables. Each circle represents the variance for that variable. Where circles overlap (the solid gray areas), shared variability is represented (i.e., $MS_{between}$). The area in the DV that is unshaded is the leftover portion, or error (MS_{error}). Part A and Part B of Figure 12.1 show how the variability is chopped up when assessing the relationship between each IV and the DV in isolation using two separate One-Way ANOVAs.

In each analysis, quite a bit of the variability in the DV is unaccounted for (or leftover). When both IVs are considered together (Part C), however, the amount of leftover variance in the DV is greatly reduced (the unshaded portion of the DV). This reduces the

Figure 12.1   Chopping the Variance for One-Way and Factorial ANOVA

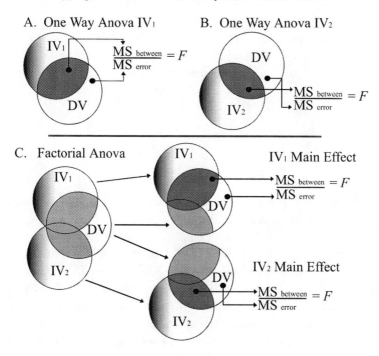

denominator of the F ratio and results in a larger F for each of the main effects. It does not always work out quite this well, but, as long as the IV's are not redundant, and both IV's are related to the DV, you should typically obtain larger main effect Fs using the factorial ANOVA, compared to the simpler one-way ANOVA procedure.

Interaction Effects

The last overall statistic obtained from the two-way factorial ANOVA is usually referred to as an *interaction effect*. Again, the interaction represents the combined influence two independent variables exert on the dependent variable. Specifically, it shows interactions when either the strength or direction of the relationship between an IV and DV depends on the value of the other IV. As in the case of the *South Park* and Cheezy Poofs example, whether watching *South Park* was associated with people eating more Cheezy Poofs depended upon whether they like *South Park*. This pattern of results suggests that there may be a significant interaction effect.

To know whether the interaction between two independent variables is meaningful the F ratio must be examined for the interaction effect. Like all F ratios, the interaction effect F is a ratio of shared variance to error variance. In this case, however, the shared variance of interest is the variability in the DV that is shared between both of the IVs. Figure 12.2

Figure 12.2   Chopping the Variance for the Interaction Effect

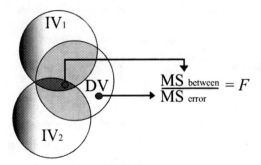

shows the interaction effect as the area where the two IVs overlap with one another within the area of the DV (the darkly shaded area).

After determining whether the interaction between two variables is meaningful (which requires a significance test that is covered later in this chapter), you then must interpret the effect. There are procedures for assessing differences between the group means at different levels of each of the IVs, which are not covered in this text, but there also are ways to quickly gain a more general understanding of what is happening with your data. One useful method is to look at the different sub-group means (as we did with our *South Park* and Cheezy Poofs example). These means give us a pretty good idea of what sort of influence each of our IVs was having on the DV, and enable us to see how the IVs were interacting with each other. However, we can make the interpretation of these effects easier simply by plotting the sub-group means in a line graph.

Figure 12.3 presents the graph of our *South Park* and Cheezy Poofs data, where each of the four sub-group means are plotted. Means connected by lines represent sub-groups with similar *South Park* attitudes. Means within columns (and not connected by lines) are sub-groups that were in the same TV viewing condition. The Y axis represents the dependent variable (the number of Cheezy Poofs eaten).

Figure 12.3   TV Condition and *South Park* Attitude Interaction

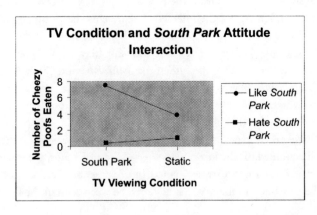

The graph of our sub-group means shows that people who liked *South Park* ate more Cheezy Poofs if they had just watched 4 hours of it than if they had just watched 4 hours of static (this is shown by the top line of the graph). There is an almost opposite pattern for people who hate *South Park,* although the effect is much less striking. This represents an interaction effect, because the two lines of the graph are not *parallel.* Any time the lines of these graphs meet or cross each other, or if extended beyond the graph they would meet at some point, then it is likely that you have a significant interaction effect.

To interpret the main effects for the data, we literally must read between the lines. First, we see that people who like *South Park* ate more Cheezy Poofs than people who do not like *South Park,* regardless of what they watched. We know this because the end points of the two lines in the graph generally are rather far apart. If the lines were very close together at both ends, then there is probably no main effect for that variable. For our data, the graph indicates a strong likelihood that the main effect for attitudes toward *South Park* is significant.

Comparing the data in the columns, we know that people who watched *South Park* ate more Cheezy Poofs than did people who watched *Saved by the Bell.* To see this, find the point within each column that falls between the two means represented in each column (i.e., the halfway point between the two points that are on the same side of the graph, but are not connected by a line). If the midpoints that located differ with respect to location on the Y axis, then it is likely that the main effect for that variable is significant. In our case, they are different but the difference is not large. This suggests that there may be a significant main effect for TV condition although it is probably small; and whether it will meet the .05 alpha cutoff will depend on the size of the sample.

When interpreting the results of a factorial ANOVA, it is important to remember that there will not always be significant main effects and interaction effects. One can exist without the other; in fact, it is possible for none of the main effects to be significant. Figure 12.4 on p. 222 presents eight basic combinations of possible effects.

- Graphs 1 through 4 demonstrate situations where the interaction effect is not significant. Notice that the lines in each graph are parallel to one another; they do not cross.
- Graphs 5 through 8 demonstrate significant interaction effects, and lines either cross or meet in each example.
- Graphs 1, 2, 5, and 7 demonstrate situations where the main effects for the second independent variable are not significant. Notice that in all cases the centers of each line are close together (1 & 2) or touching (5 & 7).
- Graphs 1, 3, 5, and 8 demonstrate situations where the main effects for the first independent variable are not significant. In each case, if you were to average the points in each column (the points that are not connected by lines) and compare them, averages would have nearly the same value with respect to the Y axis; they would be numerically equal.

Figure 12.4   Possible Types of Effects

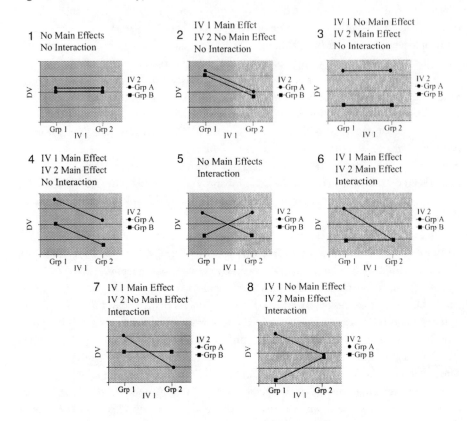

Please note that there are other ways that the means could be dispersed in the graph; however, all the other ways are simply variations on the eight patterns shown. If you do get a new pattern, simply apply what you know: (1) check to see if the lines are parallel, (2) read between the lines, and (3) read between the columns. These steps should help you know what to expect from any data set.

Two-Way ANOVA

Using the data from our Cheezy Poofs example, Table 12.2 is a data summary table that will help us perform the necessary calculations. Many of the symbols in this table are new, so let's review them. In the last chapter you were presented with the notation X_{ij}, where i = a specific person and j = a specific group of the independent variable (e.g., X_{12} = the first person in the second group).

The two-way factorial ANOVA uses an expanded form of this notation: X_{ijk}, where i = a specific person, j = a specific group for the first independent variable, and k = a spe-

Table 12.2   Cheezy Poofs Data Summary Table
2 x 2 Two-Way ANOVA Example
Number of Cheezy Poofs Eaten, Separated by
Viewing Condition and Attitude Toward *South Park*

(n = 20)				*Watched TV*		*Row*
		Watched South Park		*Static*		*Sums*
	s#	$X_{.11}$	$X^2_{.11}$	s#	$X_{.21}$	$X^2_{.21}$	
Like	X_{111}	10	.	X_{121}	6	.	
South	X_{211}	9	.	X_{221}	5	.	
Park	X_{311}	8	.	X_{321}	3	.	
	X_{411}	6	.	X_{421}	3	.	
	X_{511}	4	.	X_{521}	2	.	
		$\Sigma X_{.11}$.		$\Sigma X_{.21}$.		$\Sigma X_{.1}$.	
			$\Sigma X^2_{.11}$.		$\Sigma X^2_{.21}$.	$\Sigma X^2_{.1}$.	
	n$_{.11}$			**n**$_{.21}$		**n**$_{.1}$	
	s#	$X_{.12}$	$X^2_{.12}$	s#	$X_{.22}$	$X^2_{.22}$	
Hate	X_{112}	1	.	X_{122}	2	.	
South	X_{212}	1	.	X_{222}	2	.	
Park	X_{312}	0	.	X_{322}	1	.	
	X_{412}	0	.	X_{422}	0	.	
	X_{512}	0	.	X_{522}	0	.	
		$\Sigma X_{.12}$.		$\Sigma X_{.22}$.		$\Sigma X_{.2}$.	
			$\Sigma X^2_{.12}$.		$\Sigma X^2_{.22}$.	$\Sigma X^2_{.2}$.	
	n$_{.11}$			**n**$_{.22}$		**n**$_{.2}$	
Column	$\Sigma X_{.1.}$.			$\Sigma X_{.2.}$.		ΣX_{ijk} .	
Sums			$\Sigma X^2_{.1.}$.		$\Sigma X^2_{.2.}$.	ΣX^2_{ijk} .	
	n$_{.1.}$			**n**$_{.2.}$		**n**$_{ijk}$	

cific group for the second independent variable. For example, subject X_{311} watched *South Park*, reported liking *South Park*, and ate 8 Cheezy Poofs, while subject X_{422} watched static, reported hating *South Park*, and ate zero Cheezy Poofs. Based on this notation, the data for the people in the first group of IV1 (who watched *South Park*) and the first group of IV2 (who like *South Park*) are presented under the sub-group heading $X_{.11}$ (in the upper left-hand area of the table). Similarly $X_{.21}$, $X_{.12}$, and $X_{.22}$ represent the scores for the remaining 3 sub-groups. Returning to the upper left-hand part of the table, the column

---

Box 12.1   The Null Hypothesis for Factorial ANOVA

The null hypothesis and the research hypothesis in factorial ANOVA can be treated quite the same as they were for the One-Way ANOVA. That is, instead of statements of one mean being or not being equal, these potential relationships are stated in slightly different terms. When four or more group means, from two or more independent variables, are being compared, the null hypothesis states that none of the means is significantly different; all of them are statistically equal. Conversely, the research hypothesis holds that one or more of the means are statistically different, not equal.

If statistical significance is found for any of the effects in the factorial ANOVA, it shows that at least one mean is different from at least one other mean, but it does not tell us which means are significantly different. Follow-up tests like the LSD t-test and other related procedures help to determine which means are different from one another.

Both the null and research hypothesis for the Two-Way factorial ANOVA are mathematically represented below. Note that the subscripts on the means refer to the combinations of different groups for two independent variables with j and k levels each, and μ_{jk} refers to the final group.

Null Hypothesis

$H_0 : \mu_{11} = \mu_{12} = \ldots \mu_{jk}$

Research Hypothesis

$H_A :$ One or more group means are not equal

---

below $X^2_{.11}$ would be filled in with the appropriate squared value of each sub-group member's score for number of Cheezy Poofs eaten, as would $X^2_{.21}$, $X^2_{.12}$, and $X^2_{.22}$.

In addition to presenting the individual scores for each person within each sub-group, the table has spaces below each group's X_{jk} and X^2_{jk} columns where the sum of the observed values (ΣX_{jk}), the sum of squared values (ΣX^2_{jk}), and the number of subjects in each sub-group (n_{jk}) can be entered. Also, the very bottom row of the table (labeled Column Sums) has a place where the sum of the observed values ($\Sigma X_{.j.}$), the sum of the squared values for every member ($\Sigma X^2_{.j.}$), and the number of people ($n_{.j.}$) in of each group of IV 1 can be filled in separately.

For example, $\Sigma X_{.1.}$ includes the observed values for sub-groups X_{11} and X_{12}, and could be obtained by summing the values of ΣX_{11} and ΣX_{12}. The same holds true for $\Sigma X^2_{.1.}$ and $n_{.1.}$. The very last column of the table (labeled Row Sums) has space where the sum of each respondent's observed values ($\Sigma X_{..k}$), the sum of each respondent's squared values ($X^2_{..k}$), and number of people ($n_{..k}$) in each group of IV2 can be filled in separately. For example, $\Sigma X_{.2}$ includes the observed values for sub-groups $X_{.12}$ and $X_{.22}$. Again, this row sum could be obtained by summing the sub-group sums: $\Sigma X_{.12}$ and $\Sigma X_{.22}$. The same holds true for $\Sigma X^2_{.2}$ and $n_{..2}$.

Finally, in the last row of the last column of the table, there is space to fill in the sum of all the observed values (ΣX_{ijk} : referred to as the grand sum), the sum of all the squared values (ΣX^2_{ijk}), and the sample size (n_{ijk}) for everyone in the whole table. ΣX_{ijk} can be obtained by summing values across the bottom row ($\Sigma X_{.1.} + \Sigma X_{.2.}$) or down the

Table 12.3 Cheezy Poofs Completed Data Summary Table for 2 x 2 Two-Way Data ANOVA Revised Table with Squared and Summed Values Included

(n = 20)		Watched South Park			Watched TV Static		Row Sums
	s#	$X_{.11}$	$X^2_{.11}$	s#	$X_{.21}$	$X^2_{.21}$	
Like	X_{111}	10	100	X_{121}	6	36	
South	X_{211}	9	81	X_{221}	5	25	
Park	X_{311}	8	64	X_{321}	3	9	
	X_{411}	6	36	X_{421}	3	9	
	X_{511}	4	16	X_{521}	2	4	
	$\Sigma X_{.11}$ 37			$\Sigma X_{.21}$ 19			$\Sigma X_{.1}$ 56
		$\Sigma X^2_{.11}$ 297			$\Sigma X^2_{.21}$ 83		$\Sigma X^2_{.1}$ 380
	$n_{.11}$ 5			$n_{.21}$ 5			$n_{.1}$ 10
	s#	$X_{.12}$	$X^2_{.12}$	s#	$X_{.22}$	$X^2_{.22}$	
Hate	X_{112}	1	1	X_{122}	2	4	
South	X_{212}	1	1	X_{222}	2	4	
Park	X_{312}	0	0	X_{322}	1	1	
	X_{412}	0	0	X_{422}	0	0	
	X_{512}	0	0	X_{522}	0	0	
	$\Sigma X_{.12}$ 2			$\Sigma X_{.22}$ 5			$\Sigma X_{.2}$ 7
		$\Sigma X^2_{.12}$ 2			$\Sigma X^2_{.22}$ 9		$\Sigma X^2_{.2}$ 11
	$n_{.11}$ 5			$n_{.22}$ 5			$n_{.2}$ 10
Column Sums	$\Sigma X_{.1.}$ 39			$\Sigma X_{.2.}$ 24			ΣX_{ijk} 63
		$\Sigma X^2_{.1.}$ 299			$\Sigma X^2_{.2.}$ 92		ΣX^2_{ijk} 391
	$n_{.1.}$ 10			$n_{.2.}$ 10			n_{ijk} 20

last column $(\Sigma X_{..1} + \Sigma X_{..2})$. It is always best to check one against the other to try and catch any mistakes. ΣX^2_{ijk} and n_{ijk} also can be obtained in the same manner.

As noted earlier, this text treats the calculation of Two-Way ANOVA as a nineteen-step process; however, the steps themselves can be grouped into four parts. Part I focuses on completing the data summary table (Table 12.2). Part II presents procedures for finding the sums of squares (SS) for all the components of the factorial ANOVA. Part III includes the steps required to complete the factorial ANOVA summary tables and obtain the three F ratios (two main effects and the interaction effect). The goal of Part IV is completion of the significance tests for all three F ratios and interpretation of the results. For each step requiring calculations we first describe the procedure, then present the general formula that is applicable to any Two-Way ANOVA regardless of the number of groups, and finally we present the calculations based on the Cheezy Poofs example.

Part I: Complete the Data Summary Table

The first step has us find $\Sigma X_{.jk}$ and $\Sigma X^2_{.jk}$ for every sub-group in our data set. To find $\Sigma X_{.jk}$ we simply add together all of the observed values separately for each of our sub-groups. To find $\Sigma X^2_{.jk}$ we first must square all of the observed values, next enter them in the table, and then sum the squared values separately for each sub-group. These operations are completed in the revised data summary table (Table 12.3) and are mathematically represented and completed as follows.

Step 1.   Find:
$\Sigma X_{.jk}$ and $\Sigma X^2_{.jk}$
$\Sigma X_{.jk} = X_{1jk} + X_{2jk} + \ldots X_{ijk}$

Recall that this formula has us start with the first person in a given sub-group (X_{1jk}) and sum the scores until we get to the last person (person i) in that sub-group (X_{ijk}). Repeat this step for each sub-group.
$\Sigma X^2_{.jk} = X^2_{1jk} + X^2_{2jk} + \ldots X^2_{ijk}$
Similarly, this formula tells us to do the same as the above, but using the squared values instead.

For this example:
$\Sigma X_{.11} = 10 + 9 + 8 + 6 + 4 = 37$
$\Sigma X^2_{.11} = 10^2 + 9^2 + 8^2 + 6^2 + 4^2 = 100 + 81 + 64 + 36 + 16 = 297$
$\Sigma X_{.21} = 6 + 5 + 3 + 3 + 2 = 19$
$\Sigma X^2_{.11} = 6^2 + 5^2 + 3^2 + 3^2 + 2^2 = 36 + 25 + 9 + 9 + 4 = 83$
$\Sigma X_{.12} = 1 + 1 + 0 + 0 + 0 = 2$
$\Sigma X^2_{.12} = 1^2 + 1^2 + 0^2 + 0^2 + 0^2 = 1 + 1 + 0 + 0 + 0 = 2$
$\Sigma X_{.22} = 2 + 2 + 1 + 0 + 0 = 5$
$\Sigma X^2_{.12} = 2^2 + 2^2 + 1^2 + 0^2 + 0^2 = 4 + 4 + 1 + 0 + 0 = 9$

Step 2 requires us to find the separate group sums and squared sums for the first independent variable. For the current data set, IV1 (TV condition) has two groups, so we must obtain two sets of sums ($\Sigma X_{.1.}$, $\Sigma X^2_{.1.}$, $\Sigma X_{.2.}$, and $\Sigma X^2_{.2.}$). These can be obtained by summing all of the observed scores in the columns of the data summary table or by adding together the sub-group sums within the same columns. The completed operations for Step 2 are presented below and in the revised data summary table (Table 12.3).

Step 2.   Find:

$\Sigma X_{.j.}$ and $\Sigma X^2_{.j.}$

$\Sigma X_{.j.} = \Sigma X_{.j1} + \Sigma X_{.j2} + \ldots \Sigma X_{.jk}$ or $X_{1j1} + X_{2j1} + X_{3j1} + \ldots X_{ijk}$

$\Sigma X^2_{.j.} = \Sigma X^2_{.j1} + \Sigma X^2_{.j2} + \ldots \Sigma X^2_{.jk}$ or $X^2_{1j1} + X^2_{2j1} + X^2_{3j1} + \ldots X^2_{ijk}$

for this example:

$\Sigma X_{.1.} = \Sigma X_{.11} + \Sigma X_{.12} = 37 + 2 = 39$

$\Sigma X^2_{.1.} = \Sigma X^2_{.11} + \Sigma X^2_{.12} = 297 + 2 = 299$

$\Sigma X_{.2.} = \Sigma X_{.21} + \Sigma X_{.22} = 19 + 5 = 24$

$\Sigma X^2_{.2.} = \Sigma X^2_{.21} + \Sigma X^2_{.22} = 83 + 9 = 92$

Step 3 requires that we find the separate group sums and squared sums for the second independent variable. For our current data set, IV2 (attitude toward *South Park*) has two groups, so we must obtain two sets of sums ($\Sigma X_{..1}$, $\Sigma X^2_{..1}$, $\Sigma X_{..2}$, and $\Sigma X^2_{..2}$). These can be obtained by summing all of the observed scores in the rows of the data summary table or by adding together sub-group sums within the same rows. The completed operations for Step 3 are presented below and in the revised data summary table (Table 12.3).

Step 3.   Find:

$\Sigma X_{..k}$ and $\Sigma X^2_{..k}$

$\Sigma X_{..k} = \Sigma X_{.1k} + \Sigma X_{.2k} + \ldots \Sigma X_{.jk}$ or $X_{11k} + X_{21k} + X_{31k} + \ldots X_{ijk}$

$\Sigma X^2_{..k} = \Sigma X^2_{.1k} + \Sigma X^2_{.2k} + \ldots \Sigma X^2_{.jk}$ or $X^2_{11k} + X^2_{21k} + X^2_{31k} + \ldots X^2_{ijk}$

for this example:

$\Sigma X_{..1} = \Sigma X_{.11} + \Sigma X_{.21} = 37 + 19 = 56$

$\Sigma X^2_{..1} = \Sigma X^2_{.11} + \Sigma X^2_{.21} = 297 + 83 = 380$

$\Sigma X_{..2} = \Sigma X_{.12} + \Sigma X_{.22} = 2 + 5 = 7$

$\Sigma X^2_{..2} = \Sigma X^2_{.12} + \Sigma X^2_{.22} = 2 + 9 = 11$

In step four we must find the sizes for all four sub-groups separately and the sizes of each of the groups for each IV. For our present data, IV1 and IV2 each have two groups giving us four sub-groups. Thus, we need four sub-group sizes ($n_{.11}$, $n_{.21}$, $n_{.12}$, and $n_{.22}$) and the sizes of each of the groups for IV1 and IV2 ($n_{.1.}$, $n_{.2.}$, $n_{..1}$, and $n_{..2}$, respectively). To obtain each of the sub-group sizes, simply count the number of people in each of the four sub-groups. To find the size of each group for each IV, either count the total number of people in each group of each IV, or add the sub-group sizes in the appropriate columns or rows. The completed operations for this step are presented below and in the revised data summary table (Table 12.3).

Step 4.   Find:

$n_{.jk}$, $n_{.j.}$, and $n_{..k}$

$n_{.j.} = n_{.j1} + n_{.j2} + \ldots n_{.jk}$

$n_{..k} = n_{.1k} + n_{.2k} + \ldots n_{.jk}$

for this example:

$n_{.11} = 5$

$n_{.21} = 5$

$n_{.12} = 5$

$n_{.22} = 5$

$n_{.1.} = n_{.11} + n_{.12} = 5 + 5 = 10$

$n_{.2.} = n_{.21} + n_{.22} = 5 + 5 = 10$

$n_{..1} = n_{.11} + n_{.21} = 5 + 5 = 10$

$n_{..2} = n_{.12} + n_{.22} = 5 + 5 = 10$

This may seem rather repetitive as all the numbers are the same, but in situations where you have different sub-group sizes, these procedures are quite useful.

Step 5 instructs us to find the grand sum (ΣX_{ijk}) that represents the total of all subjects' scores. This value can be easily found by either summing the observed score (X_{ijk}) for every person in the whole data set, summing the sum of every sub-group ($\Sigma X_{.jk}$), summing across the final row ($\Sigma X_{.j.}$) of the data summary table, or summing down the final column ($\Sigma X_{..k}$) of the data summary table. We suggest using the latter two methods and comparing the answers resulting from each. The results should be the same. If they are different, then you know there is a mistake somewhere in the previous summations. The completed operations for this step are presented below and in the revised data summary table 12.3 on p. 225.

Step 5.   Find: ΣX_{ijk}

$\Sigma X_{ijk} = (\Sigma X_{.11} + \Sigma X_{.21} + \ldots \Sigma X_{.jk})$ or $(\Sigma X_{.1.} + \Sigma X_{.2.} + \ldots \Sigma X_{.j.})$ or $(\Sigma X_{..1} + \Sigma X_{..2} + \ldots \Sigma X_{..k})$

for this example:

$\Sigma X_{ijk} = \Sigma X_{.1.} + \Sigma X_{.2.} = 39 + 24 = 63$

or

$\Sigma X_{ijk} = \Sigma X_{..1} + \Sigma X_{..2} = 56 + 7 = 63$

Step 6 has us find the sum of the squared observed scores for the entire data set (ΣX^2_{ijk}). We do this by either summing the squared observed score (X^2_{ijk}) for every person in the whole data set, summing the sum of every sub-group (ΣX^2_{jk}), summing across the final row ($\Sigma X^2_{.j.}$) of the data summary table, or summing down the final column ($\Sigma X^2_{..k}$) of the data summary table. Again we suggest that you use the latter two methods and compare the answers resulting from each. The results should be the same. If they are different, then you know you have made a mistake somewhere in your previous summations. The completed operations for this step are presented below and in the revised data summary table 12.3 on p. 225.

Step 6.   Find: ΣX^2_{ijk}

$$\Sigma X^2_{ijk} = (\Sigma X^2_{.11} + x^2_{.21} + \ldots x^2_{ijk}) \text{ or } (\Sigma X^2_{.1.} + x^2_{.2.} + \ldots x^2_{.j.}) \text{ or } (\Sigma X^2_{..1} + x^2_{..2} + \ldots x^2_{..k})$$

for this example:

$$\Sigma X^2_{ijk} = \Sigma X^2_{.1.} + \Sigma X^2_{.2.} = 299 + 92 = 391$$
or
$$\Sigma X^2_{ijk} = \Sigma X^2_{..1} + \Sigma X^2_{..2} = 380 + 11 = 391$$

Step 7, the final step in Part I, has us find the total sample size (n_{ijk}). This value can be obtained several ways. You can either count all the subjects, add the individual sub-group sizes (n_{jk}), add the group sizes listed in the final row ($n_{.j.}$) of the data summary table, or add the individual group sizes listed in the final column ($n_{..k}$) of the data summary table. The completed operations for this step are presented below and in the revised data summary table (Table 12.3).

Step 7.   Find: n_{ijk}

$$n_{ijk} = (n_{.11} + n_{.21} + \ldots n_{ijk}) \text{ or } (n_{.1.} + n_{.2.} + \ldots n_{.j.}) \text{ or } (n_{..1} + n_{..2} + \ldots n_{..k})$$

for this example:

$$n_{ijk} = n_{.11} + n_{.21} + n_{.12} + n_{.22} = 5 + 5 + 5 + 5 = 20$$
or
$$n_{ijk} = n_{.1.} + n_{.2.} = 10 + 10 = 20$$
or
$$n_{ijk} = n_{..1} + n_{..2} = 10 + 10 = 20$$

Part II: Finding the Sums of Squares (SS)

As you remember from Chapter 11, the sums of squares are simply different parts of the variance in the dependent variable. We have already discussed how the factorial ANOVA chops the variance of the DV into more parts than the One-Way ANOVA does. As such, there are more sums of squares to find here than in Chapter 11. Specifically we will need to find six different sums of squares, but only four of them will be used in the calculation of the final F ratios.

Step 8 instructs us to compute the squared Grand Sum of scores divided by the total sample size, a value that is used in almost all of the sums of squares formulas presented here. This formula should be familiar to you, as it is essentially the second half of the numerator of the variance formula. Here we find the grand sum of the observed scores (ΣX_{ijk}, obtained in Step 5), square that sum, and divide it by the total sample size (n_{ijk}: Obtained in step 7). The completed operations for this step are presented below.

Step 8.   Find: $\dfrac{\left(\Sigma X_{ijk}\right)^2}{n_{ijk}}$

for this example:

$$\frac{\left(\Sigma X_{ijk}\right)^2}{n_{ijk}} = \frac{(step5)^2}{step7} = \frac{(63)^2}{20} = \frac{(3969)}{20} = \boxed{198.45}$$

In Step 9 we must compute the total sums of squares (SS_{tot}), which represents the total amount of variability in the scores for the dependent variable. The SS_{tot} is not directly used in calculating any of the F ratios for a factorial ANOVA, but it is necessary to know the SS_{tot} to find the other sums of squares, especially the SS_{error}. The formula for SS_{tot} should look familiar, as it is the numerator of the formula for variance. These calculations instruct us to (1) find the sum of the squared scores for all subjects (completed in Step 6) and (2) subtract the product of the squared sum of all subjects' scores divided by the total sample size (completed in Step 8). The completed operations for this step are presented below.

Step 9.   Find: $SS_{TOT} = \Sigma X_{ijk}^2 - \dfrac{\left(\Sigma X_{ijk}\right)^2}{n_{ijk}}$

for this example:

$$SS_{TOT} = \Sigma X_{ijk}^2 - \frac{\left(\Sigma X_{ijk}\right)^2}{n_{ijk}} = (step6) - (step8) = 391 - 198.45 = \boxed{192.55}$$

Step 10 instructs us to find the Sums of Squares for the first independent variable (SS_{IV1}), which is the variability in the DV that is shared with IV1. This step requires us to take the column sums of the observed scores for each of our IV1 groups

($\Sigma\mathbf{X}_{.j.}$: obtained in Step 2), square these values, divide them by the respective number of people in each IV1 group ($n_{.j.}$: obtained in Step 4), and sum these products across the groups of IV1. From this value we are instructed to subtract the value we obtained in Step 8. The completed operations for this step are presented below.

Step 10. Find:

$$SS_{IV1} = \Sigma\left(\frac{\left(\Sigma X_{.j.}\right)^2}{n_{.j.}}\right) - \frac{\left(\Sigma X_{ijk}\right)^2}{n_{ijk}} = \left(\frac{\left(\Sigma X_{.1.}\right)^2}{n_{.1.}} + \frac{\left(\Sigma X_{.2.}\right)^2}{n_{.2.}} + ... \frac{\left(\Sigma X_{.j.}\right)^2}{n_{.j.}}\right) - \frac{\left(\Sigma X_{ijk}\right)^2}{n_{ijk}}$$

for this example:

$$SS_{IV1} = \left(\frac{\left(\Sigma X_{.1.}\right)^2}{n_{.1.}} + \frac{\left(\Sigma X_{.2.}\right)^2}{n_{.2.}}\right) - Step8 = \left(\frac{(39)^2}{10} + \frac{(24)^2}{10}\right) - 198.45 =$$

$$\left(\frac{1521}{10} + \frac{576}{10}\right) - 198.45 = (152.1 + 57.6) - 198.45 = 209.7 - 198.45 = \boxed{11.25}$$

In Step 11 we find the sums of squares for the second independent variable (SS_{IV2}), which is the variability in the DV that is shared with IV2. This step requires us to take the column sums of the observed scores for each of our IV2 groups ($\Sigma\mathbf{X}_{..k}$, obtained in Step 3), square these values, divide them by the respective number of people in each IV1 group ($n_{..k}$, obtained in Step 4), and sum these products across the groups of IV2. From this value we are instructed to subtract the value obtained in Step 8. The completed operations for this step are presented below.

Step 11. Find:

$$SS_{IV2} = \Sigma\left(\frac{\left(\Sigma X_{..k}\right)^2}{n_{..k}}\right) - \frac{\left(\Sigma X_{ijk}\right)^2}{n_{ijk}} = \left(\frac{\left(\Sigma X_{..1}\right)^2}{n_{..1}} + \frac{\left(\Sigma X_{..2}\right)^2}{n_{..2}} + ... \frac{\left(\Sigma X_{..k}\right)^2}{n_{..k}}\right) - \frac{\left(\Sigma X_{ijk}\right)^2}{n_{ijk}}$$

for this example:

$$SS_{IV2} = \left(\frac{\left(\Sigma X_{..1}\right)^2}{n_{..1}} + \frac{\left(\Sigma X_{..2}\right)^2}{n_{..2}}\right) - Step8 = \left(\frac{(56)^2}{10} + \frac{(7)^2}{10}\right) - 198.45 =$$

$$\left(\frac{3136}{10} + \frac{49}{10}\right) - 198.45 = (313.6 + 4.9) - 198.45 = 318.5 - 198.45 = \boxed{120.05}$$

Step 12 may look quite similar to the previous two steps, but it provides an estimate of the total amount of variance shared between the DV and the two IVs. Like the SS_{tot}, the sums of squares between total (SS_{BTWTOT}) is not directly used to compute any of the F ratios, but it necessary for finding the variance attributable to the interaction between the two independent variables.

To find the SS_{BTWTOT} we must find the sum of each of the four sub-groups ($\Sigma X_{.jk}$, obtained in Step 1), square each sub-group sum, divide each squared sub-group sum by its respective sub-group size ($n_{.jk}$, obtained in Step 4), and from this value subtract the values obtained in Step 8. The completed operations for this step are presented below.

Step 12.   Find:

$$SS_{BTWTOT} = \Sigma\left(\frac{\left(\Sigma X_{.jk}\right)^2}{n_{.jk}}\right) - \frac{\left(\Sigma X_{ijk}\right)^2}{n_{ijk}} = \left(\frac{\left(\Sigma X_{.11}\right)^2}{n_{.11}} + \frac{\left(\Sigma X_{.21}\right)^2}{n_{.21}} +... \frac{\left(\Sigma X_{.jk}\right)^2}{n_{.jk}}\right) - \frac{\left(\Sigma X_{ijk}\right)^2}{n_{ijk}}$$

for this example:

$$SS_{BTWTOT} = \left(\frac{\left(\Sigma X_{.11}\right)^2}{n_{.11}} + \frac{\left(\Sigma X_{.21}\right)^2}{n_{.21}} + \frac{\left(\Sigma X_{.12}\right)^2}{n_{.12}} + \frac{\left(\Sigma X_{.22}\right)^2}{n_{.22}}\right) - Step8 =$$

$$\left(\frac{(37)^2}{5} + \frac{(19)^2}{5} + \frac{(2)^2}{5} + \frac{(5)^2}{5}\right) - 198.45 = \left(\frac{1369}{5} + \frac{361}{5} + \frac{4}{5} + \frac{25}{5}\right) - 198.45 =$$

$$(273.8 + 72.2 + .8 + 5) - 198.45 = 351.8 - 198.45 = \boxed{153.35}$$

In Step 13, we utilize the value obtained from the previous three steps, and find the sums of squares for the interaction effect (SS_{1x2}). Recall that the interaction effect represents the joint effect of the two independent variables, and that we are interested in the part of the variance that is shared with the DV, beyond the main effects for each variable. We can identify the SS_{1x2} by subtracting the sums of squares for the main effects of the two IVs (SS_{IV1} & SS_{IV2}) from the total amount variance shared between the DV and the two IVs (SS_{BTWTOT}). The completed operations for this step are presented below.

Step 13.   Find: $SS_{1x2} = SS_{BTWTOT} - SS_{IV1} - SS_{IV2}$

for this example:
SS_{1x2} = Step 12 − Step 11 − Step 10 = 153.35 − 120.05 − 11.25 = $\boxed{22.05}$

Step 14, the last step in Part II, requires us to find the variance that is left over, and attributable to error (SS_{ERROR}). This is really the same as the sums of squares within groups obtained from the One-Way ANOVA procedures. The SS_{ERROR} can easily be obtained using the sums of squares values already computed. Specifically, because we know the total variance in the DV (SS_{TOT}; Step 9) and we know the total amount of variance shared between the DV and IVs (SS_{BTWTOT}), then subtracting SS_{BTWTOT} from the SS_{TOT} will leave the SS_{ERROR}. The completed operations for this step are presented below.

Step 14. Find: $SS_{ERROR} = SS_{TOT} - SS_{BTWTOT}$

for this example:

SS_{ERROR} = Step 9 – Step 12 = 192.55 – 153.35 = $\boxed{39.2}$

Part III: Filling in the Factorial ANOVA Summary Table

Now that we have obtained all of the required sums of squares, we can begin to fill in the factorial ANOVA summary table, like the one presented in Table 12.4, with the ultimate goal of obtaining the relevant F ratios. In the case of the Two-Way ANOVA, we are concerned with obtaining two Fs for the main effects and an F for the interaction effect. As a note, we have listed Step 19 in Table 12.4, and it is considered part of the ANOVA summary table. However, we will not discuss step 19 until we present Part IV, which presents the procedures for testing the significance of the F ratios and how to interpret the results. As you become more proficient in completing the factorial ANOVA summary tables, all of these steps will become quite automatic. However, as in Chapter 11, the first few examples explicitly list all of the steps.

Step 15 has us fill in the first column of the factorial ANOVA summary table with the appropriate sums of squares. The first column of Table 12.5 (labeled SS) lists the previ-

Table 12.4   Factorial ANOVA Summary Table

	Step 15	Step 16	Step 17	Step 18	Step 19
	SS	df	MS	F	p
Main Effects					
IV1	Step 10	$j - 1$	SS_{IV1}/df_{IV1}	MS_{IV1}/MS_{ERROR}	--
IV2	Step 11	$k - 1$	SS_{IV2}/df_{IV2}	MS_{IV2}/MS_{ERROR}	--
Interaction					
1x2	Step 13	$(j-1)(k-1)$	SS_{1x2}/df_{1x2}	MS_{1x2}/MS_{ERROR}	--
ERROR	Step 14	$n_{ijk} - jk$	SS_{ERROR}/df_{ERROR}		
TOTAL	Step 9	$n_{ijk} - 1$			

Table 12.5   Cheezy Poofs Data: Intermediate Steps for Completing the Factorial ANOVA Summary Table

	Step 15	Step 16	Step 17	Step 18
	SS	df	MS	F
Main Effects				
IV1	Step 10	j - 1	SS_{IV1}/df_{IV1}	MS_{IV1}/MS_{ERROR}
	11.25	2 - 1 = 1	11.25/1 = 11.25	11.25/2.45 = 4.5918
IV2	Step 11	k - 1	SS_{IV2}/df_{IV2}	MS_{IV2}/MS_{ERROR}
	120.05	2 - 1 = 1	120.05/1 = 120.05	120.05/2.45 = 49.000
Interaction				
1 x 2	Step 13	$(j-1)(k-1)$	SS_{1x2}/df_{1x2}	MS_{1x2}/MS_{ERROR}
	22.05	(2-1)(2-1) = 1	22.05/1 = 22.05	22.05/2.45 = 9.000
ERROR	Step 14	n_{ijk} - jk	SS_{ERROR}/df_{ERROR}	
	39.20	20-(2)(2) = 16	39.20/16 = 2.45	
TOTAL	Step 9	n_{ijk} -1		
	192.55	20 - 1 = 19		

ous steps where each of the required sums of squares is obtained, and below each step the actual value for each sum of squares for the example is presented. Column one of Table 12.6 shows the appropriate sums of squares, obtained in our Cheezy Poofs example, entered into the completed factorial ANOVA summary table.

Step 16 requires that we find the degrees of freedom for each of the relevant parts of the factorial ANOVA. The second column of Table 12.5 presents procedures for finding each df. For the main effect of IV1, the df is obtained by subtracting 1 from the number of groups contained in IV1. This is represented in the formula $j-1$, where j indicates the number of groups in IV1. In our example, $j = 2$, because we have two groups, one that watched *South Park* and one that watched TV static. Thus, the df_{IV1} is $2 - 1 = 1$. Table 12.6 has this value in the first row of column two. The df for the main effect of IV2 also can be found by subtracting one from the number of groups contained in IV2, and is represented by the formula $k-1$, where k represents the number of groups in IV2. In our example, $k = 2$, because we have two groups of participants, one that likes *South Park* and one that hates *South Park*. Thus, df_{IV2} is $2-1 = 1$. This value is entered in the second row and second column of Table 12.6.

To obtain the degrees of freedom for the interaction term requires a different approach. Here we must multiply the df for each of the main effects together. This is represented by the formula $(j-1)(k-1)$, where j is the number of groups for IV 1 and k is the

Table 12.6   Cheezy Poofs Data: Complete Factorial ANOVA Summary Table

	SS	df	MS	F	p
Main Effects					
IV1	11.25	1	11.25	4.5918	$p < .05$
IV2	120.05	1	120.05	49.0000	$p < .01$
Interaction					
1 x 2	22.05	1	22.05	9.0000	$p < .01$
ERROR	39.20	16	2.45		
TOTAL	192.55	19			

number of groups for IV2. For our example, $j = 2$ and $k = 2$. Thus, $df_{1 \times 2}$ is $(2–1)(2–1) = 1$. This value is entered in the third row and second column of Table 12.6.

Although the next df on the factorial ANOVA summary table is for the error term, it clarifies where the df_{ERROR} comes from to first cover the total degrees of freedom. As in the One-Way ANOVA, we obtain the total degrees of freedom (df_{TOTAL}) by subtracting one from the total sample size (n_{ijk}, obtained in Step 7). Our example has 20 subjects, so $df_{TOTAL} = n_{ijk} – 1 = 20 – 1 = 19$. This value is entered in the last row of column two in Table 12.6. We presented this procedure first because, as indicated previously, an ANOVA error represents what is leftover. Thus, if we know the total degrees of freedom, and we know the degrees of freedom for the main effects and the interaction effects, then finding the difference between the degrees of freedom for the effects and the total should give us the degrees of freedom for the error. Thus: $df_{ERROR} = df_{TOTAL} – df_{IV1} – df_{IV2} – df_{1 \times 2}$.

Our current example has $df_{ERROR} = 19 – 1 – 1 – 1 = 16$, which is consistent with what is in the next-to-last row of column two in Table 12.6. However, this can be simplified somewhat by using the df_{ERROR} formula presented in Table 12.5: $df_{ERROR} = n_{ijk} – jk$. This formula instructs us to multiply the number of groups for IV1 by the number of groups for IV2 and subtract that product from the total number of people in the sample. For our example df_{ERROR} is $(20 -(2)(2)) = (20 – 4) = 16$. As shown, either procedure gives the same answer for df_{ERROR}. You can use whichever you find most comfortable or easiest to remember.

Step 17 has us find the mean square (MS) for each part of the factorial ANOVA. As in the One-Way ANOVA, the MS is simply the amount of variance averaged across the respective degrees of freedom. That is, we divide each sum of squares by the degrees of freedom listed in its row. Column three of Table 12.5 presents the components for each MS value for the main effects, the interaction effect, and the error term, respectively. Also, below each formula examples of the calculations are provided for the Cheezy Poofs data. Again, like One-Way ANOVA, there is no need to find the MS for the total row (if you did, however, you would simply have computed the sample variance (s^2) for the dependent variable). In our example, because each of the main effects and the interaction effect have *df*s of 1, the *MS* is the same as the *SS*. This can be seen by comparing the values in the first three rows of column 3 with their respective values in column 1 in Table 12.6.

With respect to the *MS* for the error term (MS_{ERROR}, obtained from the following computations: $SS_{ERROR}/df_{ERROR} = 39.20/16 = 2.45$), notice that the larger degrees of freedom (compared to the *df*s for the main effects and the interaction effect) have greatly reduced the value of MS_{ERROR}, compared to the SS_{ERROR} and the other *MS* values. For a researcher who wants to find significant effects (i.e., a large and significant *F* ratio), it is best when the MS_{ERROR} is small, relative to the other *MS* values. For our data, the MS_{ERROR} is about one-fifth as large as the smallest of all the other *MS* values. Thus, it is quite likely that all of our effects will be significant although, ultimately, sample size and the number of groups must be considered in the determination of significance.

Now that we have the *MS* values, Step 18 instructs us to find the *F* ratios for the main effects and the interaction effect. Again, like One-Way ANOVA, each *F* is simply the ratio of the *MS* for the respective effect divided by the MS_{ERROR} for the sample. Column four of Table 12.5 presents the computations for each of the *F* ratios. Note that each *F* ratio uses the same MS_{ERROR} in the denominator—this value does not change from *F* to *F*, although the numerator does. For our example, the numerator of the *F* for each effect (main and interaction) is 2.45. The final *F* values are in row four of Table 12.6, but these values mean little by themselves. We still must determine whether they are significant. As a general rule of thumb, however, when you have at least 10 subjects, *F*s of 5.12 or larger will be significant. Looking at our example, we can speculate that most of our effects may be significant, but it is a close call for the main effect of IV1.

Part IV: Testing the Significance and Interpreting the F Ratios

Now that we have found the *F*s for the main effects and the interaction effect, we must determine which effects, if any, are significant. We also must be able to interpret the results of any significant effects. This section first presents an overview of significance testing (Step 19), followed by a brief discussion of interpreting significant main effects and interactions.

Step 19 is the final formal step of the factorial ANOVA procedure. Fortunately, the significance testing procedures we learned for One-Way ANOVA can be directly applied to the factorial ANOVA procedure. In this case, the significance of each *F* must be tested separately. As in Chapter 11, we rely on the Table of Critical Values of *F* presented in Appendix 3. Listed at the top of each of the tables in Appendix 3 is an explanation that the first-row values are for the .05 alpha level and the second-row values are for the .01 alpha levels. Within the actual tables are column headings for the numerator and degrees of freedom (the *df* for either the main effects or the interaction effect) and row headings for the denominator degrees of freedom (the df_{ERROR}). Recall that these *df*s are values obtained in Step 16, and are listed in column two of the factorial ANOVA summary table.

For each significance test performed, the *df* of the numerator depends upon which effect's *F*-obtained you are testing. The *df* of the denominator (df_{ERROR}) will be the same, however, regardless of which *F*-obtained is being tested. For our example, because we only had two groups for each independent variable, the *df* for the numerator is 1 for each of the main effect and interaction effect *F*s. The *df* of the denominator for each *F* is 16. Thus, the critical value for all three significance tests will be the same. Looking at 1 and 16 degrees of freedom in Appendix 3 we get *F*-critical values of 4.49 and 8.53 for the .05 and .01 alpha levels, respectively.

As with all of the significance testing done thus far, we will compare the *F*-obtained with the *F*-critical to determine whether, given the number of groups and subjects we have, the *F*-obtained is large enough for us to be at least 95% confident that differences between our groups did not occur by chance alone. If the *F*-obtained is larger than the *F*-critical at the .05 alpha level, then we can conclude that the group differences meet the minimal criterion for significance.

For our present example, all of the *F*-obtained values are greater than the *F*-critical (4.49) for 1 and 16 degrees of freedom at the .05 alpha level, so we know that both main effects and the interaction effect for our Cheezy Poofs data are significant at least at the .05 alpha level. With respect to significance at the more desirable .01 alpha level, only two of the *F*-obtained values exceed the *F*-critical (8.53) for 1 and 16 degrees of freedom at the .01 alpha level. While it is significant at the .05 level, the main effect for IV1 (TV viewing condition) is not significant at the .01 level. However, both the main effect for IV2 (attitude toward *South Park*) and the interaction between IV1 and IV2 is significant at the .01 alpha level and are reported as such in the factorial ANOVA summary table. The last column of Table 12.6 presents the significance levels for each of the effects. Notice that the most desirable level (lowest alpha level) of significance obtained for each effect is reported in the table.

Now that we know which of our effects are significant, it becomes necessary to interpret these results. Interpreting a significant main effect is no different from interpreting a significant One-Way ANOVA. It's a matter of looking at the group means of the independent variable to get an idea of what is going on.

In our example, the main effect for IV1 (TV viewing condition) was significant, and the *South Park* and Static groups had means of 3.9 and 2.4 (obtained from Table 12.1), respectively. This shows that people who watched four hours of *South Park* ate a small but significantly larger number of Cheezy Poofs during a thirty-minute post-viewing session, compared to participants who watched four hours of static. Similarly, the main effect for IV2 (attitude toward *South Park*) was also significant, and the Like *South Park* and Hate *South Park* groups had means of 5.6 and .7, respectively.

In this example, the interpretation is aided by the fact that we only have two groups in each variable. When the IVs with significant main effects have more than two groups, the LSD tests (or other related tests) must be performed to find which group means are significantly different. The example in the next section demonstrates the use of LSD *t*-tests with factorial ANOVA.

When it comes to interpreting significant interaction effects, you are encouraged to plot the sub-group means in a line graph, as shown in Figure 12.3. When describing the results of an interaction, it is best to first describe the overall pattern of results, and then describe the relationship between the sub-group means in each row and each column separately.

For example, we found that the relationship between watching *South Park* and eating Cheezy Poofs depends on whether someone likes the show. Specifically, for people who like *South Park*, watching four hours of *South Park* greatly increased the number of Cheezy Poofs eaten, as compared to watching four hours of static TV fuzz. Looking at people who hate *South Park*, watching four hours of it slightly reduced the number of Cheezy Poofs they ate as compared to watching four hours of TV fuzz. With respect to the people who watched *South Park* for four hours, people who like *South Park* ate a great deal more Cheezy Poofs than did individuals who hate the show. Finally, for individuals who watched TV static, those who like *South Park* ate a few more Cheezy Poofs than did individuals who hate the show.

Cartoon 12.1   BLOOM COUNTY

As a final note, notice that the description above did not make any statements comparing people who watched *South Park* and like it and people who watched static and hate *South Park*. Nor did we make comparisons between people who watched static and like *South Park* and people who watched *South Park* and hate it. Generally, it is not necessary to make comparisons between sub-group means that do not share either a column or a row. In part, this is just standard practice, but it is also rather difficult to know what such comparisons really tell you about your sub-groups.

A Second Example: 2 x 3 Two-Way ANOVA

Next is a second example of using factorial ANOVA. Again we present a situation with two independent variables. In this example one of our IVs consists of three groups, however, giving us a 2 x 3 design with six sub-groups. Cartoon 12.1 illustrates the classic issue of subliminal priming (see Box 12.2 for some background information). Research has shown that subliminal primes can have an influence on people but, as with most relationships in the social and behavioral sciences, it depends on a variety of factors. For example, the nature of the prime is important. That is, whether you use words or pictures can influence the results. The length of time the prime is presented (100 vs. 700 milliseconds) also can affect the results. Further, the person's existing attitudes toward the target of the prime are quite influential. When people have strong feelings toward the primed target, it may be more difficult to influence them than it is when their feelings are rather vague.

For our present example, assume that our young scientist, Oliver Wendell, has decided to study whether the effect of exposing individuals to subliminal messages to put pickles up their nose and Spam on their head depends on any of the factors mentioned above.

Box 12.2   Liars

You may feel that our example of subliminal messages involving pickles and Spam may seem particularly absurd, even by this book's standards, and of little practical relevance. The area of subliminal priming has been extensively studied, however, by both social and behavioral scientists.

The results have been mixed, but there is substantial evidence to suggest that stimuli presented below the threshold of awareness can, under certain conditions, influence people's general moods, attitudes, and motivations. Obviously, subliminal priming has both potentially helpful and dangerous applications.

A poignant example of this occurred during the 2000 presidential election campaign when George W. Bush ran a television campaign ad that briefly flashed the word "LIARS" while talking about candidate Gore's healthcare reform plan. Whether these ads really influence voters is questionable, though the practice seems no less disturbing.

Table 12.7 PINASH Data Summary Table 2 x 3 Two-Way ANOVA Example, Frequency of Wearing Pickles Up One's Nose and Spam on One's Head, Separated by Stimulus Type and Attitude toward Food as a Fashion Accessory

(n = 36)		Picture			Words		Row Sums
	s#	$X_{.11}$	$X^2_{.11}$	s#	$X_{.21}$	$X^2_{.21}$	
FAFAA	X_{111}	14	.	X_{121}	7	.	
Positive	X_{211}	13	.	X_{221}	6	.	
	X_{311}	11	.	X_{321}	5	.	
	X_{411}	10	.	X_{421}	5	.	
	X_{511}	8	.	X_{521}	3	.	
	X_{611}	8	.	X_{621}	3	.	
	$\Sigma X_{.11}$.			$\Sigma X_{.21}$			$\Sigma X_{..1}$.
			$\Sigma X^2_{.11}$.			$\Sigma X^2_{.21}$.	$\Sigma X^2_{..1}$.
	$n_{.11}$			$n_{.21}$			$n_{..1}$
	s#	$X_{.12}$	$X^2_{.12}$	s#	$X_{.22}$	$X^2_{.22}$	
FAFAA	X_{112}	13	.	X_{122}	14	.	
Neutral	X_{212}	13	.	X_{222}	13	.	
	X_{312}	11	.	X_{322}	11	.	
	X_{412}	10	.	X_{422}	9	.	
	X_{512}	9	.	X_{522}	8	.	
	X_{612}	7	.	X_{622}	8	.	
	$\Sigma X_{.12}$.			$\Sigma X_{.22}$.			$\Sigma X_{..2}$.
			$\Sigma X^2_{.12}$.			$\Sigma X^2_{.22}$.	$\Sigma X^2_{..2}$.
	$n_{.11}$			$n_{.22}$			$n_{..2}$
	s#	$X_{.13}$	$X^2_{.13}$	s#	$X_{.23}$	$X^2_{.23}$	
FAFAA	X_{113}	12	.	X_{123}	6	.	
Negative	X_{213}	12	.	X_{223}	6	.	
	X_{313}	11	.	X_{323}	5	.	
	X_{413}	10	.	X_{423}	4	.	
	X_{513}	9	.	X_{523}	4	.	
	X_{613}	8	.	X_{623}	2	.	
	$\Sigma X_{.13}$.			$\Sigma X_{.23}$.			$\Sigma X_{..3}$.
			$\Sigma X^2_{.13}$.			$\Sigma X^2_{.23}$.	$\Sigma X^2_{..3}$.
	$n_{.13}$			$n_{.23}$			$n_{..3}$
Column	$\Sigma X_{.1.}$.			$\Sigma X_{.2.}$.			ΣX_{ijk} .
Sums			$\Sigma X^2_{.1.}$.			$\Sigma X^2_{.2.}$.	ΣX^2_{ijk} .
	$n_{.1.}$			$n_{.2.}$			n_{ijk}

Specifically, he is interested in looking at two independent variables: the nature of the prime (Pictures vs. Words) and people's attitudes toward wearing food as fashion accessories (Negative, Neutral, and Positive), which we will refer to as FAFAA (Food as Fashion Accessory Attitude). For the dependent variable, Oliver measured the frequency with which subjects put pickles in their noses and wore Spam on their heads during the seven-day period following exposure to the subliminal prime, referred to as their PINASH score (Pickles in Nose and Spam on Head). Table 12.7 presents the data summary table for Oliver's results.

Competing the 2 x 3 Two-Way ANOVA utilizes the same nineteen steps presented for the 2 x 2 design. Below are all nineteen steps applied to Oliver's data. For each step, we again present the general formula followed by the calculations for this example.

Part I: Complete the Data Summary Table

Steps 1 through 7 require filling in the different parts of the data summary table. For each step we have entered the result in the completed data summary table (Table 12.8).

Step 1.   Find: $\Sigma X_{.jk}$ and $\Sigma X^2_{.jk}$

$$\Sigma X_{.jk} = X_{1jk} + X_{2jk} + \ldots . X_{ijk}$$
$$\Sigma X^2_{.jk} = X^2_{1jk} + X^2_{2jk} + \ldots X^2_{ijk}$$

for this example:

$\Sigma X_{.11} = 14 + 13 + 11 + 10 + 8 + 8 = 64$

$\Sigma X^2_{.11} = 14^2 + 13^2 + 11^2 + 10^2 + 8^2 + 8^2 = 196 + 169 + 121 + 100 + 64 + 64 = 714$

$\Sigma X_{.21} = 7 + 6 + 5 + 5 + 3 + 3 = 29$

$\Sigma X^2_{.21} = 7^2 + 6^2 + 5^2 + 5^2 + 3^2 + 3^2 = 49 + 36 + 25 + 25 + 9 + 9 = 153$

$\Sigma X_{.12} = 13 + 13 + 11 + 10 + 9 + 7 = 63$

$\Sigma X^2_{.12} = 13^2 + 13^2 + 11^2 + 10^2 + 9^2 + 7^2 = 169 + 169 + 121 + 100 + 81 + 49 = 689$

$\Sigma X_{.22} = 14 + 13 + 11 + 9 + 8 + 8 = 63$

$\Sigma X^2_{.22} = 14^2 + 13^2 + 11^2 + 9^2 + 8^2 + 8^2 = 196 + 169 + 121 + 81 + 64 + 64 = 695$

$\Sigma X_{.13} = 12 + 12 + 11 + 10 + 9 + 8 = 62$

$\Sigma X^2_{.13} = 12^2 + 12^2 + 11^2 + 10^2 + 9^2 + 8^2 = 144 + 144 + 121 + 100 + 81 + 64 = 654$

$\Sigma X_{.23} = 6 + 6 + 5 + 4 + 4 + 2 = 27$

$\Sigma X^2_{.23} = 6^2 + 6^2 + 5^2 + 4^2 + 4^2 + 2^2 = 36 + 36 + 25 + 16 + 16 + 4 = 133$

Step 2.   Find: $\Sigma X_{.j.}$ and $\Sigma X^2_{.j.}$

$$\Sigma X_{.j.} = \Sigma X_{.j1} + \Sigma X_{.j2} + \ldots \Sigma X_{.jk} \text{ or } X_{1j1} + X_{2j1} + X_{3j1} + \ldots . X_{ijk}$$
$$\Sigma X^2_{.j.} = \Sigma X^2_{.j1} + \Sigma X^2_{.j2} + \ldots \Sigma X^2_{.jk} \text{ or } X^2_{1j1} + X^2_{2j1} + X^2_{3j1} + \ldots . X^2_{ijk}$$

Table 12.8   PINASH Completed Data Summary Table 2 x 3 Two-Way ANOVA Example, Frequency of Wearing Pickles Up One's Nose and Spam on One's Head, Separated by Stimulus Type and Attitude toward Food as a Fashion Accessory

(n = 36)							Row Sums
		Picture			*Words*		
	s#	$X_{.11}$	$X^2_{.11}$	s#	$X_{.21}$	$X^2_{.21}$	
FAFAA	X_{111}	14	196	X_{121}	7	49	
Positive	X_{211}	13	169	X_{221}	6	36	
	X_{311}	11	121	X_{321}	5	25	
	X_{411}	10	100	X_{421}	5	25	
	X_{511}	8	64	X_{521}	3	9	
	X_{611}	8	64	X_{621}	3	9	
	$\Sigma X_{.11}$ 64			$\Sigma X_{.21}$ 29		$\Sigma X_{.1}$	93
		$\Sigma X^2_{.11}$ 714			$\Sigma X^2_{.21}$ 153	$\Sigma X^2_{.1}$	867
	$n_{.11}$ 6			$n_{.21}$ 6		$n_{.1}$	12
	s#	$X_{.12}$	$X^2_{.12}$	s#	$X_{.22}$	$X^2_{.22}$	
FAFAA	X_{112}	13	169	X_{122}	14	196	
Neutral	X_{212}	13	169	X_{222}	13	169	
	X_{312}	11	121	X_{322}	11	121	
	X_{412}	10	100	X_{422}	9	81	
	X_{512}	9	81	X_{522}	8	64	
	X_{612}	7	49	X_{622}	8	64	
	$\Sigma X_{.12}$ 63			$\Sigma X_{.22}$ 63		$\Sigma X_{.2}$	126
		$\Sigma X^2_{.12}$ 689			$\Sigma X^2_{.22}$ 695	$\Sigma X^2_{.2}$	1384
	$n_{.11}$ 6			$n_{.22}$ 6		$n_{.2}$	12
	s#	$X_{.13}$	$X^2_{.13}$	s#	$X_{.23}$	$X^2_{.23}$	
FAFAA	X_{113}	12	144	X_{123}	6	36	
Negative	X_{213}	12	144	X_{223}	6	36	
	X_{313}	11	121	X_{323}	5	25	
	X_{413}	10	100	X_{423}	4	16	
	X_{513}	9	81	X_{523}	4	16	
	X_{613}	8	64	X_{623}	2	4	
	$\Sigma X_{.13}$ 62			$\Sigma X_{.23}$ 27		$\Sigma X_{.3}$	89
		$\Sigma X^2_{.13}$ 654			$\Sigma X^2_{.23}$ 133	$\Sigma X^2_{.3}$	787
	$n_{.13}$ 6			$n_{.23}$ 6		$n_{.3}$	12
Column	$\Sigma X_{.1.}$ 189			$\Sigma X_{.2.}$ 119		ΣX_{ijk}	308
Sums		$\Sigma X^2_{.1.}$ 2057			$\Sigma X^2_{.2.}$ 981	ΣX^2_{ijk}	3038
	$n_{.1.}$ 18			$n_{.2.}$ 18		n_{ijk}	36

for this example:

$$\Sigma X_{.1.} = \Sigma X_{.11} + \Sigma X_{.12} + \Sigma X_{.13} = 64 + 63 + 62 = 189$$
$$\Sigma X^2_{.1.} = \Sigma X^2_{.11} + \Sigma X^2_{.12} + \Sigma X^2_{.13} = 714 + 689 + 654 = 2057$$
$$\Sigma X_{.2.} = \Sigma X_{.21} + \Sigma X_{.22} + \Sigma X_{.23} = 29 + 63 + 27 = 119$$
$$\Sigma X^2_{.2.} = \Sigma X^2_{.21} + \Sigma X^2_{.22} + \Sigma X^2_{.23} = 153 + 695 + 133 = 981$$

Step 3.   Find: $\Sigma X_{..k}$ and $\Sigma X^2_{..k}$

$$\Sigma X_{..k} = \Sigma X_{.1k} + \Sigma X_{.2k} + \ldots \Sigma X_{.jk} \text{ or } X_{11k} + X_{21k} + X_{31k} + \ldots X_{ijk}$$
$$\Sigma X^2_{..k} = \Sigma X^2_{.1k} + \Sigma X^2_{.2k} + \ldots \Sigma X^2_{.jk} \text{ or } X^2_{11k} + X^2_{21k} + X^2_{31k} + \ldots X^2_{ijk}$$

for this example:

$$\Sigma X_{..1} = \Sigma X_{.11} + \Sigma X_{.21} = 64 + 29 = 93$$
$$\Sigma X^2_{..1} = \Sigma X^2_{.11} + \Sigma X^2_{.21} = 714 + 153 = 867$$
$$\Sigma X_{..2} = \Sigma X_{.12} + \Sigma X_{.22} = 63 + 63 = 126$$
$$\Sigma X^2_{..2} = \Sigma X^2_{.12} + \Sigma X^2_{.22} = 689 + 695 = 1384$$
$$\Sigma X_{..3} = \Sigma X_{.13} + \Sigma X_{.23} = 62 + 27 = 89$$
$$\Sigma X^2_{..3} = \Sigma X^2_{.13} + \Sigma X^2_{.23} = 654 + 133 = 787$$

Step 4.   Find: $n_{.jk}$, $n_{.j.}$, and $n_{..k}$

$$n_{.j.} = n_{.j1} + n_{.j2} + \ldots n_{.jk}$$
$$n_{..k} = n_{.1k} + n_{.2k} + \ldots n_{.jk}$$

for this example:

$$n_{.11} = 6$$
$$n_{.21} = 6$$
$$n_{.12} = 6$$
$$n_{.22} = 6$$
$$n_{.13} = 6$$
$$n_{.23} = 6$$
$$n_{.1.} = n_{.11} + n_{.12} + n_{.13} = 6 + 6 + 6 = 18$$
$$n_{.2.} = n_{.21} + n_{.22} + n_{.23} = 6 + 6 + 6 = 18$$
$$n_{..1} = n_{.11} + n_{.21} = 6 + 6 = 12$$
$$n_{..2} = n_{.12} + n_{.22} = 6 + 6 = 12$$
$$n_{..3} = n_{.13} + n_{.23} = 6 + 6 = 12$$

Step 5.   Find: ΣX_{ijk}

$$\Sigma X_{ijk} = (\Sigma X_{.11} + \Sigma X_{.21} + \ldots \Sigma X_{.ijk}) \text{ or } (\Sigma X_{.1.} + \Sigma X_{.2.} + \ldots \Sigma X_{.j.}) \text{ or } (\Sigma X_{..1} + \Sigma X_{..2} + \ldots \Sigma X_{..k})$$

for this example:

$$\Sigma X_{ijk} = \Sigma X_{.1.} + \Sigma X_{.2.} = 189 + 119 = 308$$

or

$$\Sigma X_{ijk} = \Sigma X_{..1} + \Sigma X_{..2} + \Sigma X_{..3} = 93 + 126 + 89 = 308$$

Step 6. Find: ΣX^2_{ijk}

$$\Sigma X^2_{ijk} = (\Sigma X^2_{.11} + \Sigma X^2_{.21} + \ldots \Sigma X^2_{ijk}) \text{ or } (\Sigma X^2_{.1.} + \Sigma X^2_{.2.} + \ldots \Sigma X^2_{.j.}) \text{ or }$$
$$(\Sigma X^2_{..1} + \Sigma X^2_{..2} + \ldots \Sigma X^2_{..k})$$

for this example:

$$\Sigma X^2_{ijk} = \Sigma X^2_{.1.} + \Sigma X^2_{.2.} = 2057 + 981 = 3038$$

or

$$\Sigma X^2_{ijk} = \Sigma X^2_{..1} + \Sigma X^2_{..2} + \Sigma X^2_{..3} = 867 + 1384 + 787 = 3038$$

Step 7. Find: n_{ijk}

$$n_{ijk} = (n_{.11} + n_{.21} + \ldots n_{ijk}) \text{ or } (n_{.1.} + n_{.2.} + \ldots n_{.j.}) \text{ or } (n_{..1} + n_{..2} + \ldots n_{..k})$$

for this example:

$$n_{ijk} = n_{.11} + n_{.21} + n_{.12} + n_{.22} + n_{.13} + n_{.23} = 6 + 6 + 6 + 6 + 6 + 6 = 36$$

or

$$n_{ijk} = n_{.1.} + n_{.2.} = 18 + 18 = 36$$

or

$$n_{ijk} = n_{..1} + n_{..2} + n_{..3} = 12 + 12 + 12 = 36$$

Part II: Finding the Sums of Squares (SS)

For steps 8 through 14 we must find the same six sums of squares values used in the 2 x 2 Two-Way ANOVA example. The results of each step's computations are found in the first column of both Table 12.9 and Table 12.10.

Step 8. Find: $\dfrac{\left(\Sigma X_{ijk}\right)^2}{n_{ijk}}$

for this example:

$$\frac{\left(\Sigma X_{ijk}\right)^2}{n_{ijk}} = \frac{(step5)^2}{step7} = \frac{(308)^2}{36} = \frac{(94864)}{36} = \boxed{2635.1111}$$

Step 9.   Find:

$$SS_{TOT} = \Sigma X_{ijk}^2 - \frac{\left(\Sigma X_{ijk}\right)^2}{n_{ijk}}$$

for this example:

$$SS_{TOT} = \Sigma X_{ijk}^2 - \frac{\left(\Sigma X_{ijk}\right)^2}{n_{ijk}} = (step6) - (step8) = 3038 - 2635.1111 = \boxed{402.8889}$$

Step 10.   Find:

The mean square (MS) between $\dfrac{SSbetween}{dfbetween} = \dfrac{Step9}{Step12} = \dfrac{645}{2} = \boxed{322.5}$

for this example:

$$SS_{IV1} = \Sigma = \left(\frac{\left(\Sigma X_{.1.}\right)^2}{n_{.1.}} + \frac{\left(\Sigma X_{.2.}\right)^2}{n_{.2.}}\right) - Step8 = \left(\frac{(189)^2}{18} + \frac{(119)^2}{18}\right) - 2635.1111 =$$

$$\left(\frac{35721}{18} + \frac{14161}{18}\right) - 2635.1111 = (1984.5 + 786.7222) - 2635.1111 =$$

$$2771.2222 - 2635.1111 = \boxed{136.1111}$$

Step 11.   Find:

$$SS_{IV2} = \Sigma\left(\frac{\left(\Sigma X_{..k}\right)^2}{n_{..k}}\right) - \frac{\left(\Sigma X_{ijk}\right)^2}{n_{ijk}} = \left(\frac{\left(\Sigma X_{..1}\right)^2}{n_{..1}} + \frac{\left(\Sigma X_{..2}\right)^2}{n_{..2}} + \ldots \frac{\left(\Sigma X_{..k}\right)^2}{n_{..k}}\right) - \frac{\left(\Sigma X_{ijk}\right)^2}{n_{ijk}}$$

$$12$$

for this example:

$$SS_{IV2} = \left(\frac{\left(\Sigma X_{..1}\right)^2}{n_{..1}} + \frac{\left(\Sigma X_{..2}\right)^2}{n_{..2}} + \frac{\left(\Sigma X_{..3}\right)^2}{n_{..3}}\right) - Step8 =$$

$$\left(\frac{(93)^2}{12} + \frac{(126)^2}{12} + \frac{(89)^2}{12}\right) - 2635.1111 = \left(\frac{8649}{12} + \frac{15876}{12} + \frac{7921}{12}\right) - 2635.1111 =$$

$$(720.75 + 1323 + 660.0833) - 2635111 = 2703.8333 - 2635.1111 = \boxed{68.7222}$$

Step 12.   Find:

$$SS_{BTWTOT} = \Sigma\left(\frac{\left(\Sigma X_{.jk}\right)^2}{n_{.jk}}\right) - \frac{\left(\Sigma X_{ijk}\right)^2}{n_{ijk}} = \left(\frac{\left(\Sigma X_{.11}\right)^2}{n_{.11}} + \frac{\left(\Sigma X_{.21}\right)^2}{n_{.21}} + \ldots \frac{\left(\Sigma X_{.jk}\right)^2}{n_{.jk}}\right) - \frac{\left(\Sigma X_{ijk}\right)^2}{n_{ijk}}$$

for this example:

$$SS_{BTWTOT} = \left(\frac{(\Sigma X_{.11})^2}{n_{.11}} + \frac{(\Sigma X_{.21})^2}{n_{.21}} + \frac{(\Sigma X_{.12})^2}{n_{.12}} + \frac{(\Sigma X_{.22})^2}{n_{.22}} + \frac{(\Sigma X_{.13})^2}{n_{.13}} + \frac{(\Sigma X_{.23})^2}{n_{.23}} \right) - Step8 =$$

$$\left(\frac{(64)^2}{6} + \frac{(29)^2}{6} + \frac{(63)^2}{6} + \frac{(63)^2}{6} + \frac{(62)^2}{6} + \frac{(27)^2}{6} \right) - 2635.1111 =$$

$$\left(\frac{4096}{6} + \frac{841}{6} + \frac{3969}{6} + \frac{3969}{6} + \frac{3844}{6} + \frac{729}{6} \right) - 2635.1111 =$$

$$(682.6666 + 140.1666 + 661.5 + 661.5 + 640.6666 + 121.5) - 2635.1111 =$$

$$2907.9998 - 2635.1111 = \boxed{272.8887}$$

Step 13.   Find: $SS_{1x2} = SS_{BTWTOT} - SS_{IV1} - SS_{IV2}$

for this example:

SS_{1x2} = Step 12 − Step 11 − Step 10 = 272.8887 − 68.7222 − 136.1111 = 68.0554

Step 14.   Find: $SS_{ERROR} = SS_{TOT} - SS_{BTWTOT}$

for this example:

SS_{ERROR} = Step 9 − Step 12 = 402.8889 − 272.8887 = 130.0002

Part III: Filling In the Factorial ANOVA Summary Table

Steps 15 through 18 involve completing most of the factorial ANOVA summary table. The steps and their computations are listed in Table 12.9, and the final answers have been entered in the completed summary table (Table 12.10). Step 15 instructs us to enter the sums of squares into the table. Step 16 involves finding the degrees of freedom for each component of variance (sums of squares). In Step 17 we must find the mean square for the three effects and the error term. (Remember that the MS is the quotient obtained by dividing each SS by its respective degrees of freedom. Also, you do not need to find the MS for the total sums of squares.) Step 18 instructs us to find the F ratio for each of the effects (two main effects and the interaction effect). Recall that the F for each effect is obtained by dividing the MS for each effect by the MS_{ERROR}.

In this example the MS_{ERROR} is 4.3333. Using our rule of thumb, we see that all the Fs are much larger than 5.12, so we know that all of our effects are significant, though we still must perform a significance test to determine at what alpha level they are significant.

Table 12.9   Pickles and Spam Data: Intermediate Step for
                  Completing the Factorial ANOVA Summary Table

	Step 15	Step 16	Step 17	Step 18
	SS	df	MS	F
Main Effects				
IV1	Step 10	$j - 1$	SS_{IV1}/df_{IV1}	MS_{IV1}/MS_{ERROR}
	136.1111	2 - 1 = 1	136.1111/1	136.1111/4.3333
			= 136.1111	= 31.4104
IV2	Step 11	$k - 1$	SS_{IV2}/df_{IV2}	MS_{IV2}/MS_{ERROR}
	68.7222	3 - 1 = 2	68.7222/2	34.3611/4.3333
			= 34.3611	= 7.9295
Interaction				
1 x 2	Step 13	$(j-1)(k-1)$	SS_{1x2}/df_{1x2}	MS_{1x2}/MS_{ERROR}
	68.0554	(2-1)(3-1)	68.0554/2	34.0277/4.3333
		= 2	= 34.0277	= 7.8526
ERROR	Step 14	$n_{ijk} - jk$	SS_{ERROR}/df_{ERROR}	
	130.0002	36-(2)(3)	130.0002/30	
		= 30	= 4.3333	
TOTAL	Step 9	$n_{ijk} - 1$		
	402.8889	36 - 1 = 35		

Part IV: Testing the Significance and Interpreting the F Ratios

In the final step of the factorial ANOVA, Step 19, we test the significance of each of the F ratios. Again, to do this we compare the F-obtained to the F-critical values for the degrees of freedom associated with each particular effect. Remember that the df for the denominator comes from the error term.

For this example, the df_{ERROR} is 30. The F for the main effect of IV1 has a df of 1 for the numerator, and the table of critical Fs in Appendix 3 shows that the critical values for 1 and 30 degrees of freedom are 4.17 and 7.56, for the .05 and .01 alpha levels, respectively. As the F-obtained for IV1 (31.4104) is substantially larger than both critical values,

Table 12.10   Pickles and Spam: Complete Factorial ANOVA
               Summary Table

	SS	df	MS	F	p
Main Effects					
IV1	136.1111	1	136.1111	31.4104	$p < .01$
IV2	68.7222	2	34.3611	7.9295	$p < .01$
Interaction					
1 x 2	68.0554	2	34.0277	7.8526	$p < .01$
ERROR	130.0002	30	4.3333		
TOTAL	402.8889	35			

we conclude that it is significant at least at the .01 alpha level. This suggests that there is less than a 1% chance that observed group difference is a random occurrence.

Turning to the remaining Fs (main effect for IV2 and the interaction effect), we see that they both have the same df for the numerator (2), so we can use the same F-critical values to evaluate each F-obtained. We still have $df = 30$ for our df denominator so we can get our F-critical from the same set of rows in Appendix 3. Use the second column rather than the first, however, due to the $df = 2$ for the numerator. The F-critical values for 2 and 30 degrees of freedom are 3.32 and 5.42, for the .05 and the .01 alpha levels, respectively. Thus, although the Fs for the main effect of IV2 and the interaction effect are substantially smaller than the Fs for the main effect of IV1, they are still significant at the .01 level because they are larger than their respective .01 F-critical. The significance levels for all the F's are in the last column of Table 12.10.

To aid in the interpretation of the main effect for stimulus type (IV1), the means for the picture group (10.5) and the words group (6.6111) have been plotted in Figure 12.5. It appears that the people who were exposed to subliminal pictures of people with cucumbers up their noses and Spam on their heads tended to wear cucumbers up their noses and Spam on their heads significantly more frequently than people who were exposed to a subliminal message telling them to "Put Pickles Up Your Nose and Wear Spam on Your Head."

For the main effect of IV2 (food as a fashion accessory attitudes) we have plotted the means for the three groups (Positive Attitude = 7.75, Neutral Attitude = 10.5, and Negative Attitude = 7.4166) in Figure 12.6. Although the main effect is significant, and we can clearly see the relationship between the means, because there are three of them we cannot be sure which means are significantly different. The significant F for the main effect only tells us that at least one group is significantly different from at least one other group. We must perform some form of follow-up test to determine which means are different.

Figure 12.5   Main Effect for IV1 (Stimulus Type)

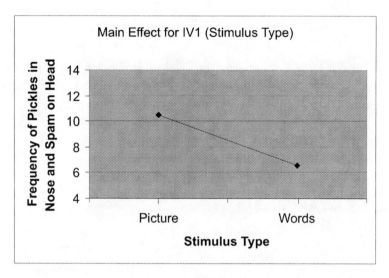

Figure 12.6   Main Effect for IV2 (Food As a Fashion Accessory Attitudes)

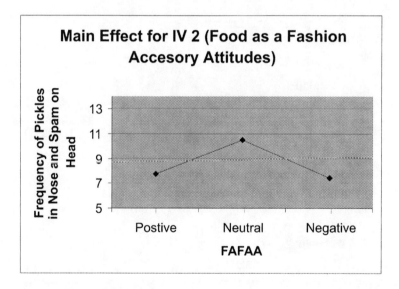

The LSD t-test (Least Significant Difference) presented in Chapter 11 can be used for testing main effects in factorial ANOVA as well as in their One-Way counterparts. As you may recall, the LSD t-test is a modified t-test that uses the MSW (mean square within subjects) in place of the standard deviation, and its significance is tested using the t-critical for the within subjects degrees of freedom.

$$\text{LSD } t \text{ test} = \frac{\bar{X}_1 - \bar{X}_2}{\sqrt{MSW\left(\dfrac{1}{n_1} + \dfrac{1}{n_2}\right)}}$$

Remember that MS_{ERROR} is the factorial counterpart to the One-Way MSW. Thus we can use MS_{ERROR} in the denominator of the LSD t-test and test its significance using the t-critical for df_{ERROR}.

$$\text{LSD } t \text{ test} = \frac{\bar{X}_1 - \bar{X}_2}{\sqrt{MS_{ERROR}\left(\dfrac{1}{n_1} + \dfrac{1}{n_2}\right)}}$$

Using the means from our current example we obtain the following.

1. Group 1 vs. Group 2

$$t_{LSD} = \frac{\bar{X}_1 - \bar{X}_2}{\sqrt{MS_{ERROR}\left(\dfrac{1}{n_1} + \dfrac{1}{n_2}\right)}} = \frac{7.75 - 10.5}{\sqrt{4.3333\left(\dfrac{1}{12} + \dfrac{1}{12}\right)}} = \frac{-2.75}{\sqrt{4.3333(.0833 + .0833)}} =$$

$$\frac{-2.75}{\sqrt{4.3333(.1666)}} = \frac{-2.75}{\sqrt{.7219}} = \frac{-2.75}{.8496} = \boxed{-3.2368}$$

2. Group 1 vs. Group 3

$$t_{LSD} = \frac{\bar{X}_1 - \bar{X}_3}{\sqrt{MS_{ERROR}\left(\dfrac{1}{n_1} + \dfrac{1}{n_3}\right)}} = \frac{7.75 - 7.1466}{\sqrt{4.3333\left(\dfrac{1}{12} + \dfrac{1}{12}\right)}} = \frac{.6034}{\sqrt{4.3333(.0833 + .0833)}} =$$

$$\frac{.6034}{\sqrt{4.3333(.1666)}} = \frac{.6034}{\sqrt{.7219}} = \frac{.6034}{.8496} = \boxed{.7120}$$

3. Group 2 vs. Group 3

$$t_{LSD} \frac{\bar{X}_2 - \bar{X}_3}{\sqrt{MS_{ERROR}\left(\dfrac{1}{n_2} + \dfrac{1}{n_3}\right)}} = \frac{10.5 - 7.1466}{\sqrt{4.3333\left(\dfrac{1}{12} + \dfrac{1}{12}\right)}} = \frac{3.3534}{\sqrt{4.3333(.0833 + .0833)}} =$$

$$\frac{3.3534}{\sqrt{4.3333(.1666)}} = \frac{3.3534}{\sqrt{.7219}} = \frac{3.3534}{.8496} = \boxed{3.9470}$$

The *t*-critical for 30 degrees of freedom at the .05 alpha level is 2.042. From these results we can conclude the people who have rather neutral attitudes concerning food as a fashion accessory are more likely to wear cucumbers up their noses and Spam on their heads after being subliminally primed to do so, compared to individuals with strong positive or negative attitudes.

With respect to the interaction effect, again, interpretation is aided by plotting the means of all the individual sub-groups, as seen in Figure 12.7.

Here we can see that the influence of the different types of subliminal priming stimulus (pictures vs. words) depends on the individuals' attitudes toward using food as accessories. Specifically, the results suggest that the effect of using pictures as subliminal primes is not affected by one's fashion attitudes. Individuals who where shown subliminal primes of people with pickles up their noses and Spam on their heads all demonstrated high levels of pickle sticking and Spam wearing, regardless of their food fashion attitudes.

The effects of using words as subliminal primes, however, seems to be highly influenced by food fashion attitudes. Individuals who were subliminally primed with the message "Put Pickles Up Your Nose and Wear Spam on Your Head" were more likely to do so if their food fashion attitudes were neutral than if they were strongly positive or negative. Further, for individuals with strong positive and strong negative food fashion attitudes, pictures seemed to be a more effective prime than were words. For individuals with neutral attitudes, however, the two types of subliminal primes appeared equally effective.

As noted earlier, there are tests available for determining which sub-group means are significantly different. These tests, usually referred to as simple effects tests, are really just modified one-way ANOVAs that compare groups in one variable across a single level of the other variable. The difference between the three attitude groups could be examined only for people who were shown words as subliminal primes. These simple effect *F*s are

Figure 12.7   Pickles and Spam Interaction Effect

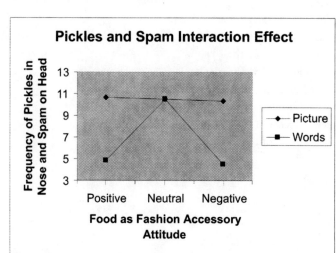

calculated like a One-Way ANOVA, however instead of using the *MSW* from that subset of data as the denominator of the *F* ratio, it uses the MS_{ERROR} term from the factorial ANOVA table.

When simple effects involve more than three groups, significant tests must be followed up with LSD *t*-tests to determine exactly which means are different.

Chapter Summary and Conclusions

This chapter presented an introduction to factorial analysis of variance, which enables testing of the relationship between two independent categorical variables and a continuous dependent variable. Specifically, this chapter distinguished between main effects (the separate influence of each independent variable) and interaction effects (the joint influence of two or more independent variables), presented a nineteen-step method for computing factorial ANOVAs by hand, and demonstrated the use of the LSD *t*-test with significant main effects. Finally, this chapter also introduced simple effects testing for significant interactions.

Key Terms to Remember

- Main Effects
- Interaction Effects
- Simple Effects
- 2 x 2 design
- 2 x 3 design
- Grand Sum (ΣX_{ijk})
- Sums of Squares (*SS*) IV1
- Sums of Squares (*SS*) IV2
- Sums of Squares (*SS*) Total Between
- Sums of Squares (*SS*) 1 x 2
- Sums of Squares (*SS*) Total
- Sums of Squares (*SS*) Error
- Degrees of Freedom (*df*) IV1 and IV2
- Degrees of Freedom (*df*) 1 x 2
- Degrees of Freedom (*df*) Error
- Degrees of Freedom (*df*) Total
- Data Summary Table
- Factorial Summary Table

Practice Exercises

1. What is a main effect in factorial ANOVA?

2. What is an interaction effect in factorial ANOVA?

3. Why is the main effect of an independent variable for a given dependent variable in factorial ANOVA generally larger than if we tested the same independent and dependent variables in a One-Way ANOVA?

4. Interpret the charts of plotted means in Figure 12.8. Determine whether the main effects and interaction effect are likely to be significant.

5. Using another example involving *South Park*, assume that a researcher wanted to know whether watching *South Park* increases the frequency with which individuals use "curse words." Further, she suspects that such a relationship may depend on whether one actually believes that such words are in fact cursed or viewed as rightfully taboo by society.

Figure 12.8   Practice Exercise 4

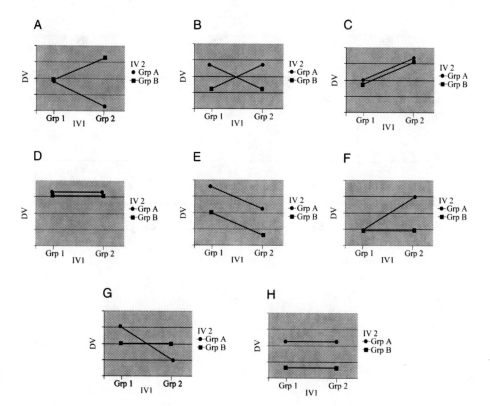

6. From a population of university freshmen, a sample of 20 students was drawn and randomly split into 2 groups of 10. Half the students were exposed to twenty-four hours of *South Park* episodes, while the other half watched reruns of *The Cosby Show*. Also, beliefs regarding cursed words were assessed and participants further were split into groups accordingly (Believers and Non-Believers). Further, after the twenty-four-hour viewing session the researcher conducted a twenty-five-minute structured interview regarding attitudes toward Cheezy Poofs, where the frequency of curse word usage was recorded. Table 12.11 presents the results in an incomplete data summary table.

Table 12.11   *South Park* and Cursing Data Summary Table
Number of Cheezy Poofs Eaten, Separate by
Viewing Condition and Beliefs Regarding Cursed
Words

(n = 20)		*Watched South Park*			*Watched Cosbey Show*		*Row Sums*
	s#	$X_{.11}$	$X^2_{.11}$	s#	$X_{.21}$	$X^2_{.21}$	
Believe	X_{111}	15	.	X_{121}	5	.	
In	X_{211}	13	.	X_{221}	2	.	
Cursed	X_{311}	12	.	X_{321}	1	.	
Words	X_{411}	10	.	X_{421}	1	.	
	X_{511}	10	.	X_{521}	0	.	
	$\Sigma X_{.11}$.			$\Sigma X_{.21}$.			$\Sigma X_{..1}$.
			$\Sigma X^2_{.11}$.			$\Sigma X^2_{.21}$.	$\Sigma X^2_{..1}$.
	n_{11}			n_{21}			$n_{..1}$
	s#	$X_{.12}$	$X^2_{.12}$	s#	$X_{.22}$	$X^2_{.22}$	
Do Not	X_{112}	6	.	X_{122}	13	.	
Believe	X_{212}	1	.	X_{222}	12	.	
In	X_{312}	1	.	X_{322}	12	.	
Cursed	X_{412}	1	.	X_{422}	11	.	
Words	X_{512}	0	.	X_{522}	11	.	
	$\Sigma X_{.12}$.			$\Sigma X_{.22}$.			$\Sigma X_{..2}$.
			$\Sigma X^2_{.12}$.			$\Sigma X^2_{.22}$.	$\Sigma X^2_{..2}$.
	n_{12}			n_{22}			$n_{..2}$
Column	$\Sigma X_{.1.}$.			$\Sigma X_{.2.}$:			ΣX_{ijk} .
Sums			$\Sigma X^2_{.1.}$.			$\Sigma X^2_{.2.}$.	ΣX^2_{ijk} .
	$n_{.1.}$			$n_{.2.}$			n_{ijk}

a. Using the nineteen steps for computing factorial ANOVA, complete the data summary table and the factorial ANOVA summary table.

b. Determine whether either of the main effects is significant. Interpret the results (i.e., if any, which group within each IV cursed significantly more or less than the other group).

c. Determine whether the interaction is significant. If so, interpret the interaction.

d. Plot the sub-group means in a line chart.

7. Returning to Cartoon 12.1, assume that Oliver Wendell Holmes is now interested in testing whether other people can be subliminally forced to put other food items on their bodies or whether the effects are limited to pickles and Spam. Further, assume that Oliver suspects that such effects may depend on the amount of time that the subliminal prime is presented (e.g., 100 milliseconds vs. 1,000 milliseconds).

8. From the population of a medium-sized Midwestern town, Oliver drew a sample of 30 participants, which was split into 6 equally sized groups. One-third of the sample was exposed to the traditional pickles-and-Spam picture primes. Another third was exposed to pictures of people putting sliced mangoes into their ears and wearing guacamole mustaches. The final third was exposed to pictures of people putting giant mackerels into their pants and wearing Canadian bacon necklaces. Half of each of these groups was exposed to the primes for only 100 milliseconds each time, a duration unlikely to trigger conscious awareness, while the other half of each group was exposed for a full second (1,000 milliseconds), a duration that people generally notice. In the seven-day period following the exposure, the frequency of wearing the relevant food items was recorded for each subject. Oliver's results are presented in the incomplete data summary table found in Table 12.12.

a. Using the nineteen steps for computing factorial ANOVA, complete the data summary table and the factorial ANOVA summary table.

b. Determine whether either of the main effects is significant. Interpret the results (i.e., if any, which group within each IV wore significantly more or fewer food items than the other group).

c. Determine whether the interaction is significant. If so, interpret the interaction.

d. Plot the sub-group means in a line chart.

Table 12.12   Subliminally Primed Food Wearing Data Summary Table
Frequency of Food Wearing, Separated by Stimulus
Duration and Type of Food Primed

(n = 36)						Row Sums
		_100 ms_			_1000 ms_	
	s#	$X_{.11}$	$X^2_{.11}$	s#	$X_{.21}$	$X^2_{.21}$
Pickles	X_{111}	14	.	X_{121}	7	.
and	X_{211}	13	.	X_{221}	6	.
Spam	X_{311}	11	.	X_{321}	5	.
	X_{411}	10	.	X_{421}	5	.
	X_{511}	8	.	X_{521}	3	.
	$\Sigma X_{.11}$.		$\Sigma X^2_{.11}$.	$\Sigma X_{.21}$	$\Sigma X^2_{.21}$.	$\Sigma X_{..1}$. $\Sigma X^2_{..1}$.
	$n_{.11}$			$n_{.21}$		$n_{..1}$
	s#	$X_{.12}$	$X^2_{.12}$	s#	$X_{.22}$	$X^2_{.22}$
Mangos	X_{112}	20	.	X_{122}	15	.
and	X_{212}	19	.	X_{222}	12	.
Guac	X_{312}	17	.	X_{322}	10	.
	X_{412}	17	.	X_{422}	10	.
	X_{512}	16	.	X_{522}	9	.
	$\Sigma X_{.12}$.		$\Sigma X^2_{.12}$.	$\Sigma X_{.22}$.	$\Sigma X^2_{.22}$.	$\Sigma X_{..2}$. $\Sigma X^2_{..2}$.
	$n_{.11}$			$n_{.22}$		$n_{..2}$
	s#	$X_{.13}$	$X^2_{.13}$	s#	$X_{.23}$	$X^2_{.23}$
Mackerel	X_{113}	13	.	X_{123}	12	.
and	X_{213}	13	.	X_{223}	12	.
Bacon	X_{313}	11	.	X_{323}	11	.
	X_{413}	9	.	X_{423}	10	.
	X_{513}	8	.	X_{523}	9	.
	$\Sigma X_{.13}$.		$\Sigma X^2_{.13}$.	$\Sigma X_{.23}$.	$\Sigma X^2_{.23}$.	$\Sigma X_{..3}$. $\Sigma X^2_{..3}$.
	$n_{.13}$			$n_{.23}$		$n_{..3}$
Column Sums	$\Sigma X_{.1.}$.		$\Sigma X^2_{.1.}$ . .	$\Sigma X_{.2.}$.	$\Sigma X^2_{.2.}$ . .	ΣX_{ijk} . ΣX^2_{ijk} .
	$n_{.1.}$			$n_{.2.}$		n_{ijk}

13

An Introduction to Chi-Square and Other Non-Parametric Statistics

Many of the statistical techniques discussed in this text drew upon two basic theoretical assumptions: (1) the use of interval-ratio level data, and (2) sample data drawn from a population that is normally distributed. As noted, the assumption of using interval-ratio data is often violated by researchers. Nevertheless, the assumption of a normal distribution is the most rudimentary of all the theoretical assumptions underlying inferential statistics that enable researchers to estimate population parameters.

Often, however, researchers are faced with situations where the use of sample data drawn from a normally distributed population and/or interval-ratio data is not available or feasible. Further, sometimes a sample drawn from a normally distributed population is not even desired. As a result, statisticians have developed an array of different statistical techniques to deal with such situations.

This chapter explores statistical techniques that utilize ordinal—or, more typically, nominal—level data and, further, that are considered *distribution-free* or *non-parametric* techniques. That is, as inferential statistics with the underlying assumption of a normal distribution are used to estimate population *parameters*, they are also called *parametric statistics*. Because distribution-free statistics, on the other hand, do not make assumptions of a normal distribution to estimate population parameters, they are considered non-parametric statistics.

The specific non-parametric statistical techniques this chapter explores are, in their order of presentation, the *chi-square test*, the *median test*, and the *Mann-Whitney U test*. While these are some of the most commonly used non-parametric statistical techniques, especially chi-square, they are just a "sampling" of the different non-parametric procedures that are available.

Chi-Square Test

While most of you may not be familiar with the actual calculations for a chi-square test (hereafter called chi-square), many of you may have discussed this technique in a research methods course or read about it in a research report. Even though the popularity of this technique (in terms of usage) has lessened somewhat in recent years with the development of more powerful alternative statistical procedures, chi-square is still a widely used technique in both the behavioral and social sciences.

Interval-ratio, ordinal, and nominal levels of measurement can all be used when undertaking chi-square (if any of these levels of measurement—types of variables—seem unfamiliar, please refer to Chapter 2 for a more detailed discussion). There are, however, other statistical techniques that were developed for the interval-ratio variables, and we have explored many of these in this text. Most of these techniques are parametric and, because parametric techniques are viewed as more powerful than, and superior to, other statistical procedures, it makes no sense to use lower-level, non-parametric tests with interval-ratio data. Moreover, although many of these techniques were developed only for interval-ratio data, they are often applied (as previously noted) to ordinal-level data. Thus, while some researchers may stretch the usage of many parametric procedures onto ordinal-level data, most will not do so with nominal-level data.

As such, non-parametric statistical techniques such as chi-square are predominantly used with nominal levels of measurement; more specifically, in cases where one nominal variable is compared to another. (Recall that we can take a nominal characteristic (e.g., breed of cow) and take an interval-ratio measurement of each group (e.g., number of times the electric fence is touched) and then use a parametric technique (independent samples t-test) to discern if there is a difference between the two groups.) Nominal variables (as discussed in Chapter 2) are qualitative characteristics that numerical values cannot be applied to in any meaningful way. Once again, variables such as gender, hair color, or your major at college are all examples of nominal characteristics.

No meaningful values are applicable per se to nominal variables, but numerical counts of rates of occurrence for different measurements of a given characteristic can be used for analysis purposes. For instance, counts of occurrence are easily applied to each of the aforementioned examples of nominal characteristics; in your statistics class you could count the number of men versus women; the number of people with blond, black, red, or brown hair; or the number of people majoring in the social versus behavioral sciences.

Gender, hair color, and major are all single counts of one nominal variable; as such, they tell nothing about potential variable relationships. When nominal characteristics are conceptualized as independent and dependent variables using counts and chi-square, however, we can test for statistically significant differences. In a limited sense, this is done in a manner similar to Pearson's r, where the expected relationship between two variables is compared to the observed one: the amount of variation in the dependent due to regression versus error. That is, nominal characteristics can also be conceptualized in terms of *expected* versus *observed* values.

Then, again, because nominal variables do not involve numerous measurements of a relationship between two variables, an alternative format for measuring expected and observed values must be utilized, specifically, measuring expected versus observed frequencies of occurrence in terms of proportions. Proportions, remember, are relative frequencies of occurrence of measurable events in predetermined categories. These categories, identical to those used in Chapter 3 to construct frequency distributions, must be *mutually exclusive* and *exhaustive*. In other words, any given occurrence can fit into only one category—no more—and there must be an available category for every observation.

Once measurements of nominal variables are viewed in proportional terms of mutually exclusive and exhaustive categories, a comparison can be made to determine if there is a statistically significant difference between expected versus observed rates of occurrence. This is exactly what chi-square does: It determines if there is a statistically significant difference between expected versus observed relative frequencies.

In other words, allowing for potential sampling error, chi-square tests to see if there is a difference between the observed and expected relative frequencies. If such a difference is found (proportionally speaking), then we can conclude that a statistically significant difference exists and that one nominal characteristic is statistically associated with (typically seen as a function of) another nominal characteristic (we accept the research hypothesis). Conversely, if a proportional difference is not found, then we conclude that the two nominal variables are not associated together (we accept the null hypothesis).

Cartoon 13.1   RUBES by Leigh Rubin

"That's it! If you kids don't start behaving, I'm taking you both to McDonald's!"

We'll use Cartoon 13.1 as a backdrop, and give some concrete meaning to what has been discussed in only abstract terms so far. Our present interests are what sort of effects disruptive behavior, such as fighting in the car, exhibited by adolescent bovines (cows) has on trips to McDonald's. That is, we want to know if disruptive behavior by adolescent bovines leads to trips to McDonald's. Or do bovine parents, like many parents, use this as an idle threat to get their offspring to behave? Especially given what a trip to McDonald's really means for cows. (Alternatively, given the cultural significance of McDonald's in our society, human parents often use trips to McDonald's as a reward for good behavior.)

The actual research question is, "Does disruptive behavior by adolescent bovines lead their parents to drop them off at McDonald's?" In other words, our independent variable is disruptive behavior and the dependent variable is a visit to McDonald's. More specifically, the independent variable is measured in the nominal terms of whether parents do or do not visit McDonald's. As such, each variable is simply operationalized as a yes or no measurement. We sample 100 bovine parents and find the data reported in Table 13.1.

Before introducing the chi-square test formula or any calculations, it is very important to discuss the above data set in terms of what it represents and in light of the previously applied terms of proportions and observed versus expected frequencies. As noted, chi-square is applicable to any level of measurement. As such, the technique itself can use an infinite number of categories for the independent or dependent variable. The above data set, however, is operationalized as a 2 x 2 (two-by-two) contingency table.

Because 2 x 2 contingency tables are, by far, the most common format used for undertaking a chi-square test, it is important to define clearly what they represent. The table is 2 x 2 in that it represents two groups (disruptive versus not disruptive adolescent bovines) in terms of two responses (visited or did not visit McDonald's). *Contingency* means that one variable is seen as dependent—contingent—upon the variability in another variable. In sum, while the notion of contingency is applicable to any size table for two variables, there are only two possible ways each nominal variable can occur in this example so it is simply called a 2 x 2 contingency table.

The categories utilized in this 2 x 2 design meet the previously discussed requirement that they are mutually exclusive and exhaustive. That is, the initial research question was

Table 13.1   Visited McDonald's by Disruptive
Behavior of Adolescent Bovines

		Disruptive Behavior	
		Yes	*No*
Visited McDonald's	Yes	38	15
	No	7	40

operationalized into four very simple response categories, and each bovine can fit into only one of these response categories. Further, for each potential response there is an available category, so the categories are mutually exclusive and exhaustive.

Several different relative frequencies—proportions—can be determined from a 2 x 2 table. For our purposes, however, column proportions are the only ones required for chi-square calculations. Any given relative frequency is derived by taking the event of interest's rate of occurrence and dividing it by the total occurrences. For example, the proportion of adolescent bovines that display disruptive behavior and subsequently visit McDonald's is 38% (38/100 = .38).

Observed values are just that, those actually reported (e.g., 7 cows are observed as undertaking disruptive behavior and not visiting McDonald's). Expected values are mathematically determined below using the observed values. What they represent is the number of events that should be found—expected—in a given category if their rates of occurrence were entirely random. Group sizes are almost always different, however, so when expected values are calculated they also take column and row totals proportionally into account.

With all this in mind, below we offer the formula for a chi-square test. An accompanying summary table (Table 13.2) is also presented as a useful step-by-step way to complete each of the calculations and, in total, to understand what they actually measure. Further, a variant of the original table that has expected values calculated is also provided (Table 13.3). Of course, because this is our first time through the calculations and not all of them are definitively found in the summary table (e.g., expected values), each step is discussed in the section that immediately follows it. While a more expedient chi-square formula is subsequently offered, because the following calculations give a better idea of what is being measured and are quite easy to complete, please review them carefully.

<u>Chi-Square Test Formula</u>

$$\chi^2 = \Sigma \left(\frac{(O_{ij} - E_{ij})^2}{E_{ij}} \right)$$

Where:
O_{ij} = the observed value for the cell in the ith row and j^{th} column.
    e.g., O_{11} = the observed value of the cell in the 1st row of the 1st column.
            O_{21} = the observed value of the cell in the 2nd row of the 1st column.

E_{ij} = the expected value (based on chance) for the cell in the ith row and j^{th} column.

First the chi-square formula tells us to take each O (observed) value and subtract its accompanying E (expected) value, square the resultant answer, and then divide this value by E. Once this is done for each observed value, all of these answers are totaled to give a final chi-square obtained value. The chi-square obtained is the compared to a chi-square critical value (found in Appendix 4) to determine whether it is significant. While Appendix 4 is discussed in detail below, statistical significance for chi-square is simply determined in

Table 13.2   Summary Table for Chi-Square test of Adolescent
                    Bovine Data

	Yes/Yes	No/Yes	Yes/No	No/No	Total
1. Observed (O_{ij})	38	15	7	40	100
2. Expected (E_{ij})	23.85	29.15	21.15	25.85	100
3. $O_{ij} - E_{ij}$	14.15	-14.15	-14.15	14.15	0
4. $(O_{ij} - E_{ij})^2$	200.2225	200.2225	200.2225	200.2225	800.89
5. $\dfrac{(O_{ij} - E_{ij})^2}{E_{ij}}$	8.395	6.8686	9.4667	7.7455	32.4758

Table 13.3   Visited McDonald's by Disruptive Behavior of
                    Adolescent Bovines. Observed Values with
                    Calculated Expected Values

| | | Disruptive Behavior | | Row |
		Yes	No	Total (R)
Visited McDonald's	Yes	38 (Observed) $E_{11} = .45 \times 53 = 23.85$ 23.85 (Expected)	15(Observed) $E_{12} = .55 \times 53 = 29.15$ 29.15 (Expected)	$R_1 = 53$
	No	7 (Observed) $E_{21} = .45 \times 47 = 21.15$ 21.15 (Expected)	40 (Observed) $E_{22} = .55 \times 47 = 25.85$ 25.85 (Expected)	$R_2 = 47$
Column total (C_j) C_j/N		$C_1 = 45$ 45 / 100 = (.45)	$C_2 = 55$ 55 / 100 = (.55)	N = 100

the same manner as all previous tests; if the obtained value is larger than critical value, then the relationship is significant.

Applying this to the bovine data set shows that, while we obviously know what the observed values are, the expected values must be mathematically determined. Expected values are derived, as reported below and in Table 13.3, by taking the column percentages and individually multiplying them by each of the row totals, as expressed in the following formula.

Formula for Calculating Expected Values

$$E_{ij} = \left(\frac{C_j}{N}\right) R_i$$

Where:
R_i = Row i Total
C_j = Column j Total
E_{ij} = Expected Value for a Cell in the ith row and j^{th} column.

Row totals (R_i) (across) are all the values found in that row (e.g., R_1 = 38 + 15 = 53), and column percentages are the column totals (C_j) (top to bottom) divided by the overall sample size (N) (e.g., C_1 = 38 + 7 = 45 and C_1/N = 45/100 = .45). Thus, for the yes/yes category (E_{11}: disruptive behavior displayed and visited McDonald's) that has an observed value of 38, its corresponding expected value is 23.85 (E_{11} = (C_1/N) × R_1 = .45 × 53 = 23.85). This and the other three expected values are reported in Table 13.3 and in the chi-square summary table (13.2).

Having determined each of the expected values, the rest of the calculations are reported in just the summary table (Table 13.2). Here, as previously outlined, each expected value (E_{ij}) is subtracted from its corresponding observed (O_{ij}) value (e.g., O_{11} − E_{11} = 38 − 23.85 = 14.15), squared ((O_{11} − E_{11})2 = 200.2225), and then divided by the expected value ((O_{11} − E_{11})²/E_{11} = (200.2225/23.85 = 8.395)). These four answers are then added together to give a chi-square obtained value of 32.4758.

Before making the determination of whether this is significant, several observations about the summary table (Table 13.2) are necessary. To begin with, as an easy way to check for potential calculation errors, the sum of expected values must always equal the sum of observed values. Thus, in the present example, the total for both observed and expected values is 100. Further, once each expected value is subtracted from its corresponding observed value ($O − E$), the sum of these values must equal zero. As such, this step is also an excellent double check of the calculations made to this point; the sum of the observed minus expected values must equal zero for subsequent steps to be correct. Finally (as the title of the test suggests), because all answers are derived through a process of squaring, one cannot have a negative chi-square value. In other words, *all* chi-square obtained values, like F-obtained values, are positive values.

With this in mind, let's make the final determination of whether the obtained value is significant. To do this, as noted, we must determine a chi-square critical value. This value is determined in a manner somewhat similar to that used in previous tests with degrees of freedom, but the manner in which df are now determined is very different. Where previous tests used sample size (or some variant of it), this technique instead uses the number of columns and rows to determine the correct chi-square critical value. More specifically, the following formula tells how many df are present in a given analysis.

Formula to Determine the df Present and the Chi-Square Critical Value

$(R-1)(C-1) = \text{df Present}$

Where: R = # of rows & C = # of Columns

The C represents the number columns whereas the R represents the number of rows; thus the present example (a 2 x 2 design) has 1 $(2 - 1)(2 - 1) = 1 \times 1 = 1$. We find in Appendix 4 that two different critical values are listed for each degree of freedom, one value for the alpha set at .05 and one value set at .01. The critical values for the present example (with 1 df) are 3.84 and 6.63. The obtained value of 32.4758 is larger than both of these values, so we report significance at the .01 level, p < .01. In other words, we report significance in the same manner that was used in ANOVA summary tables.

Thus, hypothetically speaking, if we had obtained a chi-square value of 4 (instead of the actual 32.4758), because this value is greater than 3.84 but smaller than 6.63, significance would be reported at the .05 level. Conversely, if a 2 had been obtained, then because this value is smaller than both critical values, we would report that there was not a significant difference.

Statistical significance was found, but what does that mean? First, a significant chi-square value tells us to reject the null hypothesis and fail to reject the research hypothesis, and to conclude that, proportionally speaking, there is a significant difference. In other words, more responses are being found in the yes/yes category (disruptive behavior displayed and visited McDonald's) and in the no/no category (no disruptive behavior and did not visit McDonald's) than we would expect if their rates of occurrence were random. Conversely, there are lower rates of occurrence in the yes/no category (no disruptive behavior and visited McDonald's) and the no/yes category (disruptive behavior and did not visit McDonald's) than expected.

Putting this into plain English: We can conclude that disruptive behavior apparently leads to trips to McDonald's. In fact, 84.44% (38/45 = .8444) of the disruptive adolescent bovines visited McDonald's.

Alternatively, no guarantee of not visiting McDonald's and not displaying disruptive behavior, in comparison to displaying disruptive behavior, appears to significantly reduce the probability of visiting McDonald's. Only 27.27% (15/55 = .2727) of adolescent bovines who did not display disruptive behavior visited McDonald's. In sum, a bovine who wants to grow up to become ground round instead of becoming a veal cutlet had better not display disruptive behavior.

The next example of a chi-square test is presented in a somewhat cursory manner, so if any of the steps or derived values are confusing or unclear, please refer back to this first example. For this next example, we are now interested in how the nominal characteristic of gender affects trips to McDonald's. Further, instead of the obvious beef cows that are

Table 13.4   Visited McDonald's by Gender of
                    Holstein Dairy Cow

| | | Gender | |
		Male	Female
Visited McDonald's	Yes	24	16
	No	15	30

pictured in the cartoon, we are now specifically interested in the gender of Holstein dairy cows and its effect on trips to McDonald's. We sample 85 Holstein cows (39 males and 46 females) at birth and then take our measurement at two years old to determine their status: did or did not visit McDonald's. Our findings are reported in Table 13.4.

Looking at the 2 × 2 table shows that gender apparently has an effect on trips to McDonald's, but we can more definitively make this conclusion if statistical significance is found. To this end, and as before, we offer a variant table (Table 13.5) of the original (Table 13.4) with expected values calculated in it and a summary table (Table 13.6) of the rest of the calculations with the final answer in it.

While the calculations give a chi-square obtained value of 6.0656, until this value is compared to a critical value we do not know if a significant difference is present. This is a 2 × 2 design, so the critical values again are 3.84 (.05) and 6.63 (.01) (recall that these

Table 13.5   Visited McDonald's by Gender of Holstein Dairy
                    Cow. Observed Values With Calculated Expected
                    Values

| | | Gender | | Row |
		Male	Female	Total (R_i)
Visited McDonald's	Yes	24 (Observed) E_{11}=.4588 × 40=18.352 18.352 (Expected)	15(Observed) E_{12}=.5412 × 40=21.648 21.648 (Expected)	R_1 = 40
	No	15 (Observed) E_{21}=.4588 × 45=20.646 20.646 (Expected)	40 (Observed) E_{22}=.5412 × 45=24.354 24.354 (Expected)	R_2 = 45
Column total (C_j)		C_1 = 39	C_2 = 46	N = 85
C_j/N		39 / 85 = (.4588)	46 / 85 = (.5412)	

Table 13.6   Summary Table for Chi-Square Test for Holstein
                   Data

	Male/Yes	Female/Yes	Male/No	Female/No	Total
1. Observed (O_{ij})	24	16	15	30	85
2. Expected (E_{ij})	18.352	21.648	20.646	24.354	85
3. $O_{ij} - E_{ij}$	5.648	-5.648	-5.646	5.646	0
4. $(O_{ij} - E_{ij})^2$	31.8999	31.8999	31.8773	31.8773	127.5544
5. $\dfrac{(O_{ij} - E_{ij})^2}{E_{ij}}$	1.7382	1.4735	1.5439	1.3089	6.0645

two values were determined in the previous example). With the obtained value of 6.0645 being larger than 3.84 but smaller than 6.63, we report significance at the .05 alpha level; $p < .05$. Thus, we can reject the null hypothesis and fail to reject the research hypothesis and conclude that, proportionally speaking, there is a significant difference at the .05 alpha level.

In other words, being a male Holstein cow (a bull) appears to increase the likelihood of visiting McDonald's, while being a female Holstein cow (a heifer) appears to decrease the likelihood of such visits. What sort of plausible explanations might account for this discrepancy? Are dairy farmers sexist? Well, yes. In the dairy farmers' world female cows are obviously the ones that produce milk. As such, while a few good bulls are necessary to impregnate so that the herd size is maintained and to keep the female cows lactating, beyond this, a bull's only value is how much he can fetch as a Big Mac. Of course, following this thought to its logical conclusion means that when Holsteins do have to visit McDonald's it is usually as a young bull or an old cow. Think of it—literally billions of young male and old female Holstein cows "served."

As mentioned, while the above procedure for calculating chi-square gives you the best idea of what is actually being measured, there is a simpler formula that accomplishes this task more efficiently when you are working with 2 x 2 chi-square tables. Although this formula (below) may appear to be quite different in comparison to the formula just used, in reality, after a few simple algebraic manipulations, both formulas are exactly the same.

Both formulas are measurements of how much difference exists between the observed versus expected values. The newly introduced formula, however, accomplishes this as separate calculations added together. Even so, both formulas result in the exact same final answer (sometimes, due to the rounding of fractions, the answers will be very close but not exactly the same). To demonstrate this, the calculations for this alternative formula are completed below using the previously analyzed Holstein data. Accompanying these calculations is a variant table of the original raw data with some of the required calculations reported in it (see Table 13.7).

The answer is the same as obtained using the previous formula and was discussed in detail, so the discussion is not repeated here. Nevertheless, there are still two noteworthy observations about this new formula. First, to complete the calculations the letters A through D are placed in the variant table. While the actual placement of these letters is somewhat arbitrary, for consistency purposes we suggest that you follow the above

Alternative Chi-Square Test Formula

$$\chi^2 = \frac{N(AD - BC)^2}{(A+B)(C+D)(A+C)(B+D)}$$

Calculations For Alternative Chi-Square Formula Using Holstein Data

$$\chi^2 = \frac{N(AD-BC)^2}{(A+B)(C+D)(A+C)(B+D)} = \frac{85[(24)(30)-(16)(15)]^2}{(40)(45)(39)(46)}$$

$$= \frac{85(720-240)^2}{3,229,200} = \frac{19,584,000}{3,229,200} = \boxed{6.0646}$$

Table 13.7   Visited McDonald's by Gender of Holstein Dairy Cow Lettered with Column and Row Totals

| | | Gender | | Row |
		Male	Female	Totals
Visited McDonald's	Yes	A 24	B 16	A + B 24 + 16 = 40
	No	C 15	D 30	C + D 15 + 30 = 45
	Column	A + C 24 + 15 = 39	B + D 16 + 30 = 46	
	Totals			N = 85

format. Second, having witnessed too many of our students make this calculation error we remind you to remember to square the numerator portion of the formula—failure to do so obviously results in an incorrect final answer. Finally, don't forget that this formula can only be applied when you calculate 2 x 2 chi-squares. Large matrixes (e.g., 2 x 3, 3 x 3, or 4 x 4) require you to use the more general formula.

Median Test

All of the above analyses involved relationships between two nominal characteristics. While the most typical use of the chi-square procedure is with nominal variables, as noted this statistic can be used with any level of measurement. Nevertheless, sometimes when researchers are analyzing a nominal/ordinal relationship, for simplicity purposes and often because the distribution is severely skewed—not normally distributed—they decide to use a 2 x 2 design. Because an ordinal variable can involve several, often numerous, ranked measurements of a given characteristic, some sort of procedure to collapse it into a nominal variable must be completed. One such procedure, to which we now turn our attention, is called a *median test*.

Cartoon 13.2 is presented to assist in this discussion. This is also the final cartoon in this text. Also, because this is the last chapter, and assuming your instructor has present-

Cartoon 13.2   DOONESBURY

ed the course material in the same order as found in the text, upon its completion or in the near future we assume that you will graduate. As a graduation gift to your parents, you may want to share this cartoon with them as a way of saying, "Thanks. This cartoon is an example of the type of textbook that your money purchased these last four or five years." On second thought, perhaps you shouldn't show them.

Our current research interests are what sort of an effect having paid for a daughter's or son's college education has on the parents' attitude about the quality of education their child received. To this end, at a recent graduation we asked 28 parents two simple questions: (1) did they pay for their son or daughter's education (how it was financed)? and (2) On a 20-point scale, how happy are they about the education their child received (1—really unhappy/dissatisfied to 20—really happy/pleased)?

In an attempt to keep this absurd example somewhat realistic, since most parents are happy with *any* college that their child graduated from with honors, our sample is limited to parents having children graduating with a 2.5 to 3.0 GPA. Thus, the nominal characteristic of parent paid (or did not pay) for education is conceptualized as the independent variable while degree of satisfaction with education received (an ordinal characteristic) is seen as a dependent variable. The resultant data set, collected from 28 individual parents, is found in Table 13.8.

A look at either group's score range shows two highly skewed distributions. That is, while most of the scores for either of the groups are found to occur in a range of 8 to 12,

Table 13.8   Degree of Satisfaction with Son's or Daughter's Education by Type of Financing

	How Financed	
	Parents Paid	*Other Means*
	8	9
	10	20
	2	11
	10	12
Degree of	11	8
Reported	12	19
Satisfaction	1	11
with Child's	1	10
Education	11	11
	8	12
	9	13
	11	11
	8	19
		11
		9

both groups have a set of extreme scores. For instance, the first group of parents, who paid for the education, finds 3 parents very unhappy with their child's education. Conversely, the second group, where the parents did not pay for their son or daughter's education, has several parents (3) expressing extreme satisfaction with the education the children received. In situations where one or more of the distributions is severely skewed (here both cases are), a median test is quite appropriate.

As the title of this test suggests, a median must be calculated. As shown below, it is the determination of a median that enables us to reconceptualize this ordinal variable into a nominal variable and subsequently analyze it as a 2 x 2 contingency table. In a median test, the actual median value is calculated using all of the observed values from both groups. To do this, we must first rank all of the scores into one frequency distribution. This is done in Table 13.9.

With this accomplished, a median can be calculated. Referring back to Chapter 4, we use the following formula as a first step to determine the median. This answer tells us the exact point where the median is found. While all of these calculations are found below and tell us that the median value for this data set is 10.5, following is a brief review of the definition of a median. A median, similar to a mean and a mode, is a measure of central tendency. More specifically, it gives the point where one-half of the observed values are found above and one-half of the observed values are found below (again, like the median of a road with one-half on either side).

$$\text{Median Formula} \quad \frac{N+1}{2} = \frac{28+1}{2} = \frac{29}{2} = 14.5$$

Thus we look to the 14.5 ranked observation to find it occurs between the observed values of 10 and 11. As such, we simply add these together and divide them by two to find a median value of 10.5: $(10 + 11 = 21)/2 = 10.5$. If any of this is confusing, please refer back to Chapter 4 for a more complete discussion.

$\boxed{10.5}$ = Median

Referring back to the actual test, the calculation of a median gives a point from which two nominal categories are derived: (1) above the median and (2) below the median. Reflecting these new nominal response categories and the previous categories of parent did or did not pay for education is the 2 x 2 contingency table found in Table 13.10. Found within each of the categories is the number of responses occurring in it. Thus, the number of responses above the median (10.5) in the category of parent paid for education is 4; 4 of these parents were above the median for the satisfaction level of child's education received.

With the resultant format of a 2 x 2 table, a chi-square test is all that is now left to do. So we see that a median test is actually a variant form of a chi-square test; the former just involves some preliminary calculations. While the initial format to determine the chi-square obtained could be used, we use instead the simpler lettered chi-square formula. To

Table 13.9   Rank Frequency Distribution of
             the Degree-of-Satisfaction Data

Score	Absolute Frequency	Score	Absolute Frequency
20	1	10	4
19	2	9	3
13	1	8	4
12	3	2	1
11	7	1	2

Table 13.10   Degree of Satisfaction with Son's or
             Daughter's Education (above or
             below Median) by Type of Financing

	How Financed	
	Parents Paid	Other Means
Above the Median	4	11
Below the Median	9	4

this end, the intermediate steps are shown in Table 13.11, while the formula and all remaining calculations are found below.

Instead of becoming mired in the previously explored steps, which were discussed in detail, we instead make the simple determination of whether this obtained value is significant and, if so, interpret what it means. Please review all of the calculations, however, and if any of them seem at all confusing, refer back to the previous example of this type.

This is a 2 x 2 contingency table, so we once again use the chi-square critical values of 3.84 and 6.63. Since the obtained value of 5.0727 is larger than the first critical value, it is reported significant at the .05 level, $p < .05$ or, alternatively, we reject the null and fail

Calculations for Alternative Chi-Square Formula Using College Graduate Data

$$\chi^2 = \frac{N(AD - BC)^2}{(A+B)(C+D)(A+C)(B+D)} = \frac{28[(4)(4) - (11)(9)]^2}{(15)(13)(13)(15)}$$

$$= \frac{28(16-99)^2}{38025} = \frac{28(6889)}{38025} = \frac{192892}{38025} = \boxed{5.0727}$$

Table 13.11   Degree of Satisfaction with Son's or Daughter's Education (above or below Median) by Type of Financing. Lettered with Column and Row Totals

| | How Financed | | Row |
	Parents Paid	Other Means	Totals
Above the Median	A 4	B 11	A + B 4 + 11 = 15
Below the Median	C 9	D 4	C + D 9 + 4 = 13
Column Totals	A + C 4 + 9 = 13	B + D 11 + 4 = 15	N = 28

to reject the research hypothesis and conclude that, proportionately speaking, there is a statistically significant difference.

The first conclusion that we can make is that most parents report an average amount of satisfaction with their child's education. Apparently, however, for a few parents who paid for the education of a child who did not do very well (graduating with less than a 2.5 to 3.0 GPA), there is a propensity for them to be unhappy with the education received. Conversely, not having paid for a child's education has the opposite effect for a few parents; 3 of these parents are quite pleased with their child's education. That is a few of the parents who did not have to pay are, by far, the most satisfied of either group.

While we can conclude that whether one pays for a child's education definitely appears to affect a few parents' perception about the quality of education received, any conclusion beyond this is pure speculation. For instance, we might further hypothesize that some parents who paid for their children's education appear to blame the college or university attended for their children's shortcomings. This is in direct contrast to those (few) parents who perceive the school quite favorably because they did not pay a dime, even though their children did not do very well. Then again, we could also speculate that some parents are extremely unhappy with the quality of their son's or daughter's education because, quite simply, they paid for it. Conversely, a few of the parents who did not pay may simply be proud of their children's financing their own educations—and this sentiment is reflected in their perception of the school.

The manner in which this research question was addressed, using nominal variables, therefore gives a very limited picture of the relationship found between the two variables.

While this is somewhat of a problem whenever social phenomena are quantified, this is especially true of nominal measurements.

Had we compared the variable of degree of satisfaction with an alternative variable of the actual number of dollars spent (an interval-ratio measurement), for example, a more meaningful picture of the data set might emerge. Simply speculating, we might find that it is not *whether* one pays for education, but rather *how much*. Those parents who spent the most money for their son's or daughter's education might very well be the 3 that are by far the most dissatisfied.

In sum, while nominal measurements are certainly not meaningless, such variables are limited (sometimes severely) in terms of what can be learned about a given variable relationship.

Mann-Whitney U Test

The final statistical procedure explored in this text is called a *Mann-Whitney U Test*. Like the previous two statistical tests presented in this chapter, this procedure is also non-parametric and widely used. The Mann-Whitney U Test is the non-parametric counterpart of a *t*-test and is used in situations where assumptions about the population distribution might be violated or the sample size is very small. The Mann-Whitney test does not compare means or medians, but rather measures theoretically whether there is a difference between the way two populations of numbers are distributed. Thus, the null hypothesis holds that one distribution is adequate to represent both distributions, whereas the research hypothesis holds that two distributions are required to represent the two data sets adequately. In other words, the null hypothesis for a Mann-Whitney test states that there is no difference between the two distributions, whereas the research hypothesis states that there is a difference.

Drawing upon the discussion from the end of the last section, our present research interests are whether parents who paid for their son's or daughter's education are more satisfied with the education if it was received at a private institution or if it was received at a public university. While we can expect a fair amount of variability in the amount a parent pays for a given child's education (regardless of where they graduated from), let's say that tuition, room and board, and overall costs at the public university are inexpensive, and that just the opposite is true of the private school. So it does not cost very much to attend Public U, whereas it is quite expensive to attend Private U. We use the 20-point scale previously utilized and administer it to the parents who paid for the education of children who graduated with 2.5 to 3.0 GPA. Our findings are found in Table 13.12.

Similar to the presentation format of a median test, we first offer each of the calculations required for a Mann-Whitney test and then discuss what this procedure is actually measuring in terms of the data set itself. The first step is to rank all the scores from both groups, and while we also did this, in a sense, with the median test, for a Mann-Whitney test a corresponding rank (score) is assigned to each observed value. This is done in table 13.13.

Table 13.12   Degree of Satisfaction with Son's or Daughter's Education by School of Student Whose Parent Paid Education

	Public U	Private U
	11	2
	19	8
	20	11
	18	12
Degree of	11	3
Reported	18	17
Satisfaction	9	11
with Child's	10	10
Education	11	11
	8	12
	20	2
	18	
	17	
	20	

Before proceeding, three observations are warranted. When several scores are the same—tied—their corresponding ranks are summed and then divided by the number of such observations. In other words, tied scores report the average rank of such scores. Thus, the three 20s from the data set are inferred as representing the ranks of 1, 2, and 3; however, the average of the three ranks is 2 and it is reported as such for all three scores. Be careful when determining the next rank. Often, when ranking scores in this manner, there is the propensity to use the wrong next rank (e.g., using 3 instead of the correct rank of 4 in the present example). One easy way to check that you have correctly ranked all the scores is as follows: If the very last rank is any value other than that of the sample size, you have made an error. Thus, for the present example, the last rank of 25 is correctly the same value as the sample size (25).

Second, an asterisk (*), or the lack of one, is used as a way to designate which group the score comes from. This is done to assist with the next step that must be done (see Table 13.14), where all ranks are placed back into the group from which they were drawn.

Finally, because group sizes often differ, it is important to note that the largest group must always be designated as group 1. This is necessary for a subsequent calculation.

Table 13.14 gives us two sets of rankings. These rankings are used to determine if there is a statistically significant difference in the way the two sets of numbers are distributed. The actual Mann-Whitney formula (and its sub-parts) used to make this determination

Table 13.13   Ranked Degreee of Satisfaction Data
with Corresponding Numerical Rank

Score	Rank	Score	Rank
20	2	11	14.5
20	2	11	*14.5
20	2	11	*14.5
19	4	11	*14.5
18	6	10	18.5
18	6	10	*18.5
18	6	9	20
17	8.5	8	21.5
17	*8.5	8	*21.5
12	*10.5	3	*23
12	*10.5	2	*24.5
11	14.5	2	*24.5
11	14.5		

is presented below. Also found on the following page are the corresponding calculations for the data set currently being analyzed. As always, these steps are discussed briefly in the section that immediately follows.

<u>Mann-Whitney Formula and its Sub-parts</u>

Mann-Whitney Obtained Test Value (Z) $= \dfrac{U_1 - U_E}{O_U}$

where:

$$U_1 = N_1 N_2 + \frac{N_1(N_1 + 1)}{2} - R_1$$

Where R1 = Sum of the ranks for group 1.

$$U_E = \frac{N_1 N_2}{2}$$

$$O_U = \sqrt{\frac{N_1 N_2 (N_1 + N_2 + 1)}{12}}$$

<u>Mann-Whitney Calculations for Degree-of-Satisfaction</u>

$$U_1 = (14)(11) + \frac{14(14+1)}{2} - 140 = 154 + 105 - 140 = \boxed{119}$$

$$U_E = \frac{(14)(11)}{2} = \frac{154}{2} = \boxed{77}$$

$$O_u = \sqrt{\frac{(14)(11)(14+11+1)}{12}} = \sqrt{\frac{4004}{12}} = \boxed{18.2665}$$

$$Z = \frac{119 - 77}{18.2665} = \boxed{2.2992}$$

$\alpha = .05, \quad Z \text{ Critical} = 1.96 \quad 2.2992 > 1.96; \text{ thus } p < .05$

What the Mann-Whitney test does is calculate an expected value (U_E) that represents a distribution adequate to represent both distributions. This value is then subtracted from an observed value (U_1) that represents the actual amount of variability found in group 1 (using an alternative formula, we could use group 2). The answer then is divided by a value representing the total standardized amount of variability in both groups.

Mathematically speaking, at this point we are probably correctly guessing that all of the above calculations are quite understandable. There is one value, however, that may be somewhat confusing (R_1). This value is simply obtained by totaling all of the ranked scores for 1 (i.e., 14.5 + 4 + 2 + . . . + 2 = 140). This value not withstanding, all of the remaining steps simply use an N_1 that represents the size of group 1 (14 in the present example), an N_2 that represents the size of group 2 (11 in the present example), or a fixed value of 1, 2, or 12. Nevertheless, please carefully review the above calculation.

The final answer for all of the above calculations gives an obtained value of 2.2992. As with all previous tests, this obtained value is next compared to a critical value. Fortunately, in cases where both groups' sizes are larger than 8 the critical values from a Z distribution are used. Thus, since the obtained value of 2.2992 is larger than 1.96 but smaller than 2.58, we conclude that there is a statistically significant difference at the .05 alpha level; p < .05. Further, we also reject the null hypothesis and fail to reject the research hypothesis, and conclude that one distribution is not adequate to represent both distributions.

Considering what the raw data set looked like, a finding of significance is not that surprising. Nevertheless, there are still some more meaningful things that can be said about this specific variable relationship. More specifically, this finding says that parents who paid for their daughter's or son's education at Public U are far happier with the education

Table 13.14   Ranks for Degree of Satisfaction with Son's/Daughter's Education by Where Graduated from Data

	Public U		Private U	
	Score	Rank	Score	Rank
	11	14.5	2	24.5
	19	4	8	21.5
	20	2	11	14.5
	18	6	12	10.5
Degree of	11	14.5	3	23
Reported	18	6	17	8.5
Satisfaction	9	20	11	14.5
Scores and	10	18.5	10	18.5
Corresponding	11	14.5	11	14.5
Ranks	8	21.5	12	10.5
	20	2	2	24.5
	18	6		
	17	8.5		
	20	2		

their child received than parents who paid for an education at Private U. Apparently the amount of money that parents spend for a child's education has a direct impact on how satisfied they are with the education received for average students (GPA 2.5–3.0).

One final observation about this technique is warranted. Using just the sum of the ranks from group 2, this value can be compared to a table value to determine significance. To give a better idea what the statistic is actually measuring, we have purposely not included this table.

Chapter Summary and Conclusions

This chapter reviewed three basic and widely used non-parametric statistical procedures. The first, chi-square, although applicable to every level of measurement, was discussed in terms of its most typical application: nominal characteristics using a 2 x 2 contingency table. Next, a similar procedure called a median test was discussed. This test involved a nominal/ordinal variable relationship collapsed into a 2 x 2 so that a chi-square test could be completed. Finally, a Mann-Whitney U test was discussed. This procedure determines if one or two separate distributions is necessary to represent two sets of numbers.

This is the last chapter in this text, so we wish all of you "luck" in the statistical world we reside in—one that, in all "probability," you now better understand. Of course, we are expressing this sentiment at the .05 alpha level.

Key Terms to Remember

- Non-Parametric
- Chi-Square Test
- Distribution-Free
- Median Test
- 2 x 2 (Two-by-Two) Contingency Table
- Mann-Whitney U Test

Practice Exercises

1. Instead of dairy cows, we are interested in the gender of the cow for the Angus breed in terms of visiting McDonald's. Our findings are reported in Table 13.15 below.
   a. Using the appropriate test, determine whether gender has a significant effect on visits to McDonald's.

2. Using Cartoon 13.2, say that, instead of parents and their degree of satisfaction with their sons or daughters, we are interested in these same parents' children's reported level of satisfaction. In other words, we interview the 28 children of the parents previously discussed and ask them how happy they were with the education they received. Obviously, we already know if they did or did not pay for their own educations. These new findings are reported in Table 13.16.
   a. Using a median test, is there a difference between parents' and children's scores? If so, what?

3. Instead of parents' degree of satisfaction with education at a private or public university, we want to know parents' degree of satisfaction for those who paid for their son or daughter to attend a community college versus a private college. These findings are found in Table 13.17 on p. 280.
   a. Using a Mann-Whitney U test, is there a difference between the two distributions of scores? If so, what does this mean?

Table 13.15   Visited McDonald's by Gender of Angus Cow

		Gender	
		Male	*Female*
Visited McDonald's	Yes	28	25
	No	32	31

Table 13.16   Degree of Satisfaction with Education
               Received by Type of Financing

	How Education Financed	
	Parents Paid	*Other Means*
	8	9
	10	2
	19	11
	10	12
Degree of	11	8
Reported	12	2
Satisfaction	9	11
with	18	9
Education	11	11
by Students	8	12
	20	8
	11	11
	8	1
		11
		9

Table 13.17   Degree of Satisfaction with Son's or Daughter's Education by School of Student Whose Parent Paid Education

	Community College	Private
	11	14
	11	13
	19	8
	20	11
Degree of	18	12
Reported	11	9
Satisfaction	18	17
with Child's	9	11
Education	10	10
	11	11
	8	12
	20	15
	18	17
	18	18
	17	17
	20	

Appendix 1

Table of Probabilities Under the Normal Curve

1 Z	2 Area from Mean to Z	3 The Big Part	4 The Small Part	1 Z	2 Area From Mean to Z	3 The Big Part	4 The Small Part
.00	.0000	.5000	.5000	.35	.1368	.6368	.3632
.01	.0040	.5040	.4960	.36	.1406	.6406	.3594
.02	.0080	.5080	.4920	.37	.1443	.6443	.3557
.03	.0120	.5120	.4880	.38	.1480	.6480	.3520
.04	.0160	.5160	.4840	.39	.1517	.6517	.3483
.05	.0199	.5199	.4801	.40	.1554	.6554	.3446
.06	.0239	.5239	.4761	.41	.1591	.6591	.3409
.07	.0279	.5279	.4721	.42	.1628	.6628	.3372
.08	.0319	.5319	.4681	.43	.1664	.6664	.3336
.09	.0359	.5359	.4641	.44	.1700	.6700	.3300
.10	.0398	.5398	.4602	.45	.1736	.6736	.3264
.11	.0438	.5438	.4562	.46	.1772	.6772	.3228
.12	.0478	.5478	.4522	.47	.1808	.6808	.3192
.13	.0517	.5517	.4483	.48	.1844	.6844	.3156
.14	.0557	.5557	.4443	.49	.1879	.6879	.3121
.15	.0596	.5596	.4404	.50	.1915	.6915	.3085
.16	.0636	.5636	.4364	.51	.1950	.6950	.3050
.17	.0675	.5675	.4325	.52	.1985	.6985	.3015
.18	.0714	.5714	.4286	.53	.2019	.7019	.2981
.19	.0753	.5753	.4247	.54	.2054	.7054	.2946
.20	.0793	.5793	.4207	.55	.2088	.7088	.2912
.21	.0832	.5832	.4168	.56	.2123	.7123	.2877
.22	.0871	.5871	.4129	57	.2157	.7157	.2843
.23	.0910	.5910	.4090	.58	.2190	.7190	.2810
.24	.0948	.5948	.4052	.59	.2224	.7224	.2776
.25	.0987	.5987	.4013	.60	.2257	.7257	.2743
.26	.1026	.6026	.3974	.61	.2291	.7291	.2709
.27	.1064	.6064	.3936	.62	.2324	.7324	.2676
.28	.1103	.6103	.3897	.63	.2357	.7357	.2643
.29	.1141	.6141	.3859	.64	.2389	.7389	.2611
.30	.1179	.6179	.3821	.65	.2422	.7422	.2578
.31	.1217	.6217	.3783	.66	.2454	.7454	.2546
.32	.1255	.6255	.3745	.67	.2486	.7486	.2514
.33	.1293	.6293	.3707	.68	.2517	.7517	.2483
.34	.1331	.6331	.3669	.69	.2549	.7549	.2451

Table of Probabilities Under the Normal Curve *(continued)*

1	2	3	4	1	2	3	4
Z	Area from Mean to Z	The Big Part	The Small Part	Z	Area From Mean to Z	The Big Part	The Small Part
.70	.2580	.7580	.2420	1.05	.3531	.8531	.1469
.71	.2611	.7611	.2389	1.06	.3554	.8554	.1446
.72	.2642	.7642	.2358	1.07	.3577	.8577	.1423
.73	.2673	.7673	.2327	1.08	.3599	.8599	.1401
.74	.2704	.7704	.2296	1.09	.3621	.8621	.1379
.75	.2734	.7734	.2266	1.10	.3643	.8643	.1357
.76	.2764	.7764	.2236	1.11	.3665	.8665	.1335
.77	.2794	.7794	.2206	1.12	.3686	.8686	.1314
.78	.2823	.7823	.2177	1.13	.3708	.8708	.1292
.79	.2852	.7852	.2148	1.14	.3729	.8729	.1271
.80	.2881	.7881	.2119	1.15	.3749	.8749	.1251
.81	.2910	.7910	.2090	1.16	.3770	.8770	.1230
.82	.2939	.7939	.2061	1.17	.3790	.8790	.1210
.83	.2967	.7967	.2033	1.18	.3810	.8810	.1190
.84	.2995	.7995	.2005	1.19	.3830	.8830	.1170
.85	.3023	.8023	.1977	1.20	.3849	.8849	.1151
.86	.3051	.8051	.1949	1.21	.3869	.8869	.1131
.87	.3078	.8078	.1922	1.22	.3888	.8888	.1112
.88	.3106	.8106	.1894	1.23	.3907	.8907	.1093
.89	.3133	.8133	.1867	1.24	.3925	.8925	.1075
.90	.3159	.8159	.1841	1.25	.3944	.8944	.1056
.91	.3186	.8186	.1814	1.26	.3962	.8962	.1038
.92	.3212	.8212	.1788	1.27	.3980	.8980	.1020
.93	.3238	.8238	.1762	1.28	.3997	.8997	.1003
.94	.3264	.8264	.1736	1.29	.4015	.9015	.0985
.95	.3289	.8289	.1711	1.30	.4032	.9032	.0968
.96	.3315	.8315	.1685	1.31	.4049	.9049	.0951
.97	.3340	.8340	.1660	1.32	.4066	.9066	.0934
.98	.3365	.8365	.1635	1.33	.4082	.9082	.0918
.99	.3389	.8389	.1611	1.34	.4099	.9099	.0901
1.00	.3413	.8413	.1587	1.35	.4115	.9115	.0885
1.01	.3438	.8438	.1562	1.36	.4131	.9131	.0869
1.02	.3461	.8461	.1539	1.37	.4147	.9147	.0853
1.03	.3485	.8485	.1515	1.38	.4162	.9162	.0838
1.04	.3508	.8508	.1492	1.39	.4177	.9177	.0823

Table of Probabilities Under the Normal Curve *(continued)*

1	2	3	4	1	2	3	4
Z	Area from Mean to Z	The Big Part	The Small Part	Z	Area From Mean to Z	The Big Part	The Small Part
1.40	.4192	.9192	.0808	1.75	.4599	.9599	.0401
1.41	.4207	.9207	.0793	1.76	.4608	.9608	.0392
1.42	.4222	.9222	.0778	1.77	.4616	.9616	.0384
1.43	.4236	.9236	.0764	1.78	.4625	.9625	.0375
1.44	.4251	.9251	.0749	1.79	.4633	.9633	.0367
1.45	.4265	.9265	.0735	1.80	.4641	.9641	.0359
1.46	.4279	.9279	.0721	1.81	.4649	.9649	.0351
1.47	.4292	.9292	.0708	1.82	.4656	.9656	.0344
1.48	.4306	.9306	.0694	1.83	.4664	.9664	.0336
1.49	.4319	.9319	.0681	1.84	.4671	.9671	.0329
1.50	.4332	.9332	.0668	1.85	.4678	.9678	.0322
1.51	.4345	.9345	.0655	1.86	.4686	.9686	.0314
1.52	.4357	.9357	.0643	1.87	.4693	.9693	.0307
1.53	.4370	.9370	.0630	1.88	.4699	.9699	.0301
1.54	.4382	.9382	.0618	1.89	.4706	.9706	.0294
1.55	.4394	.9394	.0606	1.90	.4713	.9713	.0287
1.56	.4406	.9406	.0594	1.91	.4719	.9719	.0281
1.57	.4418	.9418	.0582	1.92	.4726	.9726	.0274
1.58	.4429	.9429	.0571	1.93	.4732	.9732	.0268
1.59	.4441	.9441	.0559	1.94	.4738	.9738	.0262
1.60	.4452	.9452	.0548	1.95	.4744	.9744	.0256
1.61	.4463	.9463	.0537	1.96	.4750	.9750	.0250
1.62	.4474	.9474	.0526	1.97	.4756	.9756	.0244
1.63	.4484	.9484	.0516	1.98	.4761	.9761	.0239
1.64	.4495	.9495	.0505	1.99	.4767	.9767	.0233
1.65	.4505	.9505	.0495	2.00	.4772	.9772	.0228
1.66	.4515	.9515	.0485	2.01	.4778	.9778	.0222
1.67	.4525	.9525	.0475	2.02	.4783	.9783	.0217
1.68	.4535	.9535	.0465	2.03	.4788	.9788	.0212
1.69	.4545	.9545	.0455	2.04	.4793	.9793	.0207
1.70	.4554	.9554	.0446	2.05	.4798	.9798	.0202
1.71	.4564	.9564	.0436	2.06	.4803	.9803	.0197
1.72	.4573	.9573	.0427	2.07	.4808	.9808	.0192
1.73	.4582	.9582	.0418	2.08	.4812	.9812	.0188
1.74	.4591	.9591	.0409	2.09	.4817	.9817	.0183

Table of Probabilities Under the Normal Curve *(continued)*

1	2	3	4	1	2	3	4
Z	Area from Mean to Z	The Big Part	The Small Part	Z	Area From Mean to Z	The Big Part	The Small Part
2.10	.4821	.9821	.0179	2.45	.4929	.9929	.0071
2.11	.4826	.9826	.0174	2.46	.4931	.9931	.0069
2.12	.4830	.9830	.0170	2.47	.4932	.9932	.0068
2.13	.4834	.9834	.0166	2.48	.4934	.9934	.0066
2.14	.4838	.9838	.0162	2.49	.4936	.9936	.0064
2.15	.4842	.9842	.0158	2.50	.4938	.9938	.0062
2.16	.4846	.9846	.0154	2.51	.4940	.9940	.0060
2.17	.4850	.9850	.0150	2.52	.4941	.9941	.0059
2.18	.4854	.9854	.0146	2.53	.4943	.9943	.0057
2.19	.4857	.9857	.0143	2.54	.4945	.9945	.0055
2.20	.4861	.9861	.0139	2.55	.4946	.9946	.0054
2.21	.4864	.9864	.0136	2.56	.4948	.9948	.0052
2.22	.4868	.9868	.0132	2.57	.4949	.9949	.0051
2.23	.4871	.9871	.0129	2.58	.4951	.9951	.0049
2.24	.4875	.9875	.0125	2.59	.4952	.9952	.0048
2.25	.4878	.9878	.0122	2.60	.4953	.9953	.0047
2.26	.4881	.9881	.0119	2.61	.4955	.9955	.0045
2.27	.4884	.9884	.0116	2.62	.4956	.9956	.0044
2.28	.4887	.9887	.0113	2.63	.4957	.9957	.0043
2.29	.4890	.9890	.0110	2.64	.4959	.9959	.0041
2.30	.4893	.9893	.0107	2.65	.4960	.9960	.0040
2.31	.4896	.9896	.0104	2.66	.4961	.9961	.0039
2.32	.4898	.9898	.0102	2.67	.4962	.9962	.0038
2.33	.4901	.9901	.0099	2.68	.4963	.9963	.0037
2.34	.4904	.9904	.0096	2.69	.4964	.9964	.0036
2.35	.4906	.9906	.0094	2.70	.4965	.9965	.0035
2.36	.4909	.9909	.0091	2.71	.4966	.9966	.0034
2.37	.4911	.9911	.0089	2.72	.4967	.9967	.0033
2.38	.4913	.9913	.0087	2.73	.4968	.9968	.0032
2.39	.4916	.9916	.0084	2.74	.4969	.9969	.0031
2.40	.4918	.9918	.0082	2.75	.4970	.9970	.0030
2.41	.4920	.9920	.0080	2.76	.4971	.9971	.0029
2.42	.4922	.9922	.0078	2.77	.4972	.9972	.0028
2.43	.4925	.9925	.0075	2.78	.4973	.9973	.0027
2.44	.4927	.9927	.0073	2.79	.4974	.9974	.0026

Table of Probabilities Under the Normal Curve *(continued)*

1	2	3	4	1	2	3	4
Z	Area from Mean to Z	The Big Part	The Small Part	Z	Area From Mean to Z	The Big Part	The Small Part
2.80	.4974	.9974	.0026	3.05	.4989	.9989	.0011
2.81	.4975	.9975	.0025	3.06	.4989	.9989	.0011
2.82	.4976	.9976	.0024	3.07	.4989	.9989	.0011
2.83	.4977	.9977	.0023	3.08	.4990	.9990	.0010
2.84	.4977	.9977	.0023	3.09	.4990	.9990	.0010
2.85	.4978	.9978	.0022	3.10	.4990	.9990	.0010
2.86	.4979	.9979	.0021	3.11	.4991	.9991	.0009
2.87	.4979	.9979	.0021	3.12	.4991	.9991	.0009
2.88	.4980	.9980	.0020	3.13	.4991	.9991	.0009
2.89	.4981	.9981	.0019	3.14	.4992	.9992	.0008
2.90	.4981	.9981	.0019	3.15	.4992	.9992	.0008
2.91	.4982	.9982	.0018	3.16	.4992	.9992	.0008
2.92	.4982	.9982	.0018	3.17	.4992	.9992	.0008
2.93	.4983	.9983	.0017	3.18	.4993	.9993	.0007
2.94	.4984	.9984	.0016	3.19	.4993	.9993	.0007
2.95	.4984	.9984	.0016	3.20	.4993	.9993	.0007
2.96	.4985	.9985	.0015	3.21	.4993	.9993	.0007
2.97	.4985	.9985	.0015	3.22	.4994	.9994	.0006
2.98	.4986	.9986	.0014	3.23	.4994	.9994	.0006
2.99	.4986	.9986	.0014	3.24	.4994	.9994	.0006
3.00	.4987	.9987	.0013	3.30	.4995	.9995	.0005
3.01	.4987	.9987	.0013	3.40	.4997	.9997	.0003
3.02	.4987	.9987	.0013	3.50	.4998	.9998	.0002
3.03	.4988	.9988	.0012	3.60	.4998	.9998	.0002
3.04	.4988	.9988	.0012	3.70	.4999	.9999	.0001

Appendix 2

Critical Values of *t*

For any given df, the table shows the values of t *corresponding to various levels of probability.*
Obtained t *is significant at a given level if it is equal to or greater than the value shown in the table.*

(n - 1) df	Level of Significance for One-Tailed Test					
	.10	.05	.025	.01	.005	.0005
	Level of Significance for Two-Tailed Test					
	.20	.10	.05	.02	.01	.001
1	3.078	6.314	12.706	31.821	63.657	636.619
2	1.886	2.920	4.303	6.965	9.925	31.598
3	1.638	2.353	3.182	4.541	5.841	12.941
4	1.533	2.132	2.776	3.747	4.604	8.610
5	1.476	2.015	2.571	3.365	4.032	6.859
6	1.440	1.943	2.447	3.143	3.707	5.959
7	1.415	1.895	2.365	2.998	3.499	5.405
8	1.397	1.860	2.306	2.896	3.355	5.041
9	1.383	1.833	2.262	2.821	3.250	4.781
10	1.372	1.812	2.228	2.764	3.169	4.587
11	1.363	1.796	2.201	2.718	3.106	4.437
12	1.356	1.782	2.179	2.681	3.055	4.318
13	1.350	1.771	2.160	2.650	3.012	4.221
14	1.345	1.761	2.145	2.624	2.977	4.140
15	1.341	1.753	2.131	2.602	2.947	4.073
16	1.337	1.746	2.120	2.583	2.921	4.015
17	1.333	1.740	2.110	2.567	2.898	3.965
18	1.330	1.734	2.101	2.552	2.878	3.922
19	1.328	1.729	2.093	2.539	2.861	3.883
20	1.325	1.725	2.086	2.528	2.845	3.850
21	1.323	1.721	2.080	2.518	2.831	3.819
22	1.321	1.717	2.074	2.508	2.819	3.792
23	1.319	1.714	2.069	2.500	2.807	3.767
24	1.318	1.711	2.064	2.492	2.797	3.745
25	1.316	1.708	2.060	2.485	2.787	3.725
26	1.315	1.706	2.056	2.479	2.779	3.707
27	1.314	1.703	2.052	2.473	2.771	3.690
28	1.313	1.701	2.048	2.467	2.763	3.674
29	1.311	1.699	2.045	2.462	2.756	3.659
30	1.310	1.697	2.042	2.457	2.750	3.646
40	1.303	1.684	2.021	2.423	2.704	3.551
60	1.296	1.671	2.000	2.390	2.660	3.460
120	1.289	1.658	1.980	2.358	2.617	3.373
∞	1.282	1.645	1.960	2.326	2.576	3.291

Appendix 2 is taken from Table III of Fisher and Yates, *Statistical Tables for Biological, Agricultural, and Medical Research*, 6th edition, published by Longman Group UK, Ltd., 1974 (previously published by Oliver and Boyd, Edinburgh), and by permission of the authors and publishers.

Appendix 3

Critical Values of F (α = .05 first row; α = .01 second row)

df for numerator

		1	2	3	4	5	6	7	8	9	10	11	12
df for denominator	1	161	200	216	225	230	234	237	239	241	242	243	244
		4,052	4,999	5,403	5,625	5,764	5,859	5,928	5,981	6,022	6,056	6,082	6,106
	2	18.51	19.00	19.16	19.25	19.30	19.33	19.36	19.37	19.38	19.39	19.40	19.41
		98.49	99.00	99.17	99.25	99.30	99.33	99.34	99.36	99.38	99.40	99.41	99.42
	3	10.13	9.55	9.28	9.12	9.01	8.94	8.88	8.84	8.81	8.78	8.76	8.74
		34.12	30.82	29.46	28.71	28.24	27.91	27.67	27.49	27.34	27.23	27.13	27.05
	4	7.71	6.94	6.59	6.39	6.26	6.16	6.09	6.04	6.00	5.96	5.93	5.91
		21.20	18.00	16.69	15.98	15.52	15.21	14.98	14.80	14.66	14.54	14.45	14.37
	5	6.61	5.79	5.41	5.19	5.05	4.95	4.88	4.82	4.78	4.74	4.70	4.68
		16.26	13.27	12.06	11.39	10.97	10.67	10.45	10.27	10.15	10.05	9.96	9.89
	6	5.99	5.14	4.76	4.53	4.39	4.28	4.21	4.15	4.10	4.06	4.03	4.00
		13.74	10.92	9.78	9.15	8.75	8.47	8.26	8.10	7.98	7.87	7.79	7.72
	7	5.59	4.74	4.35	4.12	3.97	3.87	3.79	3.73	3.68	3.63	3.60	3.57
		12.25	9.55	8.45	7.85	7.46	7.19	7.00	6.84	6.71	6.62	6.54	6.47
	8	5.32	4.46	4.07	3.84	3.69	3.58	3.50	3.44	3.39	3.34	3.31	3.28
		11.26	8.65	7.59	7.01	6.63	6.37	6.19	6.03	5.91	5.82	5.74	5.67
	9	5.12	4.26	3.86	3.63	3.48	3.37	3.29	3.23	3.18	3.13	3.10	3.07
		10.56	8.02	6.99	6.42	6.06	5.80	5.62	5.47	5.35	5.26	5.18	5.11
	10	4.96	4.10	3.71	3.48	3.33	3.22	3.14	3.07	3.02	2.97	2.94	2.91
		10.04	7.56	6.55	5.99	5.64	5.39	5.21	5.06	4.95	4.85	4.78	4.71
	11	4.84	3.98	3.59	3.36	3.20	3.09	3.01	2.95	2.90	2.86	2.82	2.79
		9.65	7.20	6.22	5.67	5.32	5.07	4.88	4.74	4.63	4.54	4.46	4.40
	12	4.75	3.88	3.49	3.26	3.11	3.00	2.92	2.85	2.80	2.76	2.72	2.69
		9.33	6.93	5.95	5.41	5.06	4.82	4.65	4.50	4.39	4.30	4.22	4.16
	13	4.67	3.80	3.41	3.18	3.02	2.92	2.84	2.77	2.72	2.67	2.63	2.60
		9.07	6.70	5.74	5.20	4.86	4.62	4.44	4.30	4.19	4.10	4.02	3.96
	14	4.60	3.74	3.34	3.11	2.96	2.85	2.77	2.70	2.65	2.60	2.56	2.53
		8.86	6.51	5.56	5.03	4.69	4.46	4.28	4.14	4.03	3.94	3.86	3.80

(continued)

Critical Values of F ($\alpha = .05$ first row; $\alpha = .01$ second row)

					df for numerator							
14	16	20	24	30	40	50	75	100	200	500	∞
245	246	248	249	250	251	252	253	253	254	254	254
6,142	6,169	6,208	6,234	6,258	6,286	6,302	6,323	6,334	6,352	6,361	6,366
19.42	19.43	19.44	19.45	19.46	19.47	19.47	19.48	19.49	19.49	19.50	19.50
99.43	99.44	99.45	99.46	99.47	99.48	99.48	99.49	99.49	99.40	99.50	99.50
8.71	8.69	8.66	8.64	8.62	8.60	8.58	8.57	8.56	8.54	8.54	8.53
26.92	26.83	26.69	26.60	26.50	26.41	26.35	26.27	26.23	26.18	26.14	26.12
5.87	5.84	5.80	5.77	5.74	5.71	5.70	5.68	5.66	5.65	5.64	5.63
14.24	14.15	14.02	13.93	13.83	13.74	13.69	13.61	13.57	13.52	13.48	13.46
4.64	4.60	4.56	4.53	4.50	4.46	4.44	4.42	4.40	4.38	4.37	4.36
9.77	9.68	9.55	9.47	9.38	9.29	9.24	9.17	9.13	9.07	9.04	9.02
3.96	3.92	3.87	3.84	3.81	3.77	3.75	3.72	3.71	3.69	3.68	3.67
7.60	7.52	7.39	7.31	7.23	7.14	7.09	7.02	6.99	6.94	6.90	6.88
3.52	3.49	3.44	3.41	3.38	3.34	3.32	3.29	3.28	3.25	3.24	3.23
6.35	6.27	6.15	6.07	5.98	5.90	5.85	5.78	5.75	5.70	5.67	5.65
3.23	3.20	3.15	3.12	3.08	3.05	3.03	3.00	2.98	2.96	2.94	2.93
5.56	5.48	5.36	5.28	5.20	5.11	5.06	5.00	4.96	4.91	4.88	4.86
3.02	2.98	2.93	2.90	2.86	2.82	2.80	2.77	2.76	2.73	2.72	2.71
5.00	4.92	4.80	4.73	4.64	4.56	4.51	4.45	4.41	4.36	4.33	4.31
2.86	2.82	2.77	2.74	2.70	2.67	2.64	2.61	2.59	2.56	2.55	2.54
4.60	4.52	4.41	4.33	4.25	4.17	4.12	4.05	4.01	3.96	3.93	3.91
2.74	2.70	2.65	2.61	2.57	2.53	2.50	2.47	2.45	2.42	2.41	2.40
4.29	4.21	4.10	4.02	3.94	3.86	3.80	3.74	3.70	3.66	3.62	3.60
2.64	2.60	2.54	2.50	2.46	2.42	2.40	2.36	2.35	2.32	2.31	2.30
4.05	3.98	3.86	3.78	3.70	3.61	3.56	3.49	3.46	3.41	3.38	3.36
2.55	2.51	2.46	2.42	2.38	2.34	2.32	2.28	2.26	2.24	2.22	2.21
3.85	3.78	3.67	3.59	3.51	3.42	3.37	3.30	3.27	3.21	3.18	3.16
2.48	2.44	2.39	2.35	2.31	2.27	2.24	2.21	2.19	2.16	2.14	2.13
3.70	3.62	3.51	3.43	3.34	3.26	3.21	3.14	3.11	3.06	3.02	3.00

(*continued*)

Critical Values of F ($\alpha = .05$ first row; $\alpha = .01$ second row)

df for numerator

		1	2	3	4	5	6	7	8	9	10	11	12
df for denominator	15	4.54	3.68	3.29	3.06	2.90	2.79	2.70	2.64	2.59	2.55	2.51	2.48
		8.68	6.36	5.42	4.89	4.56	4.32	4.14	4.00	3.89	3.80	3.73	3.67
	16	4.49	3.63	3.24	3.01	2.85	2.74	2.66	2.59	2.54	2.49	2.45	2.42
		8.53	6.23	5.29	4.77	4.44	4.20	4.03	3.89	3.78	3.69	3.61	3.55
	17	4.45	3.59	3.20	2.96	2.81	2.70	2.62	2.55	2.50	2.45	2.41	2.38
		8.40	6.11	5.18	4.67	4.34	4.10	3.93	3.79	3.68	3.59	3.52	3.45
	18	4.41	3.55	3.16	2.93	2.77	2.66	2.58	2.51	2.46	2.41	2.37	2.34
		8.28	6.01	5.09	4.58	4.25	4.01	3.85	3.71	3.60	3.51	3.44	3.37
	19	4.38	3.52	3.13	2.90	2.74	2.63	2.55	2.48	2.43	2.38	2.34	2.31
		8.18	5.93	5.01	4.50	4.17	3.94	3.77	3.63	3.52	3.43	3.36	3.30
	20	4.35	3.49	3.10	2.87	2.71	2.60	2.52	2.45	2.40	2.35	2.31	2.28
		8.10	5.85	4.94	4.43	4.10	3.87	3.71	3.56	3.45	3.37	3.30	3.23
	21	4.32	3.47	3.07	2.84	2.68	2.57	2.49	2.42	2.37	2.32	2.28	2.25
		8.02	5.78	4.87	4.37	4.04	3.81	3.65	3.51	3.40	3.31	3.24	3.17
	22	4.30	3.44	3.05	2.82	2.66	2.55	2.47	2.40	2.35	2.30	2.26	2.23
		7.94	5.72	4.82	4.31	3.99	3.76	3.59	3.45	3.35	3.26	3.18	3.12
	23	4.28	3.42	3.03	2.80	2.64	2.53	2.45	2.38	2.32	2.28	2.24	2.20
		7.88	5.66	4.76	4.26	3.94	3.71	3.54	3.41	3.30	3.21	3.14	3.07
	24	4.26	3.40	3.01	2.78	2.62	2.51	2.43	2.36	2.30	2.26	2.22	2.18
		7.82	5.61	4.72	4.22	3.90	3.67	3.50	3.36	3.25	3.17	3.09	3.03
	25	4.24	3.38	2.99	2.76	2.60	2.49	2.41	2.34	2.28	2.24	2.20	2.16
		7.77	5.57	4.68	4.18	3.86	3.63	3.46	3.32	3.21	3.13	3.05	2.99
	26	4.22	3.37	2.98	2.74	2.59	2.47	2.39	2.32	2.27	2.22	2.18	2.15
		7.72	5.53	4.64	4.14	3.82	3.59	3.42	3.29	3.17	3.09	3.02	2.96
	27	4.21	3.35	2.96	2.73	2.57	2.46	2.37	2.30	2.25	2.20	2.16	2.13
		7.68	5.49	4.60	4.11	3.79	3.56	3.39	3.26	3.14	3.06	2.98	2.93

(continued)

Critical Values of F (α = .05 first row; α = .01 second row)

					df for numerator						
14	16	20	24	30	40	50	75	100	200	500	∞
2.43	2.39	2.33	2.29	2.25	2.21	2.18	2.15	2.12	2.10	2.08	2.07
3.56	3.48	3.36	3.29	3.20	3.12	3.07	3.00	2.97	2.92	2.89	2.87
2.37	2.33	2.28	2.24	2.20	2.16	2.13	2.09	2.07	2.04	2.02	2.01
3.45	3.37	3.25	3.18	3.10	3.01	2.96	2.89	2.86	2.80	2.77	2.75
2.33	2.29	2.23	2.19	2.15	2.11	2.08	2.04	2.02	1.99	1.97	1.96
3.35	3.27	3.16	3.08	3.00	2.92	2.86	2.79	2.76	2.70	2.67	2.65
2.29	2.25	2.19	2.15	2.11	2.07	2.04	2.00	1.98	1.95	1.93	1.92
3.27	3.19	3.07	3.00	2.91	3.81	2.78	2.71	2.68	2.62	2.59	2.57
2.26	2.21	2.15	2.11	2.07	2.02	2.00	1.96	1.94	1.91	1.90	1.88
3.19	3.12	3.00	2.92	2.84	2.76	2.70	2.63	2.60	2.54	2.51	2.49
2.23	2.18	2.12	2.08	2.04	1.99	1.96	1.92	1.90	1.87	1.85	1.84
3.13	3.05	2.94	2.86	2.77	2.69	2.63	2.56	2.53	2.47	2.44	2.42
2.20	2.15	2.09	2.05	2.00	1.96	1.93	1.89	1.87	1.84	1.82	1.81
3.07	2.99	2.88	2.80	2.72	2.63	2.58	2.51	2.47	2.42	2.38	2.36
2.18	2.13	2.07	2.03	1.98	1.93	1.91	1.87	1.84	1.81	1.80	1.78
3.02	2.94	2.83	2.75	2.67	2.58	2.53	2.46	2.42	2.37	2.33	2.31
2.14	2.10	2.04	2.00	1.96	1.91	1.88	1.84	1.82	1.79	1.77	1.76
2.97	2.89	2.78	2.70	2.62	2.53	2.48	2.41	2.37	2.32	2.28	2.26
2.13	2.09	2.02	1.98	1.94	1.89	1.86	1.82	1.80	1.76	1.74	1.73
2.93	2.85	2.74	2.66	2.58	2.49	2.44	2.36	2.33	2.27	2.23	2.21
2.11	2.06	2.00	1.96	1.92	1.87	1.84	1.80	1.77	1.74	1.72	1.71
2.89	2.81	2.70	2.62	2.54	2.45	2.40	2.32	2.29	2.23	2.19	2.17
2.10	2.05	1.99	1.95	1.90	1.85	1.82	1.78	1.76	1.72	1.70	1.69
2.86	2.77	2.66	2.58	2.50	2.41	2.36	2.28	2.25	2.19	2.15	2.13
2.08	2.03	1.97	1.93	1.88	1.84	1.80	1.76	1.74	1.71	1.68	1.67
2.83	2.74	2.63	2.55	2.47	2.38	2.25	2.21	2.16	2.16	2.12	2.10

(*continued*)

Critical Values of *F* (α = .05 first row; α = .01 second row)

df for numerator

df for denominator		1	2	3	4	5	6	7	8	9	10	11	12
	28	4.20	3.34	2.95	2.71	2.56	2.44	2.36	2.29	2.24	2.19	2.15	2.12
		7.64	5.45	4.57	4.07	3.76	3.53	3.36	3.23	3.11	3.03	2.95	2.90
	29	4.18	3.33	2.93	2.70	2.54	2.43	2.35	2.28	2.22	2.18	2.14	2.10
		7.60	5.42	4.54	4.04	3.73	3.50	3.33	3.20	3.08	3.00	2.92	2.87
	30	4.17	3.32	2.92	2.69	2.53	2.42	2.34	2.27	2.21	2.16	2.12	2.09
		7.56	5.39	4.51	4.02	3.70	3.47	3.30	3.17	3.06	2.98	2.90	2.84
	32	4.15	3.30	2.90	2.67	2.51	2.40	2.32	2.25	2.19	2.14	2.10	2.07
		7.50	5.34	4.46	3.97	3.66	3.42	3.25	3.12	3.01	2.94	2.86	2.80
	34	4.13	3.28	2.88	2.65	2.49	2.38	2.30	2.23	2.17	2.12	2.08	2.05
		7.44	5.29	4.42	3.93	3.61	3.38	3.21	3.08	2.97	2.89	2.82	2.76
	36	4.11	3.26	2.86	2.63	2.48	2.36	2.28	2.21	2.15	2.10	2.06	2.03
		7.39	5.25	4.38	3.89	3.58	3.35	3.18	3.04	2.94	2.86	2.78	2.72
	38	4.10	3.25	2.85	2.62	2.46	2.35	2.26	2.19	2.14	2.09	2.05	2.02
		7.35	5.21	4.34	3.86	3.54	3.32	3.15	3.02	2.91	2.82	2.75	2.69
	40	4.08	3.23	2.84	2.61	2.45	2.34	2.25	2.18	2.12	2.07	2.04	2.00
		7.31	5.18	4.31	3.83	3.51	3.29	3.12	2.99	2.88	2.80	2.73	2.66
	42	4.07	3.22	2.83	2.59	2.44	2.32	2.24	2.17	2.11	2.06	2.02	1.99
		7.27	5.15	4.29	3.80	3.49	3.26	3.10	2.96	2.86	2.77	2.70	2.64
	44	4.06	3.21	2.82	2.58	2.43	2.31	2.23	2.16	2.10	2.05	2.01	1.98
		7.24	5.12	4.26	3.78	3.46	3.24	3.07	2.94	2.84	2.75	2.68	2.62
	46	4.05	3.20	2.81	2.57	2.42	2.30	2.22	2.14	2.09	2.04	2.00	1.97
		7.21	5.10	4.24	3.76	3.44	3.22	3.05	2.92	2.82	2.73	2.66	2.60
	48	4.04	3.19	2.80	2.56	2.41	2.30	2.21	2.14	2.08	2.03	1.99	1.96
		7.19	5.08	4.22	3.74	3.42	3.20	3.04	2.90	2.80	2.71	2.64	2.58
	50	4.03	3.18	2.79	2.56	2.40	2.29	2.20	2.13	2.07	2.02	1.98	1.95
		7.17	5.06	4.20	3.72	3.41	3.18	3.02	2.88	2.78	2.70	2.62	2.56

(*continued*)

Critical Values of F (α = .05 first row; α = .01 second row)

df for numerator

14	16	20	24	30	40	50	75	100	200	500	∞
2.05	2.02	1.96	1.91	1.87	1.81	1.78	1.75	1.72	1.69	1.67	1.65
2.80	2.71	2.60	2.52	2.44	2.35	2.30	2.22	2.18	2.13	2.09	2.06
2.05	2.00	1.94	1.90	1.85	1.80	1.77	1.73	1.71	1.68	1.65	1.64
2.77	2.68	2.57	2.49	2.41	2.32	2.27	2.19	2.15	2.10	2.06	2.03
2.04	1.99	1.93	1.89	1.84	1.79	1.76	1.72	1.69	1.66	1.64	1.62
2.74	2.66	2.55	2.47	2.38	2.29	2.24	2.16	2.13	2.07	2.03	2.01
2.02	1.97	1.91	1.86	1.82	1.76	1.74	1.69	1.67	1.64	1.61	1.59
2.70	2.62	2.51	2.42	2.34	2.25	2.20	2.12	2.08	2.02	1.98	1.96
2.00	1.95	1.89	1.84	1.80	1.74	1.71	1.67	1.64	1.61	1.59	1.57
2.66	2.58	2.47	2.38	2.30	2.21	2.15	2.08	2.04	1.98	1.94	1.91
1.98	1.93	1.87	1.82	1.78	1.72	1.69	1.65	1.62	1.59	1.56	1.55
2.62	2.54	2.43	2.35	2.26	2.17	2.12	2.04	2.00	1.94	1.90	1.87
1.96	1.92	1.85	1.80	1.76	1.71	1.67	1.63	1.60	1.57	1.54	1.53
2.59	2.51	2.40	2.32	2.22	2.14	2.08	2.00	1.97	1.90	1.86	1.84
1.95	1.90	1.84	1.79	1.74	1.69	1.66	1.61	1.59	1.55	1.53	1.51
2.56	2.49	2.37	2.29	2.20	2.11	2.05	1.97	1.94	1.88	1.84	1.81
1.94	1.89	1.82	1.78	1.73	1.68	1.64	1.60	1.57	1.54	1.51	1.49
2.54	2.46	2.35	2.26	2.17	2.08	2.02	1.94	1.91	1.85	1.80	1.78
1.92	1.88	1.81	1.76	1.72	1.66	1.63	1.58	1.56	1.52	1.50	1.48
2.52	2.44	2.32	2.24	2.15	2.06	2.00	1.92	1.88	1.81	1.78	1.75
1.91	1.87	1.80	1.75	1.71	1.65	1.62	1.57	1.54	1.51	1.48	1.46
2.50	2.42	2.30	2.22	2.13	2.04	1.98	1.90	1.86	1.80	1.76	1.72
1.90	1.86	1.79	1.74	1.70	1.64	1.61	1.56	1.53	1.50	1.47	1.45
2.43	2.40	2.28	2.20	2.11	2.02	1.96	1.88	1.84	1.78	1.73	1.70
1.90	1.85	1.78	1.74	1.69	1.63	1.60	1.55	1.52	1.48	1.46	1.44
2.46	2.39	2.26	2.18	2.10	2.00	1.94	1.86	1.82	1.76	1.71	1.68

(continued)

Critical Values of F (α = .05 first row; α = .01 second row)

df for numerator

		1	2	3	4	5	6	7	8	9	10	11	12
df for denominator	55	4.02	3.17	2.78	2.54	2.38	2.27	2.18	2.11	2.05	2.00	1.97	1.93
		7.12	5.01	4.16	3.68	3.37	3.15	2.98	2.85	2.75	2.66	2.59	2.53
	60	4.00	3.15	2.76	2.52	2.37	2.25	2.17	2.10	2.04	1.99	1.95	1.92
		7.08	4.98	4.13	3.65	3.34	3.12	2.95	2.82	2.72	2.63	2.56	2.50
	65	3.99	3.14	2.75	2.51	2.36	2.24	2.15	2.08	2.02	1.98	1.94	1.90
		7.04	4.95	4.10	3.62	3.31	3.09	2.93	2.79	2.70	2.61	2.54	2.47
	70	3.98	3.13	2.74	2.50	2.35	2.23	2.14	2.07	2.01	1.97	1.93	1.89
		7.01	4.92	4.08	3.60	3.29	3.07	2.91	2.77	2.67	2.59	2.51	2.45
	80	3.96	3.11	2.72	2.48	2.33	2.21	2.12	2.05	1.99	1.95	1.91	1.88
		6.96	4.88	4.04	3.56	3.25	3.04	2.87	2.74	2.64	2.55	2.48	2.41
	100	3.94	3.09	2.70	2.46	2.30	2.19	2.10	2.03	1.97	1.92	1.88	1.85
		6.90	4.82	3.98	3.51	3.20	2.99	2.82	2.69	2.59	2.51	2.43	2.36
	125	3.92	3.07	2.68	2.44	2.29	2.17	2.08	2.01	1.95	1.90	1.86	1.83
		6.84	4.78	3.94	3.47	3.17	2.95	2.79	2.65	2.56	2.47	2.40	2.33
	150	3.91	3.06	2.67	2.43	2.27	2.16	2.07	2.00	1.94	1.89	1.85	1.82
		6.81	4.75	3.91	3.44	3.14	2.92	2.76	2.62	2.53	2.44	2.37	2.30
	200	3.89	3.04	2.65	2.41	2.26	2.14	2.05	1.98	1.92	1.87	1.83	1.80
		6.76	4.71	3.88	3.41	3.11	2.90	2.73	2.60	2.50	2.41	2.34	2.28
	400	3.86	3.02	2.62	2.39	2.23	2.12	2.03	1.96	1.90	1.85	1.81	1.78
		6.70	4.66	3.83	3.36	3.06	2.85	2.69	2.55	2.46	2.37	2.29	2.23
	1000	3.85	3.00	2.61	2.38	2.22	2.10	2.02	1.95	1.89	1.84	1.80	1.76
		6.66	4.62	3.80	3.34	3.04	2.82	2.66	2.53	2.43	2.34	2.26	2.20
	∞	3.84	2.99	2.60	2.37	2.21	2.09	2.01	1.94	1.88	1.83	1.79	1.75
		6.64	4.60	3.78	3.32	3.02	2.80	2.64	2.51	2.41	2.32	2.24	2.18

(continued)

Critical Values of F ($\alpha = .05$ first row; $\alpha = .01$ second row)

df for numerator

14	16	20	24	30	40	50	75	100	200	500	∞
1.88	1.83	1.76	1.72	1.67	1.61	1.58	1.52	1.50	1.46	1.43	1.41
2.43	2.35	2.23	2.15	2.06	1.96	1.90	1.82	1.78	1.71	1.66	1.64
1.86	1.81	1.75	1.70	1.65	1.59	1.56	1.50	1.48	1.44	1.41	1.39
2.40	2.32	2.20	2.12	2.03	1.93	1.87	1.79	1.74	1.68	1.63	1.60
1.85	1.80	1.73	1.68	1.63	1.57	1.54	1.49	1.46	1.42	1.39	1.37
2.37	2.30	2.18	2.09	2.00	1.90	1.84	1.76	1.71	1.64	1.60	1.56
1.84	1.79	1.72	1.67	1.62	1.56	1.53	1.47	1.45	1.40	1.37	1.35
2.35	2.28	2.15	2.07	1.98	1.88	1.82	1.74	1.69	1.62	1.56	1.53
1.82	1.77	1.70	1.65	1.60	1.54	1.51	1.45	1.42	1.38	1.35	1.32
2.32	2.24	2.11	2.03	1.94	1.84	1.78	1.70	1.65	1.57	1.52	1.49
1.79	1.75	1.68	1.63	1.57	1.51	1.48	1.42	1.39	1.34	1.30	1.28
2.26	2.19	2.06	1.98	1.89	1.79	1.73	1.64	1.59	1.51	1.46	1.43
1.77	1.72	1.65	1.60	1.55	1.49	1.45	1.39	1.36	1.31	1.27	1.25
2.23	2.15	2.03	1.94	1.85	1.75	1.68	1.59	1.54	1.46	1.40	1.37
1.76	1.71	1.64	1.59	1.54	1.47	1.44	1.37	1.34	1.29	1.25	1.22
2.20	2.12	2.00	1.91	1.83	1.72	1.66	1.56	1.51	1.43	1.37	1.33
1.74	1.69	1.62	1.57	1.52	1.45	1.42	1.35	1.32	1.26	1.22	1.19
2.17	2.09	1.97	1.88	1.79	1.69	1.62	1.53	1.48	1.39	1.33	1.28
1.72	1.67	1.60	1.54	1.49	1.42	1.38	1.32	1.28	1.22	1.16	1.13
2.12	2.04	1.92	1.84	1.74	1.64	1.57	1.47	1.42	1.32	1.24	1.19
1.70	1.65	1.58	1.53	1.47	1.41	1.36	1.30	1.26	1.19	1.13	1.08
2.09	2.01	1.89	1.81	1.71	1.61	1.54	1.44	1.38	1.28	1.19	1.11
1.69	1.64	1.57	1.52	1.46	1.40	1.35	1.28	1.24	1.17	1.11	1.00
2.07	1.99	1.87	1.79	1.69	1.59	1.52	1.41	1.36	1.25	1.15	1.00

Appendix 4

Critical Values of the Chi-Square Distribution

Critical Values of the
Chi-square Distribution
for $\alpha = .05$ and $\alpha = .01$

df	$\alpha = .05$	$\alpha = .01$
1	3.84	6.63
2	5.99	9.21
3	7.81	11.3
4	9.49	13.3
5	11.1	15.1
6	12.6	16.8
7	14.1	18.5
8	15.5	20.1
9	16.9	21.7
10	18.3	23.2
11	19.7	24.7
12	21.0	26.2
13	22.4	27.7
14	23.7	29.1
15	25.0	30.6
16	26.3	32.0
17	27.6	33.4
18	28.9	34.8
19	30.1	36.2
20	31.4	37.6
21	32.7	38.9
22	33.9	40.3
23	35.2	41.6
24	36.4	43.0
25	37.7	44.3
26	38.9	45.6
27	40.1	47.0
28	41.3	48.3
29	42.6	49.6
30	43.8	50.9

Reprinted with permission of the Biometrika
Trustees from Table VIII, Percentage Points,
Chi-Square Distribution. *Biometrika Tables for
Statisticians*, 3rd ed. (Cambridge University
Press, Cambridge, 1966) Vol. 1.

Index

CPSIA information can be obtained at www.ICGtesting.com
Printed in the USA
LVOW050745150812

294333LV00001B/5/A